Manufacturing planning systems

Manufacturing planning systems

Bill Scott

McGRAW-HILL BOOK COMPANY

London · New York · St Louis · San Francisco · Auckland
Bogotá · Caracas · Lisbon · Madrid · Mexico · Milan
Montreal · New Delhi · Panama · Paris · San Juan
São Paulo · Singapore · Sydney · Tokyo · Toronto

Published by
McGRAW-HILL Book Company Europe
Shoppenhangers Road, Maidenhead, Berkshire SL6 2QL, England
Telephone 0628 23432
Fax 0628 770224

British Library Cataloguing in Publication Data

Scott, Bill
  Manufacturing Planning Systems
  I. Title
  658.503

  ISBN 0-07-707743-1

Library of Congress Cataloging-in-Publication Data

Scott, Bill
    Manufacturing planning systems / Bill Scott.
        p.   cm.
    Includes bibliographical references and index.
    ISBN 0-07-707743-1
    1. Production planning.   I. Title.
TS176.S385   1994
658.5—dc20

1 2 3 4 5   CUP   9 8 7 6 5 4

Typeset by Paston Press Ltd, Loddon, Norfolk
and printed and bound in Great Britain at the University Press, Cambridge

Contents

Preface

This book is about integrated manufacturing planning systems. Many books on this subject read as if they were written for the systems designer. This book is for users of the systems, particularly those who may be about to implement, or re-implement, such a system.

The typical user is likely to be in that manufacturing sector normally described as discrete batch production, which is a generic pseudonym for anything between the continuous process industries at one extreme of the spectrum and complex one-off engineering projects at the other. The typical user is also likely to be small or medium-sized, and will almost certainly buy and install proprietary software packages as opposed to designing and commissioning bespoke computer software.

Pathway

Part One of this book serves as an introduction to the subject. The essential manufacturing equation is defined, and the major components of the systems needed to satisfy it are outlined. One component is the material planning system, for which a widely accepted standard tool, material requirements planning (MRP), exists. The other component is the wider manufacturing planning system. The problem of how to reconcile a generic systems framework with the heavily prescriptive standard system of MRPII (manufacturing resource planning) is tackled head on by adopting MRPII as the generic framework, and redefining the detail to accommodate a wide variety of production environments. The justification for this, together with a critique of MRPII in relation to the reality of manufacturing strategy in the 1990s, is provided in Appendix A.

Parts Two and Three address the major components of an integrated manufacturing planning system in detail. Part Two deals with the materials planning system—MRP, and Part Three covers the wider production management system, of which MRP is itself a component part.

In Part Four the problems of planning, implementation and management of the system are addressed. Reasons for failure and factors for success are examined. The constraints on selection of software are explored, and this part concludes with an analysis of the benefits that may be expected from the system. The underlying message is that benefits accrue from manufacturing strategy and not from the system *per se*.

Throughout the detailed parts of this book a very simple but fictitious company is used as an example to provide continuity as each component of the system is explained. Birdhomes may strike many readers as a relic of the past. It does however serve to provide a basis for the exercises in Appendix B, and the exercises and answers in that appendix address all of the significant aspects of an integrated manufacturing planning system. The critical reader is invited to formulate a manufacturing strategy which will bring Birdhomes into a competitive position in the 1990s.

A glossary of terms is to be found in Appendix D, and a short but worthwhile bibliography is in Appendix E.

Terminology

In any work of this type there is difficulty in the terminology. There is the problem of an emerging jargon, some of which may pass into common use, and some of which may not. For this reason 'customer delight', 'vendor delinquency' and the like are discarded in favour of more conservative terminology.

Certain words can mean one thing in the UK and something different in the USA. That many systems techniques and a great deal of the currently available software originate in the USA compounds this problem. The key differences in meaning are outlined below.

Requirements and orders

One example is requirements and orders. Many systems from the USA use the term *requirements* when describing the demand side of the supply and demand equation, and use *orders* to denote the supply side. The term orders is, at least on this side of the Atlantic, typically associated with a real transaction—a customer or sales order, a supplier (or vendor) order, or a works order, and that is the terminology used in this book. Requirements are used to denote the intermediate calculations lying between the representation of demand and the generation of orders on suppliers or the works to satisfy that demand.

Vendor and supplier

Vendor is the same as *supplier*. Both terms are today in the UK vocabulary, and both may appear in this work.

Backlog

Great confusion exists over the term *backlog* when used in the context of order backlog. In the UK this typically refers to overdue orders (or past due orders in American parlance), whereas in the USA it refers to all orders on the open order book. Where it is necessary to differentiate between all orders and those which are overdue, then the terms *outstanding orders*, and *order arrears* or *overdue orders*, are used.

Jobbing shop

Similar confusion exists over the term *job shop*. American parlance uses this term to describe what Browne *et al.* (1988) refer to as a process-oriented plant layout, or one in which work moves through different work centres each associated with a particular type of machine or operation. The job shop is the opposite of a *flow shop*, in which work moves along an assembly line or through a work cell using group technology.

In the UK, and in this book, the term *jobbing shop* has the specific connotation of a business that makes no standard product but instead manufactures a wide variety of different products or components, usually to bespoke customer specification. The problems of a jobbing shop are those of thousands of small subcontractors, very often caught between the two stools of larger and more powerful customers on the one hand and all powerful multinational material suppliers on the other. Jobbing businesses are all too often ignored by software systems designers, and their specific needs and problems feature equally in this book with those of original equipment manufacturers. To avoid confusion the American term job shop is discarded in favour of *process-oriented*.

MRP, MRP1 and MRPII

To distinguish between materials requirements planning (MRP) and manufacturing resource planning (MRPII), it has become fashionable sometimes to refer to MRP as MRP1. Wight (1984) added to the confusion between MRP, closed loop MRP and MRPII by his assertion that we could simply call it MRP, and that the context in which the acronym MRP was used would adequately define which level was implied. He used the analogy of New York to justify that. New York can mean the state of New York, the city of New York (the five boroughs), or sometimes more narrowly just Manhattan, but which of these definitions is implied is always clear from the context in which New York is used.

In this book, MRP denotes materials requirements planning, and the acronym MRP1 is studiously avoided. MRPII is used to denote not only manufacturing resource planning—the standard system—but also a generic manufacturing planning system framework which is widely applicable but non-prescriptive. Where it becomes necessary to avoid confusion, the term *MRPII standard system* is used, and this fits with a generic classification applied by the author to the commercially available MRPII software packages:

- *Standard system*: a system which conforms to the concept of closed loop MRP described in Wight (1984).
- *Part standard system*: a system which broadly conforms to Wight's concept of closed loop MRP, but which fails to provide for the balancing of supply and demand at or above the level of master production scheduling, or which does not cater for the customized product specifications typical of an assemble-to-order environment.
- *Non-standard system*: a system addressing the central objectives of MRPII, but which is founded on planning and scheduling principles that differ from those adopted by the advocates of the MRPII standard system. The most important of these include alternatives to order-based scheduling, the incorporation of scheduling to finite capacity, and the use of variable planning leadtimes.

Process oriented and business process re-engineering

The term 'process oriented' refers to a specific physical manufacturing process organization and is defined clearly in Browne *et al.* (1988). This is not to be confused with *business process re-engineering*, which is concerned with making improvements in the business processes, especially the flow of information.

These are the most important subtleties of terminology to recognize. There are others, and the glossary of terms in Appendix D will clarify for the reader exactly what meaning is associated with which term.

Acknowledgements

This book is an expanded version of delegate notes prepared for a training programme on manufacturing planning systems, and the assistance of Michael Seymour-Jones in that previous task was invaluable. In addition, the help and cooperation of a number of companies in assembling case study material was of enormous value; particular thanks are due to Boss Trucks Ltd, British Aerospace plc, C&K Switches Ltd, Fourth Shift (UK) Ltd, Pattison Mitchell, Quantel Ltd, Sara Lee Household and Personal Care, and Thurne Engineering Ltd.

The cooperation of the following, in agreeing to permit reproduction of material or in assisting with case study material, is also acknowledged: Addison-Wesley Publishing Ltd, ASK Computer Systems (UK) Ltd, AT&T Istel Ltd, Dr M. M. Barekat, Cassel Educational Ltd, Department of Trade and Industry, KPMG Management Consultants, IBM United Kingdom Ltd, Industrial Technology, Institute of Materials Management, A. T. Kearney Ltd, McGraw-Hill Inc, Oliver Wight Publications Inc, Thames Valley Enterprise Ltd, and Xerox Computer Services Ltd.

PART ONE
INTRODUCTION

In Chapter 1 the manufacturing equation is defined in terms of a simple model, and its two main components—the materials planning system and the manufacturing planning system—are briefly defined. Chapters 2 and 3 then examine the function and evolution of these two component parts in greater depth. Chapter 2 addresses the materials planning system, and Chapter 3 the wider production management system of which the materials management system is itself a constituent part. The detailed mechanics of these system components are themselves the subjects of Parts Two and Three of this book.

Chapter 4 of this first part sets the scene for that by examining the variables of the manufacturing environment. These are the constraints with which a system has to fit in order to be successful in operation and to yield benefits to an organization.

Finally, in Chapter 5, the subject of manufacturing strategy is introduced. Benefits accrue from the adoption of an appropriate manufacturing strategy, not a planning tool, and the brief overview in Chapter 5 helps put the manufacturing planning system in a proper context.

1
The manufacturing equation

1.1 Introduction

A very simple model of the manufacturing process and the systems needed to drive it is shown in Figure 1.1. This is almost as close as we can come, without major argument, to a concept of the *universal manufacturing equation* claimed by Wight (1984).

The process begins and ends with customers. Customers create demand for a product, and this demand is satisfied by the shipping of the product to the customer. The customers may be third parties, or they may be downstream manufacturing plants or work cells within the company. The product may be shipped from an inventory of the finished product or it may be manufactured to order.

Either way, the customer demand translates directly (in the form of a sales order) or indirectly (by a need to replenish finished inventory) into the need to manufacture the product. In order to plan ahead, the firm demand represented by real, live, customer orders may have to be supplemented by a forecast of what customers can be expected to order in future periods for which demand has not yet been confirmed.

The manufacturing equation or process is summed up in the central box of Figure 1.1:

$$\text{Materials} + \text{value-adding work} = \text{product}$$

In short, to make the product we need two distinct elements:

- materials and component parts
- manufacturing or assembly capacity

Materials and component parts

These may be procured from external suppliers or they may be manufactured within the company. *Materials planning systems* are concerned with planning the procurement and availability of these materials in a way that reconciles

3

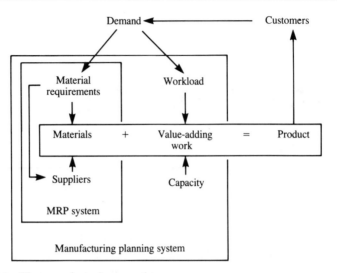

Figure 1.1 The manufacturing equation

the potentially conflicting requirements of end-customer demand and the necessity of organizing the flow of materials to minimize or optimize the investment in inventories.

Manufacturing or assembly capacity

Production capacity is the means of converting the materials into the inter-mediate component part or the end product. This involves balancing work-load and capacity, and is no use if the necessary materials are not available. The wider task of planning this process is the task of the whole *manufacturing planning system*, which therefore includes the materials planning system.

This is what it is all about, and it is best to begin with as simple an overview as possible. That way we avoid making simple things complex.

Later in Part One we will examine the many factors that appear to make things more complex. In reality, what adds to the complexity is quite simply the attempt to cope within one universal or standard system framework with the wide diversity of differing manufacturing environments that occur in real life.

We have already noted several variables of the overall manufacturing environment:

– whether to make to stock or make to order;
– whether or not demand forecasting is needed to supplement firm customer orders through the planning horizon;
– whether components are sourced in-plant, in-company, or externally;

- whether the end product is shipped to third parties or whether it is for consumption within a finished product in other factories or departments within the organization.

Among the major variables we will note later are these:

- The manufacturing process may produce one product, or it may produce many products.
- The product technology may be simple or it may be complex.
- The products may be standard products, they may be original equipment manufacturer (OEM) products tailored to customer specification, or they may be specifically manufactured to customer specification.
- The products may be produced in volume, they may be produced in small to medium-sized batches, or they may be unique one-off products.
- The manufacturing resource may be organized in different ways—as flow lines, work cells, or as a collection of process-related work centres through which work may pass in many different sequences depending upon individual product structures.
- Within the major resource centre the nature of the work associated with different products may be similar or homogeneous, or it may differ widely from one product specification to another.
- At shop-floor level, manufacturing strategy may have resulted in the introduction of a *kanban system*.

1.2 The materials planning system

The primary objective of the materials planning system is the balancing of supply and demand for component parts and materials, to ensure that the correct parts or materials for manufacture or assembly are available

- in the correct quantities
- at the right time
- in the right place

The well-defined technique of *material requirements planning* (MRP) is almost universally accepted as the standard materials planning system. Over the years it has yielded a high success rate as a planning tool.

1.3 The manufacturing planning system

Within the wider production management system, or manufacturing planning system, is included the materials planning system together with its extension into *capacity requirements planning* (CRP), which is essentially the balancing of production workload and production capacity.

Systems evolution has tended towards the integration of these functions with higher-level business planning as well as with systems functions at execution and feedback level on the shop floor. Lateral integration links the production management system with sales order processing systems, financial accounting systems, and with the design engineering process.

Manufacturing resource planning (MRPII) has been widely promoted as a standard system. The MRPII standard system has a much lower success rate than MRP, and is not appropriate in many manufacturing environments. In this book MRPII is used both as an example of a specific manufacturing planning system, and also as a generally valid systems framework to indicate where variants, hybrids or alternatives should be considered. The justification for this, along with an objective assessment of the MRPII standard system, is given in Appendix A.

This justification is similar to one offered by Luscombe (1993), who is on balance more sympathetic towards MRPII than this author. Luscombe addresses the question of an OPT/MRPII hybrid and poses the question as to whether or not such a system would still be MRPII. His answer is an unequivocal yes:

> Manufacturing resource planning is not dependent upon MRP and CRP. It merely requires the use of procedures for planning materials and capacity that are under the control of top management through a structured closed loop methodology.

In summary, we are dealing with two major components of a planning tool or system:

1. The materials planning system—in which the almost universally applicable technique of MRP serves the purpose.
2. The wider production management system, of which MRP is a constituent part, and in which MRPII is not a prescriptive standard but rather a generic framework that should be adapted to fit the manufacturing environment.

2

The materials planning system

The materials planning system is one of the two major components of the manufacturing planning system outlined in Chapter 1. MRP is the most widely used materials planning method. This chapter briefly reviews the evolution of material planning methods. The nature of demand is then addressed; central to the MRP concept is the differentiation between dependent demand and independent demand, and the role of demand forecasting in a material planning system. The advantages of MRP compared to other planning methods are noted, and the chapter concludes with a brief review of the evolution of MRP as a technique.

2.1 Materials planning methods

The historical evolution of materials planning methods has been:

– two-bin system
– order-point system
– MRP
– kanban system

Two-bin system

In a two-bin system, each bin holds an empirically determined quantity of parts, and issues are made from only one bin at a time. When the first bin is empty it is replenished. Issue of parts then switches to the second bin.

This system was typical of the past, when no records of inventory were available for more logically based inventory control methods. Bin quantities, being empirically determined, were almost always subject to a belt-and-braces approach, with overstocking being the norm, and shortages being frequent when demand or product specifications altered.

Two-bin systems are still commonly in use as the controlling mechanism for very low value and very high usage consumable items, such as fasteners, for which the cost of record keeping outweighs the benefits of inventory management.

Order-point system

In an order-point system, stock replenishment is triggered by stock falling below a re-order point, which is calculated based upon the expected demand over the replenishment leadtime. To this calculation is normally added a safety stock, which is intended to give protection against the variability in the demand pattern.

Both the expected demand and the safety stock are typically derived from historical usage data. The major pitfall in this is that historic usage does not very often correspond to future demand, especially where there is randomness in the demand pattern, where demand is rising or falling, or where the content of the product's component parts changes.

When reorder is triggered, there are various formulae for determining the reorder quantity. One of the most common is the economic order quantity, a mathematical calculation which is based on an algebraic trade-off between the costs of carrying inventory and the costs of reordering.

A readable account of the order-point inventory model is given by Wight (1984: Appendix 2).

MRP

The detailed mechanics of MRP is the subject of Part Two. In essence, MRP can be summed up as a form of time-phased order-point system which recognizes that demand for component parts is dependent on the demand for the components or products of which they are constituent parts.

MRP is the process by which component parts or materials are:

– planned to be manufactured or purchased and delivered,
– to satisfy the known or forecast demand,
– so that material shortages are eliminated,
– and excess stocks are not allowed to build up.

Kanban system

The kanban system associated with *just-in-time* (JIT) is no more than the application of order-point replenishment techniques to the short-term supply chain. It may even be regarded as an extension of a two-bin system controlling the replenishment of shop-floor buffer stock.

The crucial difference, however, between the re-order point kanban system and earlier order-point systems is that an MRP-type planning system will normally overlay the kanban system, thus ensuring that forward planning information is founded on future visibility as opposed to a knowledge of the past. This will be enlarged upon in Chapter 21. For the moment, however, we will accept MRP as the core building block of the materials planning system.

2.2 Demand

MRP recognizes that demand may be either dependent or independent. The distinction is fundamental to a proper understanding and choice of materials planning methods, and the definitive explanation may be found in Orlicky (1975: 22).

Independent demand

By independent demand is meant the demand for a part which is not dependent on the demand for any other part. Finished goods and service spares, therefore, are examples of independent demand. Demand forecasting techniques may be applied to the forecasting of independent demand parts, in order to provide a form of simulated visibility for forward planning purposes beyond the horizon of real customer orders.

In MRP the balancing of demand and supply of independent demand items is conventionally the function of a *master production schedule* (MPS) which drives the MRP system. There are alternative system drivers, which will be explored in Chapter 12, and which may be more appropriate in certain manufacturing environments.

Dependent demand

Dependent demand exists where the demand for an item is dependent on the demand for a higher-level component part or end product. The demand for component parts and raw materials is dependent on the demand for the assemblies or subassemblies of which they are components. Such dependency of demand implies a relationship in terms of both quantity and time.

It is therefore not sensible to forecast demand for such items as if they were independent of each other, as the earlier order-point systems did. Common sense suggests that such demand should be generated instead from the known or forecast demand of the parent components, of which they are integral component parts.

In MRP, dependent demand for component items is generated from the actual or forecast demand for the independent end products of which they are component parts. This is a major function of the MRP system, and one that differentiates MRP from an order-point system. The mechanism used in the process of converting the higher-level or parent demand into the lower-level or child demand is the *bill of materials*.

An order-point system regards all demand as independent demand. Therefore it is not an appropriate materials planning method for dependent demand items. The full reasoning is given by Orlicky (1975: 22). A detailed explanation of the order-point system itself may be found in Wight (1984: Appendix 2).

2.3 Demand forecasting

It is fundamental to MRP that forecasting of demand is relevant only in the case of independent demand items. Future demand for independent demand items may be forecast from their known historical demand. Demand forecasting detects and takes account of trends. These trends may typically be seasonal or cyclical, or they may be related to market-place activity.

A safety stock may be calculated to cater for the randomness or variability of demand. Forecasting has the effect of smoothing a real-life discontinuous demand into a fictitious continuous demand pattern, which may be comfortable for planning purposes but is unlikely to be mirrored as the real forward demand pattern gradually reveals itself.

2.4 Comparison of MRP and order-point systems

Dependent demand is discontinuous. Orlicky (1975) describes it as *lumpy*. A continuous or smooth high-level independent demand pattern will translate into a lumpy dependent demand pattern as a result of:

- The lot-sizing method in use. Many lot-sizing methods are concerned with minimizing the total of inventory carrying costs and ordering or production setup costs. The general effect is to group together into one order the demand from several discrete planning time periods. This leads to lot-sized demand lumping together in specific time periods, often in a pattern that bears no superficial resemblance to the original demand pattern.
- The fact that dependent demand may be generated from more than one higher-level product, each with a different demand pattern, with a similar outcome of lumping together. Because of this Orlicky correctly concludes that order-point systems are not appropriate for the management of the dependent demand elements of manufacturing inventories.

MRP respects the characteristics of discontinuous dependent demand by the technique of time phasing. This preserves the discrete attributes of quantity and date of a real requirement, in contrast to an order-point system which is concerned primarily with *when* to order a replenishment quantity, which is often predetermined.

The essential differences between MRP and an order-point system are as follows. In MRP:

− The calculation of material requirements is derived from the known or forecast demand for a higher-level product.
− Component parts are ordered in balanced product sets.
− The order interval is normally fixed.
− The order quantity is varied to control the flow of materials.
− New orders are typically released in accordance with a master production schedule.
− The date and quantity dependency on the higher-level product generating the independent demand for an item is therefore preserved.

In an order-point system:

− Demand is projected forwards from the known historical usage.
− Each part is normally treated in isolation from all other parts.
− The order quantity is normally fixed according to an *economic order quantity* (EOQ) calculation, to the usage over a given period of time, or to order coverage analysis.
− The order interval is varied to control the level of inventory.
− New orders are released when stock falls to a mathematically calculated re-order point.

2.5 MRP in perspective

The move from order-point systems to MRP equates to a move from control of inventory levels to the control of the flow of materials. MRP is equally applicable to the planning of:

− purchased parts
− parts manufactured in company

MRP is more responsive to dynamic market demand than the order-point systems it replaced, and it enables management to look to the future and plan receipts in line with the available visibility of requirements. Provided it is stable and properly managed, MRP is more likely than an order-point system both to eliminate shortages and reduce inventory levels of dependent demand items.

2.6 The development of MRP

The basic technique of MRP was developed before the Second World War. MRP was in use on a manual basis by the 1950s, but its large-scale use followed the development of computer processing technology in the 1960s. MRP became recognized as the standard technique in the late 1960s with the advent of second-generation computers and their associated proprietary software—for example, IBM System 360 and BOMP (Bill of Materials Processor). High interest rates in the 1970s focused attention on inventory financing costs, and prompted APICS (American Production and Inventory Control Society) to launch its MRP crusade.

MRP is today a standard technique, applicable over a wide range of materials planning and control environments. With certain provisos, it is also fully compatible with a JIT philosophy.

3

The manufacturing planning system

In this chapter the evolution from MRP, the materials planning system, into MRPII, the wider manufacturing planning system, is described. The MRPII standard system is open to criticism on a number of points, and this is put in perspective. The objectives of MRPII are then noted, and this chapter concludes with a review of what benefits can reasonably be expected from an MRPII system.

3.1 The evolution from MRP to MRPII

Wight (1984) describes the evolution of manufacturing planning systems as comprising three steps:

– MRP
– closed loop MRP
– MRPII

The original MRP systems comprised three levels (Figure 3.1):

– *system driver*: master production schedule (MPS)
– *planning module*: material requirements planning (MRP)
– *execution level*: ordering system

These were supported by bills of materials and inventory records.

The subsequent evolution to MRPII expanded the scope of MRP to six levels (Figure 3.1):

– business planning
– production planning (later renamed sales and operations planning)
– MPS
– MRP
– CRP
– ordering

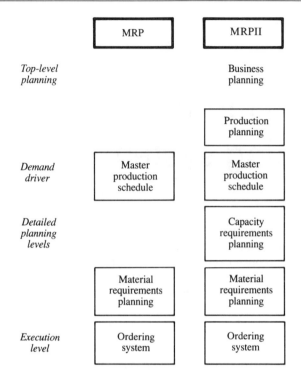

Figure 3.1   From MRP to MRPII

In addition to bills of materials and inventory records these were also supported by production activity control (PAC), production routings and shop-floor data collection (SFDC) modules.

The overview of closed loop MRP given by Wight (1984) is shown in Figure 3.2, and his overview of MRPII is shown in Figure 3.3. These two overviews scarcely differ, and Wight made the point that the real differences between closed loop MRP and MRPII were technically very small. The major technical feature is the tying together of the manufacturing planning system with the financial planning system. The other major difference lies in the way that management uses the system: it becomes a company-wide planning system and not merely the manufacturing function's planning system. What you are likely to buy as MRPII software is therefore a closed loop MRP system; whether or not you have an MRPII system depends much more on how you make use of the closed loop MRP system.

The evolution from MRP to MRPII was gradual and can be viewed from several perspectives:

– The original MRP recognized priorities but ignored several important constraints, in particular the constraint of production capacity. It told

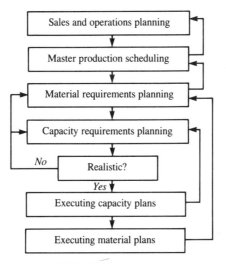

Figure 3.2   Closed loop MRP (Wight 1984)

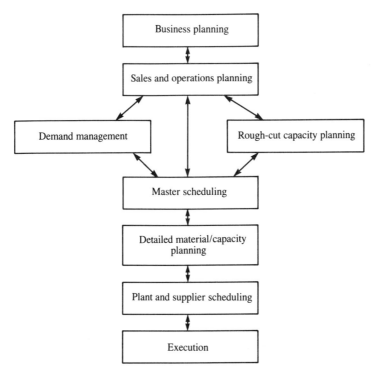

Figure 3.3   Manufacturing resource planning (MRPII) (Wight 1984)

the planners what should be done, and not what could be done. MRPII evolved to correct this by the addition of capacity requirements planning modules. These were available as extensions to MRP by the late 1960s.
- MRP was a tool solely for the use of production management and inventory management. MRPII evolved to address the need of other business functions to be involved in the manufacturing planning process, especially the financial planning function. In this way it could be ensured that different functions within a business all used the same sets of numbers for planning purposes.
- There was a prima facie case for systems integration. MRPII addressed this need by presenting a closed loop system.
- The evolution was made possible by additional computer power at lower cost in the late 1970s.
- The definitive version of MRPII evolved within IBM in the 1960s and was promoted in the 1980s as a standard system by the evangelists of MRPII in support of the APICS MRP crusade.
- MRPII has since become heavily promoted by both computer manufacturers and third-party software suppliers for commercial reasons.

3.2 MRPII in perspective

Whereas the original MRP can legitimately be regarded as a standard system, the textbook version of MRPII must be viewed more cautiously:

- Despite the claims of its promoters, it is primarily a systems technique, and not a standard.
- It is only one of several competing techniques.
- It is essentially a hierarchy of planning and control systems.
- At execution level, MRPII is becoming superseded by the kanban system of JIT. At the strategic and tactical level, MRPII is more compatible with, and can support, a JIT philosophy.
- It is primarily a decision-support tool, not a decision-making tool. In its principal planning modes it assumes infinite production capacity, disregards scheduling to finite capacity on the grounds that decision making must lie with the production planners, and leaves the balancing of demand and capacity to the planner or master scheduler.
- The standard MRPII technique is at its most appropriate within the OEM assemble-to-order manufacturing environment where it evolved. In other environments it may not be the most appropriate technique.
- MRPII evolved before the widespread understanding of state-of-the-art manufacturing strategy, such as JIT, and does not address many of the critical strategic manufacturing objectives.

– MRPII is a planning tool, not a strategy. Strategically its role is passive, rather than reactive or proactive. It accepts as user-defined parameters such fundamental items as leadtime, setup time and queue time, which a manufacturing strategy would seek to reduce.

All these points have major implications for potential MRPII users, depending on their manufacturing environment and the specific benefits they are seeking. Some of the more important points the reader should note are:

– There is a need to match the manufacturing planning system to the real-life manufacturing environment. This may necessitate a non-standard system or some variant from the textbook approach, especially where the manufacturing environment is far removed from MRPII's original environment.
– Many software packages support only the textbook approach of the MRPII standard system. Many users of these packages do not use all of the MRPII modules. Because of this, MRPII might possibly be regarded as a modular integrated computer system, comprising a standard core module (MRP) plus optional extras. This view would encompass many software packages not adhering to the standard system.
– The major concession by MRPII has been to interface with JIT by the *post facto* addition of a module supporting repetitive manufacturing.
– For many users in a jobbing environment, software packages that differ from textbook MRPII may be more accommodating, particularly those that allow system drivers other than the conventional MPS, and that cater for the non-homogeneity of product work content by transferring the balancing of demand and supply instead to the scheduling to finite capacity of process operations in discrete work centres.
– To maximize the benefits from MRPII, it becomes critical to understand the effect that underlying assumptions within MRPII may have on the end results, especially key parameters such as planning leadtime, queue time and move time.

3.3 The objectives of MRPII

The objectives of MRPII can be summed up as:

– respecting order priorities and delivery promises;
– providing decision support for capacity planning;
– scheduling the flow of materials;
– ensuring the accuracy of the database via closed loops;
– supporting differing planning horizons within a complex manufacturing environment.

3.4 What can we expect the MRPII system to achieve?

The key management issues surrounding the application of MRPII are addressed fully in Part Four, but an overview at this stage will help establish the context for that. The impact of MRPII on the following should be considered:

– inventories
– leadtimes
– delivery performance

In general, the impact of MRPII is quite limited in these areas, and attaining the performance levels associated with global competitiveness depends on much wider aspects of manufacturing strategy. This is amplified in Chapter 5, and again in Chapter 29. For the moment we will consider only the direct impact of MRPII, the planning tool.

Inventories

– *Finished inventories*: the level of finished inventory will generally be subject to the accuracy of forecasts, the level of safety stock, and/or the performance of distribution resource planning (DRP) systems rather than the MRPII system itself.
– *Materials inventories*: provided everything goes according to plan, then there will be no shortages and no excess stocks. The actual level of inventory will, however, depend on:
  the ordering system
  the lot-sizing method
  the level of safety stock
  the planning time buckets
  the frequency of planning
  the physical flow of materials.
– *Work in process*: inventory levels will mainly be determined by leadtime and queue parameters given to MRPII.

The reader is referred to Appendix C for a more detailed discussion of what drives inventory.

Leadtimes

Actual leadtimes will be determined by both the planning leadtime and queue parameters given to MRPII. A management objective of maximizing throughput will normally encourage planned queuing, and this will tend to increase leadtimes.

Delivery performance

Delivery performance will be determined by:

- The availability of materials. An MRP system will normally reduce the incidence of shortages.
- The availability of manufacturing capacity. This depends on decisions made by the production planner. The role of MRPII is confined to providing decision support to the planner.
- Order prioritization, which will be respected to differing extents by different MRPII software packages. This will be amplified in Chapters 17 and 21.

4

The manufacturing environment

Some very fundamental points made and substantiated by Bertrand *et al.* (1990) are these:

- Different manufacturing situations require different control systems.
- Different control systems require different information systems.
- The production management system is the key to the competitive manufacturing operation, and its choice may influence success or failure.

We will therefore review briefly the spectrum of those differing manufacturing situations to set the scene for Parts Two and Three of this book. The result will be that we identify major differences in the manufacturing environment, and these differences will have an important bearing on how well any particular systems technique or planning tool fits that particular environment.

4.1 Different manufacturing situations

A simplified spectrum of production processes is illustrated in Table 4.1. It is in the middle of this spectrum—discrete parts production—that manufacturing planning systems apply. Wight claimed that MRPII was universally applicable, and predicted (1984: 280) that MRPII would supersede project management systems. It has not happened, for the simple reason that what we generically accept as project management systems are better adapted as both information systems and control systems to the management of complex one-off engineering projects.

Table 4.1   Spectrum of production processes

Type of operation	Example	Management method
Continuous process	Oil refinery	Process management
Discrete parts production	Motor car	Production management
Complex one-off	Channel tunnel	Project management

Table 4.2   Discrete parts manufacture

Type of operation	Volume	Variety	Plant layout
Assembly line	High	Low	Product based
Repetitive manufacturing			Product based
Batch production			Process based
Jobbing shop	Low	High	Process based

Table 4.2 indicates the spectrum of discrete parts production. The manu-facturing planning system must fit the characteristics of these. Despite the claim of a standard system, it will be seen in Part Three that the MRPII stan-dard system is not always fully sympathetic to a jobbing type of business. It will also be noted that in repetitive manufacturing situations the standard-system foundation block of master scheduling is often discarded in favour of rate-based scheduling.

Browne *et al.* (1988) explain how the nature of the specific manufacturing environment is typically characterized by:

- the degree of process decoupling—any decoupling of processes implies inter-process inventories or queues of work ahead of each process;
- the degree of product orientation within the plant layout.

The implications of these are illustrated in Tables 4.3 and 4.4.

Table 4.3   Process decoupling

Degree of decoupling	High	Low
WIP inventory	High	Low
Control of WIP	Complex	Simpler
Production leadtime	Long	Short
Response to market	Low	Higher
Management task	Difficult	Easier

Table 4.4   Product orientation

Product orientation	High	Low
Product mix management	Difficult	Easier
New product introduction	Difficult	Easier
Labour skills needed	Lower	Higher
Labour flexibility	Higher	Lower
Management task	Easier	Difficult

4.2 Product structure

The complexity of the manufacturing process will be influenced by the product structure. Three broad categories can be recognized:

1. A standard product, specified and designed in company.
2. A standard product with customized features or options.
3. A customized product, typically specified and designed by or for a specific customer.

While wholly customized products are by far the most difficult to live with, much of the complexity of MRPII addresses the second of these—the standard product with customized options. This is also the scenario in which the full range of features of the MRPII standard system is most appropriate. It is also the manufacturing environment in which MRPII was conceived.

Just as important as the distinction between these three categories of products is the degree of homogeneity of work content between the products sharing a manufacturing resource. This is the main determinant of the form of scheduling needed. We can distinguish three situations:

– High homogeneity of work content, normally also in conjunction with stable high-volume production and minimal production leadtimes. In this case, rate-based scheduling will be preferable to the MRPII method of order-based master scheduling.
– Medium homogeneity of work content. The MRPII standard form of order-based master scheduling will be an appropriate technique in this instance.
– Low homogeneity of work content, typically associated with a jobbing shop, where a wide variety of subcontract work is carried out to unique customer specification, much of it with widely differing production routings and operation times. The result is a high contention between workload and capacity at individual work centres, which is not easily resolved by the conventional rough-cut capacity planning linked to master production scheduling. In this situation detailed scheduling to finite capacity, by operation and work centre, at least on bottleneck work centres, will normally be required, and may be the only feasible means of balancing supply and demand.

A further important distinction, of significance in determining the material flow systems and its supporting material planning systems, is between what Johnson (1991) described as runners, repeaters and strangers:

– *Runners*: the same product or key features manufactured regularly.
– *Repeaters*: the same product or key features manufactured periodically.
– *Strangers*: products or key features manufactured infrequently.

Table 4.5   Make to stock or make to order

	Make to stock	*Make to order*
Customer demand	Continuous	Discontinuous
	Predictable	Unpredictable
Product customization	Low	High
Customer delivery need	Short	Undemanding
Production leadtime	Long	Short

4.3 The production drivers

The fundamental distinction in terms of what drives production is between *make to stock* and *make to order*. Table 4.5 summarizes the key elements underlying this decision.

Make-to-stock environments may comprise two distinct elements:

– finished inventory in the manufacturing plant;
– distributed inventories in a distribution network.

Finished inventory is a mechanism for decoupling the satisfaction of customer service needs from what the production system is capable of achieving. Finished inventories have the advantage of adding stability to production plans, and are controlled either by MRP or by an order-point system driven by demand forecasting.

Distributed inventories are a means of reducing delivery leadtimes and increasing the level of customer service. They are controlled by either a distribution resource planning (DRP) system or an order-point system, which will normally also be driven by demand forecasting.

Most reference works on MRPII, and therefore many of the software packages, recognize three basic types of driver environment:

– make to stock
– assemble to order
– make to order

None of these three adequately addresses JIT which, upstream of final assembly, is more correctly a *make-to-replenish* situation. *Assemble to order* by definition relates to a standard product with customized options. Make to stock can also involve options or variants of a base product. Make to order is typically assumed, for example by Wight (1984), to apply to complex long leadtime products which are typically being designed as they are manufactured. That is more correctly *design to order*, while make to order is what most jobbing businesses do most of the time.

A more realistic set of production driver environments, and one that is typical of many software packages, would therefore be:

- make to stock
- assemble to order
- make to replenish
- make to order
- design to order

For all of these environments the standard MRPII system has as its driver the order-based master production schedule. Two alternative drivers that will be examined in later chapters are:

- rate-based scheduling
- direct drivers, such as sales or works order files

4.4 The production management task

The complexity or difficulty of the production management task is influenced by the following:

- the degree of product complexity;
- the degree of process decoupling;
- the degree of product orientation;
- the presence or absence of finished inventories;
- the stability of plans over a cumulative manufacturing leadtime.

The first four of these have been described as *four walls constraints* because they are mainly determined within the business.

Plan stability, on the other hand, is subject to external constraints and is likely to be influenced by:

- *Market-place dynamics*: for example, customer service expectations or the variability of demand.
- *Supplier performance*: for example, leadtimes, and delivery and quality performance.

These are constraints placed on the business from outside the four walls.

The task of production management is also set in the context of a fundamental shift in emphasis during the past three decades. The salient features of this are shown in Table 4.6. It is worth bearing in mind that MRPII systems essentially reflect the emphasis of the 1960s—the decade of their conception—rather than the 1990s.

Table 4.6   Change of manufacturing emphasis

	1960s	1990s
Philosophy	Production led	Market led
Techniques	Simple	Complex
Product range	Narrow	Wide
Tooling	Dedicated	Flexible
Fixed costs	Low	High
Labour costs	High	Low
Product life cycle	Long	Short
Competition	National	Global
Customers	Stable	Demanding
Inventory	Order point	Just-in-time
Pricing	Cost plus	Market driven

Source: *Industrial Technology* (March 1991)

4.5 The birthplace of MRPII

The manufacturing environment in which MRPII originated can best be summed up as one with the following characteristics:

– a demand-driven environment;
– batch production;
– relatively complex feature-dependent OEM products;
– a product-oriented plant layout,
– but with a high degree of process decoupling;
– a Western push philosophy.

4.6 Repetitive manufacturing

In contrast to MRPII's birthplace is the original environment of repetitive or continuous flow manufacturing as we know it today:

– a Japanese pull philosophy,
– which evolved from the JIT philosophy.

The more widespread adoption of a JIT philosophy has caused a migration towards continuous flow manufacturing from both automated assembly lines and batch production. This led *post facto* to the development of a repetitive manufacturing module within MRPII. MRPII as a planning tool supports continuous flow manufacturing but, as we shall see in Chapter 21, the methods of implementation vary greatly.

4.7 The jobbing shop

What Wight (1984) defined as a jobbing shop is a process-oriented plant layout. What we recognize in the UK as a jobbing shop is the make-to-order environment that works to customer specification and design. A jobbing shop has specific divergences from the textbook MRPII environment which must be carefully considered before selecting MRPII computer software:

- a lack of visibility of medium- to longer-term demand;
- typically an exclusively make-to-order environment;
- normally a high incidence of order-specific materials;
- a much greater contention between workload and capacity;
- priorities at operation level may not mirror priorities at end-product order-book level.

4.8 Manufacturing objectives

What are the objectives sought by manufacturing management today? A revealing insight is given by the comparison of American, European and Japanese manufacturing objectives compiled by the Boston University Manufacturing Round Table in 1988, and summarized in Table 4.7.

For UK readers, conscious of the need to seek and achieve global competitiveness, what is often problematical is which of the two dominant manufacturing cultures to emulate:

1. *The USA*: with a philosophy very frequently centred on maximizing productivity; or

Table 4.7   Comparison of US, European and Japanese manufacturing objectives

Rank	Europe	USA	Japan
1	Outgoing quality	Incoming quality	Manufacturing leadtime
2	Unit manufacturing costs	Inventory accuracy	Direct labour productivity
3	Unit material costs	Direct labour productivity	WIP turnover
4	Overhead costs	Manufacturing leadtime	Incoming quality
5	On-time delivery	Vendor leadtime	Vendor leadtime
6	Incoming quality	Setup times	Indirect staff productivity
7	Direct labour productivity	WIP turnover	Material yield
8	Material yield	Material yield	Finished inventory turnover
9	Unit labour costs	Outgoing quality	Inventory accuracy
10	Forecast accuracy	Indirect staff productivity	Absenteeism

Source: *Industrial Technology* (March 1991)

Table 4.8   Which objectives does MRPII address?

The goals of JIT	What does MRPII do?
Zero defects	Does not manage quality
Zero setup times	Accepts given setup times
Zero inventories	Manages the flow of materials
Zero handling	Accepts given move times
Zero breakdowns	Accepts given production efficiency
Zero leadtimes	Accepts given leadtimes
Lot size of ONE	Accepts given lot-sizing rules

2. *The Japanese*: with a JIT philosophy founded on the elimination of waste, and with an implicit intent to maximize a competitive marketing advantage.

The reader should bear in mind that MRPII originated in the USA. What is revealing is to look at the goals of JIT and to compare these to the role played by MRPII. Table 4.8 indicates only too clearly the difference between a manufacturing strategy (JIT) and a planning system (MRPII).

4.9 Major constraints on the production management system

Despite the wide diversity of manufacturing environments there are certain elements in common. These common constraints within which a production management system must work are:

- *Demand*: the known or forecast demand from which a production plan or MPS is derived, and which in turn drives the other modules of the MRPII system.
- *Material availability*: having all component parts available to satisfy that demand. This includes parts made in plant as well as parts sourced on external suppliers. This is the role of MRP.
- *Capacity*: having sufficient capacity to make both the end product and also lower-level parts made in plant. This is supported by CRP.

Demand

The major constraints of demand are:

- the end product to be made;
- the quantity to be made;
- the due date of each order for the end product.

Production

The major constraints on making the product are:

– product technology—the lower level or component parts or materials content of the end product
– process technology—the manufacturing operations involved in converting the component parts or materials into the end product. This is also the value-adding process;
– production capacity.

These are the basics at the heart of the manufacturing equation. How they are welded together by a system to address the key variables of the manufacturing environment is what determines whether or not that system has a fit with the manufacturing environment. To recap, the major divergences are:

– whether the products being manufactured are runners, repeaters or strangers;
– whether scheduling is rate-based or order-based, and in the case of order-based scheduling whether the system is driven by a conventional master schedule or an alternative driver;
– the degree of customer options or feature dependency in the product structure;
– the presence or absence of finished inventories;
– whether or not a JIT kanban system is in use;
– at the other end of the spectrum, to what extent the many problems associated with a jobbing shop environment have to be addressed.

5
Manufacturing strategy

In this chapter we examine first why MRPII is *not* itself a manufacturing strategy, then we will consider the process by which a manufacturing strategy is developed. The classical approach to strategic planning is described, as is the newer technique of benchmarking. The chapter concludes by reviewing the principal features of modern competitive manufacturing strategies and the key attributes of world-class manufacturing status.

5.1 Why MRPII is not a manufacturing strategy

The point has already been made in Chapter 4 that the real benefits in terms of manufacturing performance accrue from the wider manufacturing strategy, and not from the more confined realm of the manufacturing planning system. When MRPII systems first developed in the 1960s the manufacturing environment was more complex, less flexible and less lean than today, and a system to control those complex environments was without doubt a strategic necessity.

Without such a system there was no practical means of managing inventory and production throughput. As computer systems became more complex, and more costly, the financial justification for their implementation switched from the direct benefits of savings in people costs to the indirect benefits of savings in inventory carrying costs. This subsequently became the cardinal selling point of MRPII, especially as interest rates escalated, and is exemplified by the typical gains quoted by Wight (1984: 69ff) when analysing the impact of MRPII on productivity.

Despite the many documented success stories, there are just as many instances where the benefits accruing from MRPII have failed to live up to expectation. What the reader must note is that the claims made on behalf of MRPII as a tool for enabling inventory reductions are not borne out by simple a priori reasoning.

Appendix C applies a priori reasoning to the question of what drives inventory and leadtimes, seeking to establish the most direct link between cause and effect. What is clear from that analysis is that almost all of the factors actually driving inventory levels, manufacturing leadtime and delivery performance are user-given parameters in an MRPII system, and that the direct influence of the system itself is minimal.

In its most elemental form, inventory level is a function of demand over leadtime. For different levels of demand, what therefore *primarily* determines the level of inventory is the leadtime, particularly the manufacturing leadtime. Within MRPII, leadtime is a user-given system parameter. The real driving force behind inventory level is clearly the factor or factors determining that leadtime, and not the system using that predetermined leadtime parameter.

The point is made very succinctly by Ralston and Reddy (1993):

> MRPII, like any other package, is not endowed with magical powers. It does not, by itself, reduce leadtime, nor does it tell you how to cut them. The only way to reduce leadtime—is to reduce leadtime. The world-class MRP expert knows that by tackling the leadtime issues, he solves most of his problems.

The solution to the leadtime issue is twofold:

1. Simplify bills of materials.
2. Eliminate all wasted and non-value-adding activities.

These arguments support the comparison between JIT and MRPII given in Table 4.8, and lead to a number of very basic conclusions:

- Achieving a competitive manufacturing advantage depends on manufacturing strategy, and not on the planning system.
- The manufacturing strategy must therefore be addressed *before* the manufacturing planning system is put in place.
- The manufacturing planning system must be supportive of whatever wider manufacturing strategy is adopted.
- The selection of the most appropriate manufacturing planning system should not be constrained by any perception of a universally applicable standard system.

5.2 The strategic planning process

Planning a competitive manufacturing strategy cannot be done in isolation. It is part and parcel of the much wider strategic planning process for the entire business. The manufacturing operation exists to satisfy customer demand. Correctly planned and operated, it will be a major contributor to customer satisfaction or delight.

But what causes customers to buy in the first place will depend on whether or not the company's products or services address the needs of the marketplace, and whether they offer product or service benefits to the market at a price commensurate with the perceived worth of these benefits, taking account of the alternative or competitive products on the market.

The strategic planning process is founded, therefore, on an understanding of the market and of the company's position in that market. In many instances there will not be a single market; there will instead be several discrete product markets that the company is competing in, each with different market needs, different customer expectations and different competitors, depending on the product group or product family.

The manufacturing operation is key to a competitive advantage, and its strengths and weaknesses will to a very large extent be constraints on how the company may exploit or develop its market position. To attain a viable market position, on the other hand, may often require fundamental changes to the manufacturing operation. There is therefore a proactive interrelationship between marketing strategy and manufacturing strategy. In the end, however, the manufacturing strategy exists to support the company's chosen marketing strategy, and not vice versa.

The process of fact finding and analysis behind the classical approach to strategic planning is by now well documented and understood, and comprises a number of key steps:

- Identifying the key criteria that will determine whether or not the company occupies a competitive market position. These may differ depending on specific product/markets.
- Assessing how well or how badly the company's actual performance matches these criteria.
- Identifying the areas where substantial improvement or change is required in order to satisfy the criteria of competitiveness. The major objective of the planning process will be to attain excellence in all areas, but with a focus on those areas where performance is critical but presently weak.
- Analysing the alternative options for change or improvement, and selecting the best combination. These will become the key elements of the strategic plan.
- Implementing the plan and monitoring its outcomes.

In undertaking this process, the spotlight will fall not only on the manufacturing operation, but also on other functions within the company, and particularly on product design and development, quality assurance, marketing, distribution, and after-sales service. The chosen manufacturing strategy will therefore be a subset of a whole strategic plan embracing the entire business.

A workable guide to the strategic planning process, with emphasis on the manufacturing operation, may be found in the DTI publication, *Competitive Manufacturing*. By completing the seven fairly simple worksheets listed in Table 5.1, as the analysis and planning process is described, the reader with no experience of what can be a complex task should be able to arrive at a sound and logically based plan for the future. The overall logic of the planning process is indicated in Figure 5.1.

Table 5.1 Strategic planning worksheets

1. Profiles of market requirements and achieved performance	Juxtaposition of the two identifies areas of weakness
2. Basic information by product family	Relative contribution; market share; growth/vulnerability; product life cycle
3. Competitive edge by product family	In terms of features, quality, delivery, flexibility, and price
4. Current performance by product family	Also in terms of features, quality, delivery, flexibility, and price
5. External opportunities and threats	
6. Assessment of the current manufacturing strategy	Facilities, capacity, span of process, process technology, human resources, quality, control systems, suppliers, product development
	Ranked in terms of detrimental to or supportive of competitive performance
7. Identifying policy areas needing change or improvement and identifying possible strategic options	

5.3 Benchmarking

An alternative technique for developing business or manufacturing strategy is that of *benchmarking*, a technique that has been steadily growing in use from the early 1980s onwards. The technique centres on the identification and implementation of industry best practice, with an emphasis thereafter of aiming to maintain continuous improvement at a pace that outstrips the competition.

The main advantage of benchmarking is that it forces a direct comparison between the company and the industry leaders, as distinct from the largely inward-looking assessment that takes place with the classical approach to strategic planning described in Figure 5.1. The technique is applicable to most functional areas within a business, and not solely to manufacturing.

The key steps in the process of benchmarking are:

1. Identify the processes and their possible measures of performance. For example, within a small manufacturing operation these could be as shown in Table 5.2.
2. Collect comparative performance measures. Establish the company's own measures, and obtain comparative external data. The external data must relate to direct competitors. This is unlikely to be given voluntarily by competitors, and may therefore have to be sought from a combination of

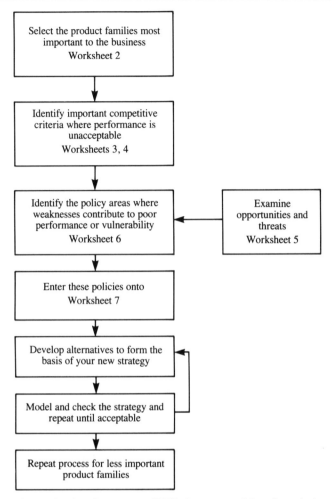

Figure 5.1 Strategic planning process (DTI, *Competitive Manufacturing*)

Table 5.2 Benchmarking process and performance measures

Process	Possible measures
Customer quotation	Response time
Pre-production	Leadtime
Material supply	Inventory level, material cost of sales
Manufacturing	Leadtime, WIP inventory, delivery reliability
	Internal reject rate, customer return rate

data in the public domain (for example, company accounts or published intercompany comparisons), and/or from suppliers, former employees, or customer surveys. From analysis of this data there will emerge a picture of where performance gaps exist, and how big a gap in performance currently exists, between the company and the industry leaders.

3. Identify and implement strategies to close the gap. This comes from identifying, and where possible improving on, established best practice. As direct competitors are unlikely to cooperate, the best approach is to seek the partnership of dissimilar companies, or other companies using similar core-process technologies but competing with different products and in different markets. Benchmarking is not just about copying industry best practice, it is about seeking to improve on the best that exists. The ability to be sufficiently innovative is therefore of key importance in attaining a step improvement in performance.

In companies where historical performance has been poor, benchmarking is more likely than more classical methods to lead to a winning strategy. In such cases a sea change in performance is normally required in order to gain a competitive position for future survival. This implies both a willingness and the resources to make the change possible. The change will be of only temporary benefit unless management subsequently focuses on a culture of never-ending improvement.

Business process re-engineering

A technique increasingly utilized in conjunction with benchmarking is that of *business process re-engineering*. It has much in common with what used to be the province of the organization and methods specialist, but has acquired a new aura as a result of becoming widely applied at a strategic level.

In essence, business process re-engineering addresses an objective but radical rethinking of the company's business processes. As an enabler of the business process, information technology (IT) normally features prominently, often leading to downsizing and decentralization of the IT facility. The technique is being applied to three types of problem-solving situations:

- companies faced with the need for substantial cost reductions, or business downsizing;
- companies faced with the prospect of external change over the forward horizon;
- companies in a strong present position, but who wish to strengthen their competitive position.

The practitioners of the technique emphasize, just as the former organization and methods (O&M) specialists did, that staff reductions are not the only goal: improvements in competitiveness are also sought, and these will lead to business growth and enhanced employment opportunities.

5.4 Competitive manufacturing strategies

Both benchmarking and the conventional strategic planning process are essentially analytical techniques. They help focus on where substantial improvement is required. Once options for change or improvement have been identified they can be evaluated by conventional financial planning techniques based on payback period and/or discounted future value formulae, while taking due account at the same time of the probability of success or risk of failure. What the planning techniques cannot themselves identify is that vital part in the middle—what the options for change, the actual elements of a future manufacturing strategy, should be. This is where knowledge or experience of best practice, combined with innovative ideas and a vision of how the business and its manufacturing base should be developed, becomes all-important. It is the difference between real understanding, vision and innovation on the one hand, and the focus on the management process, the heart of modern management education and training, on the other.

The most profitable sources of help at this stage will be: ˜

- companies in similar product/markets, but competing in sufficiently removed geographical markets;
- companies utilizing a similar process technology, but competing in different product/markets. The fortunate reader may well be able to identify supply chain partners—customers as well as suppliers—whose technology has sufficient similarity to be a useful source of established good practice.

The method is extremely simple—go and visit them, learn from their example, and then brainstorm until a leap forward can be found. That is the difficult part.

The concluding part of this chapter sets out some of the key features of competitive manufacturing strategies which have been adopted over the past decade. Such a list cannot be totally comprehensive, and the reader is urged to gain firsthand exposure to industry best practice and to use it to supplement the growing volume of published material on the subject.

The key strategies leading to a competitive manufacturing position will include:

- JIT
- synergy between marketing and manufacturing
- synergy between product development and manufacturing
- CIM
- focused manufacturing units

- control systems
- competitive process technologies
- supply chain partnership
- highly skilled flexible employees
- total quality management
- leadtime reduction

JIT

The Japanese concept of JIT is almost an overarching strategy, encompassing within itself many of the other strategies in our list. The fundamental distinction between the JIT philosophy—focused on the elimination of waste in all its forms—and the JIT kanban system is enlarged upon in Chapter 21, and the more specific use of the kanban system more properly falls within the subject of control systems (page 40). One of the most important aspects of a JIT approach is the impact it will have on leadtimes, and this is critical to a competitive manufacturing strategy. This brief overview of manufacturing strategies therefore concludes by returning to this theme of leadtime reduction (page 47).

Synergy between marketing and manufacturing

The most destructive clash within a business will exist when top management fails to bring about total synergy between the needs of marketing and the needs of manufacturing. The seeds of conflict lie in the diametrically opposed needs of the two functions:

- The needs of marketing are founded on what is desirable: what the customer wants and expects in terms of product delivery and, as every production planning manager knows only too well, this rarely occurs in the form of equal quantities of a product over successive time periods.
- The needs of manufacturing are founded on what is feasible. Production resources are relatively fixed and finite, and cannot easily be increased at short notice to cater for a rapidly growing customer demand pattern. A falling demand pattern causes fewer logistical problems, but leads instead to the pest factor of adverse variances in the recovery of fixed overhead costs, a scenario less stressful but no more comforting.

Of the many ways in which this conflict can be reduced the key ones will be:

- Better market knowledge and better knowledge of key customers' future plans will assist demand forecasting, and will bring increased stability to a forward production plan.

- Even better, becoming part of customers' supply chain partnerships should lead to single sourcing and forward delivery schedules, with a much greater degree of commitment from the customer to accept deliveries according to the agreed schedules.
- Redesigning product structures, so that individually customized product specifications are replaced by semi-standard products with customized features, will make demand more forecastable and therefore more stable. The Quantel case study (Chapter 16) illustrates how great the benefits of this can be.
- Reducing the manufacturing leadtime will do more than anything to eliminate conflict. As leadtimes decrease the operation's flexibility increases. This topic is addressed in greater detail later in this chapter (page 47).
- Formal sales and operations planning will result in an agreed plan to which both function become committed. It will be more likely to succeed if all or most of the previous strategies have first been implemented. It is significant that between the original depiction of the MRPII closed loop system and the version published in Wight (1984), the production planning module had become renamed sales and operations planning. This was indicative of a move by the early 1980s towards healing the long-standing rift between marketing and manufacturing.

Synergy between product development and manufacturing

In the beginning product design was undertaken in isolation from production engineering. Product structures were seemingly complex, and many of the features of MRPII systems reflect this early complexity. Very often, products coming from design engineering had to be redesigned by production engineers for build or assembly purposes, and there was enormous scope for error as data passed along the chain from designer to production engineer and onwards to the materials and production planners.

The strategies which overcome such problems include the following:

- *Quality function deployment* (*QFD*): a systematic process whereby marketplace reaction to the company's and its competitors' products is collected and analysed, and then used as the basis for establishing the technical specification of new products or product enhancements.
- *Simultaneous engineering*: a major objective of which is to reduce product development leadtimes—the 'time to market'. Product design is organized around the manufacturing process, involving all relevant company functions such as marketing, product design, production engineering, quality assurance, etc. This is as opposed to sequential engineering, where the product in its various stages from concept through design to production bills of materials and routings was shunted in sequence from department to

department, through what has been described as a series of management silos. The concept of supply chain partnership implies that suppliers be involved in the design process from a very early stage.

The 'time to market' concept of simultaneous engineering is now being extended to other areas of the organization, on the simple but basic premise that time is money. This is now known as *time-based competition*, and embraces within its scope savings in time of a more general nature, including time saved from inventory, time reductions in distribution chains, and time saved in administration tasks.

– *Design for assembly (DFA), or design for manufacture and assembly (DFMA)*: a design concept in which typically one designer will design the product using computer-aided design (CAD) technology and then move to an adjacent workstation and design the manufacturing process using computer-aided manufacturing (CAM) technology. The emphasis in this concept is on four primary aspects:

establishing single-level bills of materials

reducing the number of parts

making them easier to handle

making them easier to fit or to fix

Single-level bills of materials are a key feature in making MRP more manageable, particularly when adopted in conjunction with work cells and a distributed form of MRP.

– *Engineering data management (EDM)*: powerful software programs have been developed to monitor and control data generated in an engineering project. This includes automated links between CAD systems and the bill of materials module of an MRP system. Inaccurate bills of materials are frequently cited as a reason for failure of MRPII systems. More importantly they are primary causes of products not conforming to specification. Capturing data at source in this way helps eliminate both data errors and the resulting quality loss.

Computer-integrated manufacturing (CIM)

The vision offered by CIM is of the factory of the future, where the application of computer technology will lead to the integration of all processes from design to despatch. Its scope, if achieved, would place it alongside JIT as one of a limited number of overarching strategies.

In describing CIM, Browne *et al.* (1988) pointed out that recent historical application of computer methods had led to 'islands of automation' and that CIM is concerned with the integration of these islands of automation. The truth is that the concept of CIM is currently at the stage of interfacing systems which were developed independently of each other.

Browne *et al.* also note a divergence between design engineering's concept of CIM and that of manufacturing management. The scope of CIM as seen from the design engineering viewpoint encompasses product design, manufacturing process planning and product test programmes, leading to the downloading of the programme to the manufacturing function. By contrast, manufacturing management regards CIM as a process that integrates manufacture, assembly, testing and despatch. There is therefore still a fundamental gulf to be bridged before CIM evolves from simply being a concept to becoming the reality.

Focused manufacturing units

The historic approach to planning a manufacturing facility was to organize it by process. Different products moved through a maze of discrete work centres, and the total leadtime through the system was typically 20 times the technological leadtime, the time that value-adding work was being performed. The differences—queue times and move times—were, and are, a prime source of quality loss.

The strategies that lead to simplification and greater flexibility, and to an overall leadtime reduction and quality gain are firstly: the subcontracting out of all processes that are not critical to end-product integrity. In many cases the result may be to concentrate on final assembly only, or even—in the case of niche products—the customization of a bought-in product made in high volume at a low cost by a supplier to a mass market. One example of the latter is the modification of a domestic refrigerator for use in hospital blood banks, an operation that modifies rather than manufactures, but that results in a very considerable amount of value added as more advanced technology is applied in order to achieve an altogether different level of product performance.

A second strategy is to create, with the remaining processes, focused departments. These focused departments will be oriented towards producing a family of parts, in which the rate of production of the discrete processes within the department will be balanced towards a uniform throughput rate. Three distinct concepts have evolved over time:

1. *Group technology*: which focused on families of geometrically similar parts.
2. *Flexible manufacturing system* (*FMS*): which added the element of computer control to group technology.
3. *Cellular manufacturing*: in which production equipment, materials handling equipment and computer control were integrated.

By applying the concept of cellular manufacturing it becomes possible to conceive of the complete factory as a series of mini-factories, each accepting orders and producing and delivering to its immediate upstream work cell or customer. Management may be devolved, and in turn the control systems can become devolved, with significant gains in simplification and flexibility. The application of distributed MRPII (DMRP) systems to such an environment is described in Chapter 24.

Within the physical layout or grouping together of focused departments in a factory there are some basic objectives:

- The product should physically move the shortest possible distance through the factory, and this covers the total route of travel from goods inwards, through the focused departments, to end-product despatch.
- Wherever possible it should travel in a straight line between work cells, although there may be distinct advantages in adopting a U-shaped flow within each work cell.
- The logistics chain should be simplified by eliminating as much as possible of the materials handling associated with receiving, storage, inspection and despatch. Packing and despatch should become an end-of-line function, not a separate function to which goods have to be moved.
- Wherever possible the transfer from one department to another should be automated. For many decades UK industry focused on the core process and ignored materials handling, and this was a major shortcoming relative to competing national economies in the 1970s and early 1980s.

Control system

Part of the control system is, of course, the manufacturing planning system—the subject of this book. The conventional approach would typically be to offer MRPII, the JIT kanban system, and a selection of other methodologies as alternative strategies. The real issue, however, is much more fundamental than that, and centres on the clash of cultures identified in Chapter 4 between:

- the drive to maximize productivity as an objective *per se*;
- the drive to eliminate waste—the JIT philosophy, which both directly and indirectly enhances productivity.

Much emphasis has been placed on the role that material handling and tracking systems occupy in a manufacturing strategy, and handling and tracking are frequently bracketed in this way to imply a single strategy. The case can be made that material tracking systems are a feature of environments seeking to maximize productivity, in which the classical MRPII type of system will be used, and in which reliable material tracking systems are therefore vital to the integrity of the MRPII system itself. The reader should note that the kanban system is largely a paperless system (see Chapter 21), and may therefore question the importance of material tracking systems as a prima facie element of manufacturing strategy.

Johnson (1991) offers pertinent advice, depending on whether the products being made are runners, repeaters or strangers (see Chapter 4). Of runners or repeaters, he says: 'A [work] cell which predominantly contains runners and repeaters is eminently suitable for the application of kanban for materials flow control. This requires a demand to final assembly [schedule] and MRP style procurement'. This combination of kanban and MRP leads to simplification when compared to MRPII.

Of strangers, he comments: 'When the percentage of strangers is so high that kanban cannot be used, advantage can be taken of the cellular product units to treat them as small "factories" which each have their own order book.' In this case Johnson advocates the use of a distributed or DMRP type of control system.

Competitive process technologies

Despite the enormous variety of process technologies from one industry to another, many of the key elements of manufacturing competitiveness are inherent within the process itself, whether these be:

- technological leadtime
- process cost
- quality loss (or process scrap)

Minimizing all three is the key to a competitive manufacturing strategy, and should form the objectives against which choices of process technology are evaluated.

There are a number of salient points to note in this context:

- Depending on production batch sizes, reducing the setup element of the technological leadtime may be more important than the actual production element.
- The key to reducing setup time is to distinguish between the elements of setup which are inherently *internal* within the process, and those which are external. Production engineering solutions should be capable of divorcing the two, so that external elements do not indent on process or machine time.
- Statistical techniques such as *process failure modes and effect analysis* (PFMEA) exist to determine the basic capability of a process to perform within specific tolerance limits, and *statistical process control* (SPC) techniques may be used to monitor that the process in operation is performing within these control limits. These are the best tested strategies for controlling and reducing quality loss (or scrap costs).

- The human operator has an inherently low basic process capability. Where existing processes are manual or semi-automated, automating these can lead to very significant improvements in process capability, and in turn to a reduction in quality loss (or scrap costs).
- Computer-assisted manufacturing (CAM)—by removing the setup and control of a process, as opposed to simply the operation itself, from the random element of operator performance, the basic process capability will be further improved.
- The principle of self-inspection is in turn an integral part of the company's quality culture. In parallel with this should be the incorporation of in-line product testing to avoid the need for subsequent inspection and test.

Supply chain partnership

In reality the supply chain extends from the manufacturer of original equipment or consumer products, right back to the manufacturers of all component parts and raw materials used to make such products. For most businesses, therefore, the total supply chain encompasses not only its suppliers, but also its customers. The fundamental difference between relationships based on partnership and the historic norm are illustrated in Table 5.3.

Table 5.3 Supplier relationships in the 1990s

| *Supplier relationships in the 1990s* | |
will be based on	*and not on*
Partnership	Conflict
Mutual trust	Mutual suspicion
Single sourcing of families of parts	Multiple sourcing of individual parts
Visibility of the future	Ignorance of the future
Sharing information	The mushroom syndrome[†]
Design involvement	A purely commercial relationship
Forward schedules	*Ad hoc* orders
Local suppliers	Lowest price suppliers
Electronic data interchange	Communication by post
Supplier quality assurance	Incoming inspection
Inspection by the supplier	100% inspection in goods receiving
Daily deliveries	*Ad hoc* deliveries
Direct line feed	Delivery to goods inwards
High performance	Take it or leave it
Flexibility	Inflexibility
Demand led	Production led

[†] Being kept in the dark and covered with fertilizer.

The benefits of supply chain partnership accrue both on the supply side and on the demand side. On the supply side the benefits are improved quality and a more reliable delivery performance. On the demand side the primary benefit is an improved and more stable visibility of demand.

The practice of supply chain partnership in the context of MRP systems is discussed in Chapter 10.

Highly skilled flexible employees

People are the key to any business, and for people to perform effectively and efficiently they must be well led and well motivated. Above all they must have, must acquire or must be given the skills needed to carry out their job of work. The level of skills training has a direct impact on a person's ability to perform a task correctly every time, and this in turn directly affects both quality and productivity.

In the UK the level of skill training over the past century or so has not only fallen far behind its international competitors, but has historically been concentrated into specific skills acquired for life. Manufacturing flexibility depends on a multi-skilled workforce, free from restrictive practices, so that people can be moved from one workstation to another depending on the prevailing workload on different machines or in different focused departments. Above all, the possession of multiple skills is crucial to the concepts of group technology and cellular manufacturing, where the correct balancing of the cell may require one operator to perform more than one process.

One example worthy of note is the Production Employee Programme (PEP) of IBM Greenock, described by McKenzie (1991):

> The programme moves away from many workers doing one job, machines always busy, complex controls and high engineering involvement, to one where workers are trained to do a number of different jobs, take responsibility and ownership of quality . . . and only build to requirement.

With 2500 employees the plant spending on education and training in 1989 was £2.5 million, an average of £1000 per employee per annum.

Investment in skills training affects both productivity and quality, and is therefore a key manufacturing strategy. In the case of IBM Greenock, the benefits cited by McKenzie (1991) as accruing from their programme were:

- output increased by 76 per cent
- inventory turnover improved by 230 per cent
- productivity increased by 105 per cent

Among the tools more generally available to address a skills training strategy are these:

- *Investors in People*: a UK standard that defines a system for the systematic and ongoing identification of skills needed in the business, the skills possessed by individual employees, and the planning, implementation and monitoring of training plans for individuals to meet the company and individual skill needs. A case study of the successful combination of MRPII and Investors in People is reported in Chapter 28.
- *Lifelong learning*: a parallel concept that is encapsulated in the National Education and Training Targets, which were conceived jointly by industry, trade unions and government. This encourages individuals to accept that the process of learning does not end with their statutory education.
- *National Vocational Qualifications* (*NVQs*): a national qualification system, which ensures ready comparability of the level of competence possessed by individuals in specific skill areas.
- *Management Charter Initiative* (*MCI*): which is developing occupational skill standards for general managers. One of these emerging standards is directly relevant to management of the manufacturing planning function, and is the responsibility of the Purchasing and Supply Lead Body.
- *Accreditation of Prior Learning* (*APL*): a means that may be used by employers to enable individuals to gain all or parts of an NVQ by qualification of work experience, as opposed to formal training. For individuals not possessing formal qualifications this may then serve as a basis for the objective assessment of their skill level.

In addition to investment in skills training, a management culture that focuses on team-based organization and workforce empowerment contributes to flexibility and to the acceptance of responsibility, which in turn leads to improvements associated with a total quality culture. In a manufacturing context these both support, and are supported by, the introduction of work cells and a distributed form of manufacturing planning (see Chapter 24).

Total quality management (TQM)

For several years TQM has been the fashionable buzzword. What may be especially relevant to readers is the perception that systems such as MRPII are more easily implemented in organizations that have already espoused the practice of TQM. Luscombe (1993) makes the recommendation to implement TQM first before proceeding to MRPII.

The earliest quality concepts and systems were focused on product quality. The ethos of TQM is founded on two concepts:

1. Acceptance of the need for continuous improvement—what the Japanese know as *kaizen*. From this has stemmed the popular misconception that

TQM is therefore unattainable, because as we move towards it the strive for continuous improvement should be moving the goalposts further and further all the time.

2. Striving towards excellence in *every* aspect of the business operation, including internal and external relationships, as well as the more tangible aspect of product or service quality.

The process of implementing TQM typically follows four distinct phases, and is documented by Nicholls (1993). The four phases he identifies are:

– *Conformance to specification*: the emphasis is on quality assurance systems such as BS 5750. In this phase the systems tend to focus on the contractual obligation to the customer, with the contract review requirements of BS 5750 forming the cornerstone.

– *Fitness for purpose*: this involves the whole organization in error-free work, and embodying the well-proven focus on getting it right, first time, every time, and on time. The focus in some respects has shifted from the purely contractual to the much wider context of product liability, for example.

– *What customers want*: the emphasis moves more and more to that of customer satisfaction, going beyond the purely contractual or legal obligations. All functions within the business must become integrated, in a way that allows them to focus on the customers' needs. In the process, emphasis is placed not only on the external customer, but also on the 'internal' customer and on the supply chain partnership.

– *Value to the customer*: in the fourth stage the focus is on customer *delight*, as opposed to just satisfaction, a process which Nicholls describes as 'engaging everyone in the competitive delivery of value to the customer'. The wide-ranging scope of this final phase of TQM is summed up in Nicholls' description of the evolution of TQM within Ford Motor Co: 'you must constantly strive to do a better job for the people who receive the work you do, whether they are inside or outside the company'.

In a mission such as this, human resource development is of paramount importance. A corporate culture of striving towards excellence is a *sine qua non*, and this in turn implies management vision, leadership, and the motivation of a highly skilled and highly trained workforce, all striving in unison towards the corporate goal of excellence.

Apart from benefiting from the quite extensive published work on the subject, the reader should note that the most certain recipes for success are:

– learning and adopting the best practice of industry leaders;
– communicating the goals clearly, leading by example, and so motivating the entire workforce to learn by example and derive both pride and satisfaction by so doing.

At the centre of a TQM strategy will be the elimination of quality loss, and this involves a concerted attack on four areas where quality loss may originate:

1. In product design, where the design has to be right first time.
2. At the source of supply of raw materials and component parts, where external suppliers must have the capability of delivering 100 per cent good product every time.
3. In process, where the process capability must be established and then operate under controlled conditions.
4. In the people, where the responsibility for quality must be accepted by those performing the work.

The essential strategies leading towards TQM are themselves encapsulated in a series of standards or concepts:

– *Just-in-time*: the central JIT philosophy, as opposed to the more widely observed kanban system, concentrates on the elimination of waste in all its aspects. In a manufacturing operation there is an extremely high level of synergy not only between JIT and TQM, but between JIT and a winning manufacturing strategy itself. JIT has proven over more than two decades to be capable of sustaining a management and company culture in sympathy with the objectives of TQM, in a way that the remaining list of standards (below) has not as yet succeeded in attaining.
– *BS 7850*: the total quality management standard, first published in 1992. It is too early to assess BS 7850 objectively. In its present form it appears overly superficial and appears to fall very far short of the TQM standards of industry leaders; it falls far short, for example, of the Q.1 standard of Ford Motor Company.

Unlike the other standards listed here it is not intended that companies should become accredited to BS 7850; it is quite simply a set of guidelines. BS 7850 therefore may or may not become the overarching standard welding together, as it seeks to do, the list that follows.

– *ISO 9000*: an international standard defining a quality assurance system applicable to the manufacture of a product or the delivery of a service. It is identical to BS 5750 (the British standard) and EN 29000 (the European standard). The standard is onerous for very small companies, and the British Standards Institute have appointed (in 1993) a committee to consider how the standard should be applied to small businesses.
– *BS 7750*: a standard for environmental management systems. Although this standard defines the green environmental management policy demanded by 1990s legislation, its relevance to the reduction in waste management and energy costs should not be overlooked.

– *Investors in People*: a UK standard relating to human resource development, correctly perceived in BS 7850 as being a keystone of TQM.

All of these standards are relatively recent and they gain widespread acceptance only very slowly. After more than a decade, less than 20 000 companies in the UK had been accredited to BS 5750 by 1992, although the number of accreditations from now on is likely to grow by that amount year on year. Accreditations to the Investors in People standard were still newsworthy early in 1993, and the very first accreditation to BS 7750 was under dispute at the time of writing.

The reader should recognize that very often the lead in implementation and accreditation is taken by large companies, who in turn sooner or later demand that their subcontractors, however small, must also gain accreditation. The perceived expectation of major customers will therefore be vital when considering the company strategy. Pre-empting such customer pressure, and acting sooner, can yield both a marketing advantage and internal cost and quality benefits. Very often, postponing action until customer pressure builds up leads simply to cosmetic adherence to the standard for defensive reasons, rather than to genuine benefits for the business.

The essence of TQM is encapsulated in the good practice of many organizations. One example is that of Eli Lilly & Co. Ltd of Basingstoke, for which the company vision is described as follows: 'Recognition as a centre for excellence for: manufacturing, employment, and supply. Where quality is a way of life' (Gough, 1992). The company's TQM strategy is founded on four key managing principles:

– never-ending improvement
– the total elimination of waste
– total employee involvement
– a positive work environment

Leadtime reduction

The key to leadtime reduction is given by Ralston and Reddy (1993). There are two key elements:

1. Simplify the bills of materials. The key to simplification is to reduce the number of levels in the product structure, and where possible to subcontract entire subassemblies. This is also a core concept of DMRP, which is described in Chapter 24. Ralston and Reddy also recommend the adoption of an options and variants product structure as a high priority, and the benefits of this are demonstrated by the Quantel case study in Chapter 16.

2. Eliminate all wasted non-value-adding activity. This is the core principle of JIT. Ralston and Reddy identify six areas where attention must be focused: logistics, production, quality, suppliers, design, and shipping and distribution. The key actions they recommend have already been noted earlier in this appraisal of manufacturing strategies.

A two-stage plan for leadtime reduction is identified by Ralston and Reddy as follows.

STAGE ONE

- Establish work cells at subassembly levels; this will normally eliminate three levels in the manufacturing process.
- Establish direct line feed to the work cells for all manufactured components or subassemblies. This implies the elimination of kitting lists for these parts.
- Use a kanban system to pull components and subassemblies into the work cell, in line with the needs of the final assembly schedule.
- Establish the principle of self-inspection at each operation in the work cell. This must be preceded by training of the operators in quality methods.
- Establish in-line product testing in the work cell. This is crucial to the guarantee that downstream cells receive 100 per cent good parts.

STAGE TWO

- Eliminate all planning or safety buffers included in the MRPII system.
- Integrate final assembly into the work cell.
- Establish direct line feed by key suppliers.
- Move to rate-based scheduling, based on a smoothing of demand.
- Move to a lot-for-lot ordering policy, and use kanbans to pull all materials forward into the work cells.

5.5 World-class manufacturing

The concerted application of all of these manufacturing strategies enumerated should, if coupled with a significant element of innovation, lead to what has become known as world-class manufacturing status. The joint DTI/CBI report, *Innovation: The Best Practice* (1993) reminds us that the UK ranks only number 13 out of 22 OECD countries in terms of the world competitiveness scoreboard. Among the messages conveyed by this report are these:

- Successful companies accept change.
- They regard change as an opportunity.
- They foster a culture which supports innovation.

- They focus on managed risk taking as a complement to innovation.
- They develop the business process to implement the culture of innovation.
- These business processes are both sensitive to and supportive of external influences, including their customers.

Merke (1993) identifies more specifically what makes a world-class manufacturer:

- Product technology that combines high performance with a competitive price.
- A clear focus on the company's internal strengths.
- Exploitation of economies of scale, and Merke counsels manufacturing companies *not* to confuse this with the production lot size.
- Economies of scope, which are the application of the same technology in more than one product area.
- Becoming technologically advanced. In world-class companies, research and development (R&D) has a high priority.
- Belonging to international or even global long-term networks. World-class companies are not 'islands'.
- Having the advantage of speed of reaction. Merke suggests that it is not the biggest company that will survive, but the quickest, and this is an area in which medium-sized companies will possess a great advantage.

To achieve this position of world-class status, Merke identifies five basic attributes the organization must possess:

- a high level of employee competence
- the training programmes to foster that
- a decentralized organizational structure
- the pride, solidarity and loyalty of its employees
- visionary leaders.

PART TWO
MATERIALS PLANNING SYSTEMS

Chapter 6 acts as an introduction to the remainder of Part Two by first defining what material requirements planning is, then examining the major components of the MRP system, and finally providing an overview of the MRP system process. The various elements in that process—bills of materials, the MRP analysis logic, and ordering systems and lot-sizing methods—are then explained in Chapters 7, 8 and 9. The question of the supply chain, and the changing supplier relationships implied by supply chain partnership, is the subject of Chapter 10. In Chapter 11 are explained the parameters and techniques used in the management of an MRP system, and Part Two concludes with a review in Chapter 12 of the different ways in which demand may drive the materials planning system.

6
Materials requirements planning

6.1 Definition

MRP is the process by which component parts or materials

- are planned to be manufactured or purchased and delivered,
- to satisfy the known or forecast demand,
- so that material shortages are eliminated,
- and excess stocks are not allowed to build up.

MRP is demand driven, not usage driven, because the component parts of an end product represent dependent demand, not independent demand. This distinction between dependent and independent demand is fundamental in accepting the logic of MRP, and has been covered in Chapter 2.

6.2 Objective of MRP

The essential objective of MRP is to have:

- the right part
- in the right place
- at the right time
- and in the minimum quantity to satisfy the service criteria of the business.

Achieving this poses a number of questions, articulated by Wight (1984):

- What are we going to make, and when?
- What and how much is needed to make it?
- What have we got?
- What do we need to get, and when and how?

The key objective of the MRP system is to provide the answers to these questions, on a regular basis and taking account of

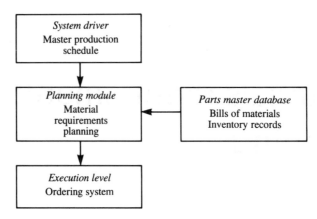

Figure 6.1 MRP system components

- the changing or evolving pattern of customers' independent demand;
- the result of executing previous plans for manufacture and/or procurement, not all of which may have been executed according to plan.

6.3 MRP system components

Figure 6.1 illustrates the key components of the MRP system. These are:

- a material requirements planning module—MRP itself,
- driven by a master production schedule (MPS),
- using information from both bills of materials and inventory records, to generate net requirements,
- for execution by an ordering system.

6.4 The basic steps in MRP logic

The basic steps in the MRP processing logic are shown in Figure 6.2, and can be summarized as follows:

- The MPS is a balancing of demand and supply at independent demand level and is a statement of what is going to be manufactured over future periods of time.
- The MPS is converted to its component part content by the technique of time-phased parts explosion, using a product structure defined by bills of materials. The result of this process is a schedule of gross requirements over future periods of time needed to satisfy the MPS.
- These gross requirements are netted off against inventory and orders in hand to arrive at the net requirements—the quantity that must now or at a later date be ordered so as to satisfy the gross requirements.

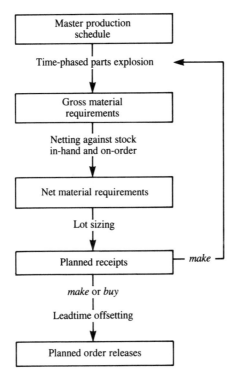

Figure 6.2   Steps in MRP process

- The net requirements are grouped into planned order receipts by a lot-sizing technique, and the planned order receipts are then offset by a planning leadtime to arrive at the date on which the orders must be released to suppliers or to production.
- In the case of component parts manufactured in company, the process then repeats itself, using planned receipts instead of the MPS quantities, until all manufactured component parts down to the lowest level in the product structure have been accounted for.
- The planned orders must then be approved by the material planner, after which their status changes from that of planned order to that of scheduled receipt.

7
Bills of materials

The bill of materials is the key to the product structure within a materials planning system. In this chapter we begin with an overview describing what a bill of materials is and how it is structured. This is followed by a summary of the data requirements of a bill of materials structure, and the different categories of components which it may comprise. An example of a bill of materials serves as a model for illustrating a number of important concepts, such as cumulative manufacturing leadtime. Useful options such as phantom subassemblies are then described. We go on to examine how the process of engineering change is catered for. Because the reader may encounter different types of bills of materials, these are summarized, and the chapter concludes by examining the more specific options applicable in a configure-to-order situation, where the bill of materials may depend on specific customized options on an incoming sales order.

7.1 Overview

Products to be made or assembled are represented by a bill of materials. The bill of materials describes the component part content in terms of the *parent/ child relationships* or linkages between an item and its immediate lower-level component parts. The structure is hierarchical, allowing many levels of sub-assembly.

The parent/child relationship defines the quantity of each child component required to make one unit of the parent component. Purchased items will normally appear at the lowest level on each limb of the hierarchical structure.

The bill of materials allows the requirements of the master production schedule to be exploded to give the gross requirements of subassemblies and component parts at each successive lower level in the structure.

A part numbering system which adequately identifies the differences between end products, subassemblies, and the various types of component parts is a prerequisite to an understandable bill-of-materials database.

7.2 Essential data

The essential data at each level in the product structure are as follows.

Parts master data

- part number
- description
- material category: make or buy
- unit of measure
- planning leadtime

Bill of materials data

- part number
- linkages to child relationships:
    child part number
    quantity per unit of parent part

Material categories

The typical material categories present in most manufacturing product structures will include the following:

- end product: *make*
- subassembly: *make*
- component part manufactured in plant: *make*
- component part purchased externally: *buy*
- raw material: *buy*

The end product will always be an item appearing on the master production schedule. *Make* items will always have lower-level children. *Buy* items will normally not have lower-level children, but a major exception could be a subcontract item for which component parts or raw materials are supplied to the subcontractor on a free-issue basis.

7.3 Example

In exercise B1 (Appendix B) Birdhomes' products are described, and the reader wishing to apply his own logic to the problem is invited to construct the parts master file and the bills of materials, instead of following the text that follows. The same example used in exercise B1 is used here to illustrate the concept of bills of materials.

Birdhomes Ltd manufacture luxury accommodation for garden birds, and the characteristics of their product are as follows:

1. They make both wall mounting and freestanding models.

2. Both models comprise a common basic housing unit, which consists of a house base, three sides, a front, and a roof. These components are all externally purchased, and are sourced in a standard colour. The house base is a plastic moulding which incorporates a twist clip fitting for a stalk.
3. On both models there is a choice of red roof or green roof. The painting of the roof is done in plant.
4. Freestanding models also comprise a stalk and a ground base. There is a choice between a short stalk (1000 mm) and a long stalk (2000 mm). The ground base is purchased and is common to both stalk heights. The stalk is cut in plant from aluminium tube which is purchased in standard four metre lengths.
5. Fixing of the roof to the sides and front is by clip-on assembly. The sides, front and house base are glued together using a bird-friendly glue which has an extensive curing time.
6. On freestanding units, one end of the stalk is machined in plant to give a twist clip fit to the base of the housing unit. The other end is welded to the ground base to comply with RSPB safety regulations.

Birdhomes' parts master file is given in Table 7.1 and the corresponding bills of materials in Table 7.2. In the Birdhomes' example the following points should be noted:

Table 7.1 Birdhomes' parts master file

Part no.	Description	Level	Unit of measure	Make/buy
A123	Wall mounting, red roof	2	Each	Make
A124	Wall mounting, green roof	2	Each	Make
A125	Freestanding, red roof, short stalk	1	Each	Make
A126	Freestanding, red roof, long stalk	1	Each	Make
A127	Freestanding, green roof, short stalk	1	Each	Make
A128	Freestanding, green roof, long stalk	1	Each	Make
B234	House subassembly	3	Each	Make
B235	Red roof	3	Each	Make
B236	Green roof	3	Each	Make
B237	Short stalk subassembly	2	Each	Make
B238	Long stalk subassembly	2	Each	Make
C345	Roof	4	Each	Buy
C346	Side	4	Each	Buy
C347	Front	4	Each	Buy
C348	House base	4	Each	Buy
C349	Short stalk	3	Each	Make
C350	Long stalk	3	Each	Make
C351	Ground base	3	Each	Buy
C352	Tube	4	Each	Buy

Table 7.2   Birdhomes' bills of materials

Parent part no.	Child part no.	Quantity per unit of parent
A123	B234	1
A123	B235	1
A124	B234	1
A124	B236	1
A125	A123	1
A125	B237	1
A126	A123	1
A126	B238	1
A127	A124	1
A127	B237	1
A128	A124	1
A128	B238	1
B234	C346	3
B234	C347	1
B234	C348	1
B235	C345	1
B236	C345	1
B237	C349	1
B237	C351	1
B238	C350	1
B238	C351	1
C349	C352	0.25
C350	C352	0.50

– Part numbers A123 and A124 have both dependent and independent demand. The independent demand arises from the MPS requirements for these parts. The dependent demand arises from their usage within part numbers A125, A126, A127 and A128, and will be in addition to the MPS requirements for part numbers A123 and A124.
– Would it be better to specify metres as the unit of measure for part number C352, and for the parent/child relationships of part numbers C349 and C350 to specify quantities of 1000 and 2000 respectively? The answer is that it is generally better to recognize discrete parts wherever possible. Metres (or perhaps even kilograms) may be used as the purchasing unit of measure for tube, but the stock-keeping unit of measure is better treated as one length.
– Note that the consumable items—glue, welding wire, etc.—have been omitted from the bills of materials. This is common practice in the case of materials for which it is either impractical or not cost-effective to measure out precisely the quantities consumed, and would typically apply to minor fixing or fastening items and to materials consumed by a manufacturing process.

Level

The Birdhomes' example also illustrates the concept of level. The level of any part number is the lowest level at which it appears in any bill of materials structure of which it is a component part. The deepest structures in the Birdhomes' bills of materials, part numbers A125, A126, A127 and A128 (see Table 7.1), stop at the fourth level down.

This concept of level is primarily intended as a mechanism for grouping together multiple end-product sources of demand for an item in order to help simplify the computer systems logic and to minimize computer processing time in the MRP system.

Bill-of-materials maintenance modules should provide for the automatic recalculation of levels after updates, and should also check that there are no loops, i.e. no lower-level item specifying a higher-level item as its child.

Product structure

The composition of each product can be depicted as a tree structure, as shown in Figure 7.1. It will be noted that the buy items appear at the ends of each limb of the tree, and that all higher-level items in the structure are make items.

How the bill of materials differs from a parts list

The bill of materials is more than a parts list. This is best illustrated by comparing an exploded bill of materials for Birdhomes part number A125 (Table 7.3) with a parts list for the same part number (Table 7.4). Tables 7.3 and 7.4 also illustrate other points worth noting:

- The bill of materials for part number A125 (Table 7.3) is an example of an indented bill. It shows the quantities at each level in the hierarchy for one unit of part number A125. It is produced by exploding the bill of materials structure, level by level, until there are no further parent/child relationships.
- The parts list (Table 7.4) does not show subassemblies or component parts finished in plant. It includes only the components at the lowest level in each limb of the product structure, i.e. the externally purchased parts. The parts list could be used only for calculating the gross requirements of these lowest-level purchased parts.
- The bill of materials offers much more than this parts list does:
  it also makes possible the calculation of gross requirements of subassemblies and component parts made in plant;

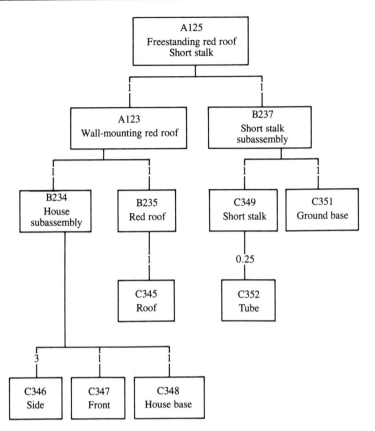

Figure 7.1   Product structure. Example: Birdhomes' part number A125

where there is commonality of material content, it avoids repetition of data, and makes changes easier and less prone to error;
it allows for the time phasing of requirements at each level in the structure, by offsetting from due date the planning leadtime for assembly, manufacture or procurement at these levels.

7.4 Cumulative manufacturing leadtime

The bill of materials can also be used to show the effect of offsetting leadtimes throughout the product structure. In Table 7.3 the longest leadtime from top to bottom of the hierarchy is 13 time periods.

This is known as the *cumulative manufacturing leadtime* (CMLT). It is the shortest delivery promise that could be offered for part number A125 if the stock and on-order position of every item in the bill of materials was zero.

Table 7.3 Exploded bill of materials: Birdhomes' part no. A125

Level	Part no.	Description	Quantity	CMLT[†]
1	A125	Freestanding, red roof, short stalk	1	1
2	A123	Wall mounting, red roof	1	2
3	B234	House subassembly	1	8
4	C346	Side	3	13
4	C347	Front	1	13
4	C348	House base	1	13
3	B235	Red roof	1	5
4	C345	Roof	1	10
2	B237	Short stalk subassembly	1	5
3	C349	Short stalk	1	7
4	C352	Tube	0.25	9
3	C351	Ground base	1	8

[†] CMLT: cumulative manufacturing leadtime

Table 7.4 Parts list: Birdhomes' part no. A125

Part no.	Description	Quantity
C345	Roof	1
C346	Side	3
C347	Front	1
C348	House base	1
C351	Ground base	1
C352	Tube	0.25

The relationship between CMLT, freeze periods in the MPS, and/or safety stocks within the system is of paramount importance to the stability of an MRP system.

7.5 Where-used listing

Envisage the indented bill of materials in Table 7.3 as the Christmas tree structure depicted in Figure 7.1, leading from an end-product item down through all its limbs to each and every lowest-level component item. A *where-used* is the converse of this. The tree leads from a low-level item back up through all the branches or structures of which it is part, and ends with all the highest-level end products of which it is a component item.

Table 7.5 illustrates the where-used list for part number C345 (roof) in Birdhomes' parts master file.

Table 7.5 Where-used list: Birdhomes' part no. C345

Level	Part no.	Description
4	C345	Roof
3	B235	Red roof
2	A123	Wall mounting, red roof
1	A125	Freestanding, red roof, short stalk
1	A126	Freestanding, red roof, long stalk
3	B236	Green roof
2	A124	Wall mounting, green roof
1	A127	Freestanding, green roof, short stalk
1	A128	Freestanding, green roof, long stalk

The use of this where-used list would include:

– identifying which bills of materials would be affected by the replacement of part number C345 by another part;
– identifying which end products would be affected by shortages of part number C345, or by quality problems associated with part number C345.

7.6 Phantom subassemblies

Most bill-of-materials processing modules make provision for phantom or ghost subassemblies. The original purpose of phantoms was to cater for discrete subassemblies that flowed directly to an upstream assembly operation where they were consumed, as opposed to moving in and out of stock between the two processes.

For example, on an engine assembly line the production of crankshafts and camshafts may be carried out on subassembly lines that transfer directly onto the engine final assembly line, and the rate of production of these subassembly lines is normally balanced with that of the final assembly line. In these circumstances the finished crankshafts and camshafts do not pass in and out of a discrete store. The MRP process of netting against inventory is therefore not relevant and should be bypassed, although Orlicky (1975) makes the point that this is important only in a net change MRP system.

Depending on the processing logic of specific MRP software packages, there are other uses that can be made of the concept of phantom subassemblies:

1. To cater for network operations. In the example given above of subassembly lines transferring directly to a final assembly line, the combination of final assembly and subassembly lines can be regarded as a network,

and the concept of phantom subassemblies can therefore be applied in any manufacturing operation involving networks. This may be useful where MRPII production routing structures do not support network operations.

2. Where a product or subassembly has a commonality of parts content with other products or subassemblies, but only up to a certain stage in the manufacturing process. The parts that are common could be treated as a phantom subassembly in order to avoid repetition of data in the respective bills of materials.

    For example, suppose that Birdhomes' sides, front and house base were designed to clip together rather than be glued together. The short assembly time would then tend to obviate the need for manufacturing these as a discrete subassembly. Suppose also that the roof was purchased already painted, and that there was a choice of 10 colours rather than only two. There would then be 10 different part numbers for the house unit, each comprising a different roof, but with commonality of the sides, front and ground base. These common parts could be regarded as a phantom subassembly to avoid repeating the same parent/child relationships on 10 different bills of materials. The C&K Switches case study (Chapter 28) also illustrates the use of phantoms in this context.

3. Where a manufacturing leadtime is lengthy, and the provisioning of materials by the planned start date of manufacturing would lead to excess stock for a period of time. The separation of a discrete manufacturing process into fictitious or phantom subassemblies will enable the leadtime to be similarly separated, with the result that the material need date will be based on the start of the operation for which the material is used, rather than the start date of the first operation in the process.

7.7 Alternative part numbers

A bill of materials structure may allow for the specification of alternative part numbers. These alternatives could then be invoked in the following circumstances:

- If an addition or increase to the MPS is made within the cumulative manufacturing leadtime, and if the alternative part provided a shorter leadtime.
- If, at works order release date, a part is not available but the alternative part is available. Issue of the alternative would prevent a delay in putting the order into production. The inference of this, however, is that either:
    there is excess stock or safety stock of the alternative part, or
    material provisioned for another lower priority order will be diverted to this higher priority order.

7.8 Engineering change

The bill of materials' content or structure may change from time to time, and the change may originate from a number of sources:

- Design or product engineering, which may make changes to the component parts content in order to:
    enhance product benefits
    reduce material costs
    incorporate new materials
    correct quality defects
    facilitate repair and maintenance
- production engineering, which may make changes to the structure in order to:
    reduce production costs
    reduce manufacturing leadtimes
    take advantage of new process technology
- purchasing, which may substitute compatible component parts, approved as alternatives by design engineering, so as to:
    re-source on an alternative supplier offering better price, quality or delivery performance.

Engineering changes have elements of both scope and timing, as follows.

Scope

The scope of an engineering change may be:

- *Specific*: the change is confined a specific parent/child relationship.
- *Global (or mass replacement)*: the change must take place wherever the part number previously appeared as a child in any parent/child relationship.

Timing

The timing of an engineering change may be:
- *Immediate*: implement immediately, without consideration of any stock redundancy, for instance, to correct a major quality defect.
- *Stockout*: implement the change when inventory of the old component is exhausted.
- *Future dated*: implement the change on a specific future date. In this case the former parent/child relationship will be tagged with a supersede date, and the new relationship will be tagged with an effective date.

There may also be provision for a cross-reference:

– The old relationship may be tagged with 'superseded by ⟨new relationship⟩'.
– The new relationship may be tagged with 'supersedes ⟨old relationship⟩'.

7.9 Types of bills of materials

There are three types of bills of materials in common use today:

– engineering bills of materials
– production bills of materials
– planning bills of materials

Engineering bills of materials

These are the bills of materials being worked on by design engineering. For any product structure there may be several versions not yet released to manufacturing.

A state-of-the-art MRP system should have provision for an automated interface with a CAD system in order to capture this data at source when it becomes released to production. This technique eliminates data transcription errors, and helps to ensure accuracy of the production bills of materials—a vital prerequisite to an MRP system that works.

Production bills of materials

These are the bills of materials currently being used for materials planning and production purposes. They will normally have been released by design engineering, and may contain future engineering changes within the planning horizon. The structure of the production bill of materials may differ from the equivalent engineering bill of materials, but the lowest-level parts and material content should not.

The structure may differ as a result of production engineering deciding how the product should be made or assembled. The practice of *design for manufacture* (DFM) will prevent such differences arising, and ensure that engineering bills of materials take account of the way in which the product will be manufactured or assembled.

Planning bills of materials

In the case of feature-dependent products, i.e. products with a variety of customer options (see section 7.10), planning bills of materials have a very specific use in master scheduling. They are used to create planned orders of a representative product-feature mix from the potentially infinite variety of order specifications contained within the known historical demand data.

Early versions of MRP included two other types of bills of materials, applicable to feature-dependent products, which have largely been made redundant by advances in both product design and computer processing technology:

– *Manufacturing bills of materials*: these were originally used to link together the basic product and all its optional features into a consolidated top-level bill of materials for final assembly purposes.
– *Pseudo bills of materials*: these functioned like manufacturing bills, but for forecasting purposes.

7.10 Configure to order

Many end products comprise a basic product plus a selection of optional features. The possible combination of options may be too many for it to be sensible or possible to create a highest-level part number and parent/child relationships for all valid combinations.

For example, a typical model of motor car may offer a choice of power unit, a choice of trim, many combinations of internal and external colour, plus a wide range of optional features such as alloy wheels, anti-lock braking and automatic transmission, to name but a few. The total number of valid combinations of basic model and customer options is likely to be numbered in the thousands.

The common-sense alternative, offered by the configure-to-order option in a bill of materials package, is to allow a customer order to be specified in terms of:

– master part number, plus
– list of feature numbers or optional part numbers.

The most common convention within sales order processing modules is to present each feature group selection as either:

– *Optional*: one or none may be selected.
– *Mandatory*: one and only one feature must be selected.

In some cases there may be additional logic constraints on the combinations of features. This requires extensive and often complex sales-order entry validation procedures, which may be so user-specific they have to be carried out in the appropriate sales-order entry system using bespoke software or customized modifications to a standard software package.

In the case of a feature-dependent product, the master part number will lead to the standard bill of materials. Each optional feature or part number will lead to an additional bill of materials specific to that feature. The combination of standard and all feature-dependent bills of materials thus represents the total bill of materials for that specific order combination.

Alternatively each feature could invoke additions or amendments to the standard bill of materials, but this is more characteristic of the relatively unsophisticated product design concepts of the 1960s:

- Add an additional relationship.
- Delete an existing relationship.
- Replace an existing relationship with an alternative one.

The configure-to-order option is normally only available in MRPII software packages that have been designed with an assemble-to-order manufacturing environment in mind. Where general-purpose configure-to-order options do exist, the systems logic is normally at two levels of details:

1. For each highest-level product, a table of permissible optional part numbers. For example, in the context of personal computers the highest-level product might be a 486 system complete with monitor, printer, mouse and external modem. The table entry for the part number corresponding to the complete system would include all of the permissible independent units, for example, printer A, printer B, monitor X, monitor Y, etc. There would also be a table entry for the PC itself, which would include the permissible options, such as 200 Mb fixed disk, 50 Mb fixed disk, 3.5 in floppy disk drive, 5.25 in floppy disk drive, etc.
2. There would in addition be a facility for describing the permissible interrelationships of these features. This would normally be provided in a form resembling a simple programming language which allows the user to define the rules, for example:
   IF modem MUST HAVE RS233 channel
   IF mouse AND modem MUST HAVE *two* RS233 channels
   IF 200 Mb drive CANNOT HAVE 50 Mb drive
   MAXIMUM 3.5 in floppy disk drive IS *two* etc.

Table 7.6 Feature-dependent bills, e.g. Birdhomes' product range

Basic model		Wall mounting unit (minus roof)	Part no. A122	
plus two sets of product feature groups:				
Roof	Mandatory	Red roof	Part no. B235	Qty 1
		Green roof	Part no. B236	Qty 1
Stalk	Optional	Short stalk	Part no. B237	Qty 1
		Long stalk	Part no. B238	Qty 1

Table 7.7 Birdhomes' complete bills of materials

Parent part no.	Description	Child part no.	Quantity per parent
A122	Basic model	B234	1
B234	House subassembly	C346	3
		C347	1
		C348	1
B235	Red roof	C345	1
B236	Green roof	C345	1
B237	Short stalk subassembly	C349	1
		C351	1
B238	Long stalk subassembly	C350	1
		C351	1
C349	Short stalk	C352	0.25
C350	Long stalk	C352	0.50

Example of feature-dependent bill of materials

Consider the Birdhomes example. Instead of six highest level products (part numbers A123 to A128), this could instead be specified as shown in Table 7.6. The bills of materials for Birdhomes' products would then be as shown in Table 7.7, a considerable simplification when compared to the original bills of materials (Tables 7.1 and 7.2).

8
The MRP process

8.1 Objectives of the MRP process

The primary objective of the MRP process is to generate a schedule of net requirements and planned order releases for the component parts and materials that are needed to satisfy the end-product demand represented by the master production schedule. An overview of the MRP process logic is shown on the flow diagram in Figure 6.2, and each step in that process is described in detail in the remainder of this chapter and in Chapter 9.

The requirements at each level in the product structure have two primary attributes:

- quantity
- time

8.2 Time buckets and bucketless systems

Within MRP there are two ways of handling the time attribute:

- time buckets
- bucketless systems

Time buckets

With time buckets the system provides a fixed number of buckets, each corresponding to future successive spans of time, for example weeks or months. The time period spanned between the first (or earliest) and the last (or latest) buckets is known as the planning horizon. In a typical system the buckets' spans of time can vary and can be determined by user parameters—for example, weeks over the earlier part of the planning horizon, months over the medium term, and perhaps even quarters towards the latter part of the horizon.

The choice of time spans in practice would reflect the firmness of demand over the future horizon, for example:

- a short span, perhaps weeks, over the period where demand is firm and represented on the MPS by firm customer orders;

- a medium span, perhaps months, over the further forward periods where demand is only beginning to firm up, and where demand is represented on the MPS by a mixture of firm customer orders and forecast orders;
- the longest span, perhaps quarters, towards the limit of the planning horizon, where there are no firm customer orders and demand is represented on the MPS only by a forecast.

When MRP uses time buckets, any order or requirement is slotted into the bucket within which the due date or required date falls. For practical purposes such as order release it is therefore necessary to decide which day within the time bucket is the effective day. The typical practice is either the first day or the last day. The most important aspect is to abide by whatever convention is decided upon.

Bucketless systems

The concept of time buckets was adopted in the early days of MRP as a means of limiting the amount of computer processing time required for the MRP run. The alternative, made feasible by increases in computer power, is a bucketless system.

With a bucketless system each order or requirement is processed as a discrete entity, thus preserving visibility of the discrete day on which it is due or required. In a bucketless system there are, therefore, no constraints on either the spans of time nor on the extent of the planning horizon. A bucketless system is therefore typical of a state-of-the-art MRP system.

8.3 The basic technique of time-phased explosion

The explosion is carried out level by level within the bill of materials structure, beginning with the highest level. The requirements of all lower-level child component items are consolidated, and are not themselves exploded until the level designated on the part master record as the lowest level of these items.

For example, part number C349 (short stalk) in the Birdhomes example (Tables B1.1 and B1.2, Appendix B) is a level 3 item. Suppose that in another Birdhomes end product part number C349 was the child of an end product at level 1. In that product example the requirements for part number C349 could be exploded at level 2, but would instead be deferred until level 3, which is the lowest level at which it occurs in any bill of materials structure, and is therefore the earliest point at which the requirements arising from the different end-product demand can be aggregated.

During explosion, two important things happen:

1. Quantity requirements are grossed up. The quantity of the parent item is multiplied by the quantity per unit of parent specified on the bill of materials' parent/child relationship to give the quantity requirement of the child item.
2. Requirements are time phased. The due date of the parent item is offset by the manufacturing leadtime of the parent item to give both its planned order release date and the required date of its child components. This off-setting or time phasing is also known as backward scheduling.

For example, suppose that Birdhomes have a firm order on the MPS for 16 units of part number A128 required for week 23, and there is no inventory and no production orders in the pipeline. The release date for the works order for part number A128 will be week 23 less the leadtime of one week, i.e. week 22, and the child components (part numbers A124 and B238) will also be required in week 22. The quantity required of part number A124 will be 16 times 1, i.e. 16, and for B238 it will also be 16 times 1, i.e. 16. The requirement for

Part no: A128   Quantity: 16   Due date: week 23

has been exploded into requirements for

Part no: A124   Quantity: 16   Required date: week 22
Part no: B238   Quantity: 16   Required date: week 22

and there will also be requirements for these two part numbers, but with differing quantities and due dates, generated by a similar explosion of all other firm or planned orders for part number A128 on the MPS. The arithmetic and logic of time-phased explosion is also illustrated in Figure 8.1, using as an example a net requirement for part number B234.

8.4 Gross material requirements

The gross requirements for an item will be the sum of:

- All requirements to satisfy independent demand. These will normally derive directly from the MPS. In the case of lower-level items this independent demand could relate to spare parts requirements.
- All requirements to satisfy dependent demand. These will have been derived as a result of a time-phased explosion from all the MPS items of which this part is directly or indirectly a component.

In the case of a make item, these gross requirements will in turn lead to a subsequent explosion into further lower level items, but not until the level is reached that is specified as the lowest level of this part number, i.e. the lowest level at which it occurs in any of the structures of which it is part.

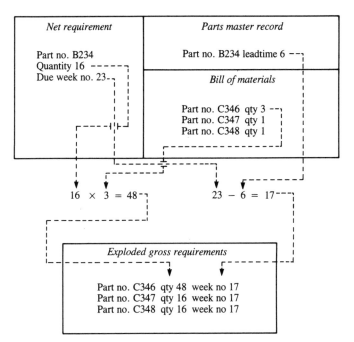

Figure 8.1   Time-phased explosion

Gross requirements have four attributes:

– part number
– quantity required
– date required
– source—the higher-level requirement generating this requirement.

Where time buckets are being used, these gross requirements will be aggregated into the appropriate time bucket, depending on the required date. The source of the requirement is therefore not directly preserved whereas, in a bucketless system, the gross requirements are preserved in full as discrete data records.

8.5 The MRP netting-off calculation

The process of *netting off*, or the calculation of net requirements, is as follows:

	Gross requirements
+	Allocated inventory
−	Projected inventory
−	Scheduled receipts
=	Net requirements

There is a net requirement only if this calculation results in a number greater than zero. Where the result is a negative number there is no net requirement, and the net requirement is therefore shown instead as zero.

This calculation of net requirements is performed item by item, beginning at the highest level and including MPS items. It is the net requirements that are subsequently exploded into gross requirements of lower-level constituent components.

MRP works down all the bills of materials, level by level, and component by component, until the net requirements for all parts have been planned. For each part number the sequence of steps is:

1. Accumulate gross requirements until the part's lowest level is reached.
2. Do the gross-to-net calculation.
3. In the case of a make item, carry out the time-phased explosion to give the gross requirements for its immediate component parts.

8.6 Planning order releases

The various lot-sizing methods in common use are described in Chapter 9. With the simplest lot-sizing method—lot for lot—the planned order-receipt date would coincide with the date on which the corresponding net requirement had been established. This is the method that would minimize inventory carrying cost, and is also the method most compatible with a JIT philosophy.

The general effect of other lot-sizing methods is to group together a number of different planned receipts and therefore bring forward some planned receipt dates in advance of the net requirements date, in order to achieve a trade-off between inventory carrying cost and the cost of ordering.

The final calculation in the MRP process is to offset the planned order-receipt date by the procurement leadtime, in order to arrive at a planned order-release date.

8.7 MRP analysis

The net requirements by part number are typically summarized on an MRP analysis report similar in format to that shown in Table 8.1. An exercise and worked examples of this can be found in Appendix B2. The following points should be noted.

Gross requirements

In some MRP systems, the gross requirements will be split into the two components of MPS requirements (i.e. independent demand) and the generated requirements (i.e. dependent demand).

Table 8.1 MRP analysis

Part no. C346
Planning leadtime 5

									Week no.										
	0	1	2	3	4	5	6	7	8	9	10	11	12	13	14	15	16	17	18
Gross requirements		0	0	0	0	0	0	60	369	429	114	54	0	0	0	0	0	0	0
Actual inventory	350																		
Allocated inventory	300	0	0	0	0	0	0	0	0	0	0	0	0	0	0	0	0	0	0
Scheduled receipts	0	0	0	0	0	0	196	0	0	0	0	0	0	0	0	0	0	0	0
Projected inventory	50	50	50	50	50	50	246	186	0	0	0	0	0	0	0	0	0	0	0
Net requirements	0	0	0	0	0	0	0	0	183	429	114	54	0	0	0	0	0	0	0
Planned order receipts	0	0	0	0	0	0	0	0	183	429	114	54	0	0	0	0	0	0	0
Planned order releases	0	0	0	183	429	114	54	0	0	0	0	0	0	0	0	0	0	0	0

Allocated inventory

In MRP, inventory is allocated only when an order is released. In the case of component parts this would be the works order, and it would be accompanied by a kitting list, picking list or stores issue list authorizing the issue of the items to the works. In the case of finished inventory or spares requirements it would be a despatch list authorizing the issue for packing and despatch to a customer. Allocated inventory is therefore the inventory needed to cover orders released but not yet issued from stores.

Scheduled receipts

These are those due to be received as a result of planned works orders or purchase orders that have already been approved and released.

Projected inventory

At the end of each period or time bucket, the projected inventory calculation is:

$$\begin{array}{ll} & \text{Brought forward inventory} \\ + & \text{Scheduled receipts} \\ - & \text{Gross requirements} \\ = & \text{Projected inventory} \end{array}$$

8.8 Summary of MRP data requirements

The following data is required to arrive at net material requirements:

- Master production schedule:
    the source of independent demand
- Parts master file:
    physical inventory level
    make or buy
    planning leadtimes
- Bills of materials:
    product structure and parts content
- Open works orders:
    scheduled receipts of make items
    inventory allocated but not yet issued
- Open purchase orders
    scheduled receipts of purchased items

9
The ordering system

This chapter first describes the different lot-sizing techniques in use with MRP systems, and then goes on to consider alternative delivery schedules, how allowance is made for material yield or reject rates, and ordering options, including make *or* buy and multiple sourcing. The question of safety stock is deferred until the next chapter.

9.1 Lot-sizing techniques

In MRP the default option for order lot size is lot for lot. In a system based on time buckets the lot will be the net requirements for each bucket of time— a week, for example. In a bucketless system, each lot will relate directly or indirectly to one specific MPS requirement. There will therefore usually be more lots generated by a bucketless system, and it follows that the average lot size will be smaller.

With both bucketed and bucketless systems there may be situations where lot for lot is not the most appropriate lot-sizing method, for example:

- For manufactured parts there may be a setup time which makes small lot sizes uneconomic, especially where the setup time is lengthy.
- For purchased parts there may be a supplier-dictated minimum order quantity or there may be arrangements for delivery at fixed intervals.

The more common lot-sizing methods in use today, and offered by proprietary software packages, are as follows:

- economic order quantity (EOQ)
- part-period balancing
- fixed order quantity
- fixed order periods or fixed order cycle
- non-stock method

It is always necessary to check which alternatives are supported by specific MRP software packages.

Economic order quantity (EOQ)

An EOQ lot-sizing method, sometimes referred to as *economic batch quantity* (EBQ), may be appropriate where setup costs are high in relation to manufacturing times and costs. In the case of purchased parts it may be appropriate where ordering costs are high in relation to order value—for example, where costs of transport are considerable and where elements of these are order related rather than quantity related. In the case of parts manufactured to order by the supplier, the purchase price may vary depending on quantity ordered, because the supplier will have taken account of the element of setup cost in the price list.

Larger production batch quantities will reduce setup costs per unit of production but will increase inventory, and therefore inventory carrying costs. Larger orders of externally purchased parts will reduce the overall cost of procurement, but will similarly lead to an increase in inventory carrying costs.

The EOQ calculation algebraically balances setup costs, or costs of ordering, against inventory carrying costs in order to minimize total costs of setup or ordering and inventory carrying cost.

The formula for calculating EOQ is:

$$Q = \sqrt{2SD/C}$$

where

Q = EOQ
S = setup cost (or ordering cost) per batch
D = demand over unit time
C = inventory carrying cost over unit time

Demand in the formula may be represented by:

- an average of historical usage taken from inventory records—this will indicate what the EOQ would have been at some point in the past, and is a frequent option in MRP software packages;
- or an average of net requirements over the planning horizon. Very few software packages offer this an option. This will indicate what the EOQ would be in the future, assuming that demand is continuous. If demand is not continuous but 'lumpy', then the true EOQ will vary from period to period depending on the demand over discrete future time periods. The technique for taking account of this is part-period balancing.

Some MRP software packages incorporate only the EOQ technique used in earlier order-point systems, the technique based on historical usage, and have not yet been adapted to supporting the central MRP concept of taking account of future visibility of demand in the case of dependent demand items.

Part-period balancing

This also calculates an economic batch size, to satisfy the trade-off between setup cost and inventory carrying cost, but in a different way from the EOQ formula. It seeks to place an order for a lot size where the two costs will be approximately equal over each discrete part of the planning horizon.

The actual calculation is done in a step-by-step manner, beginning with the first week on the new net requirements schedule. The steps in this calculation are as follows:

1. The setup cost is calculated.
2. The cumulative inventory carrying cost is calculated for each successive week, stopping at the week (week n) where cumulative carrying costs first exceed setup cost.
3. The difference between the two costs at week n is compared to the difference at the previous week (week $n - 1$) and the optimum week is the one in which the two costs are closest to being equal.
4. The lot size will then be the cumulative net requirements from week 1 through to either week n or week $n - 1$.
5. The calculation then begins over again, moving forward from week $n + 1$ or week n, and is repeated until the end of the planning horizon is reached.

With this method, variable economic batch quantities are generated in line with the specific forward demand pattern.

COMPARISON OF EOQ AND PART-PERIOD BALANCING

Consider the following example, in which demand over the future is higher than demand over past periods:

Part number	X3456
Value	45.00 per unit
Inventory cost	25.0% per annum
Carrying cost	0.22 per unit per week
Setup time	5.50 hours
Machine rate	35.00 per hour

Multiplication of the setup time by the machine rate gives the setup cost, in this case:

Setup cost	192.5 per batch

Table 9.1   Part no. X3456: usage and net requirements

Week	1	2	3	4	5	6	7	8	9	10
Usage	250	300	220	300	175	364	196	226	286	175
Week	11	12	13	14	15	16	17	18	19	20
Net requirements	350	412	365	475	500	396	575	463	569	512
Week	21	22	23	24	25	26	27	28	29	30
Net requirements	397	216	148	273	85	585	576	792	698	835

Suppose we are at the end of period 10, and that the past 10 weeks' usage and the next 20 weeks' net requirements are as shown in Table 9.1. Average usage and average net requirements may then be calculated as follows:

Average 10 weeks' historical usage   249.2

Average 10 weeks' net requirements 461.7

Average 20 weeks' net requirements 461.1

Applying the EOQ formula yields the following economic order quantities:

Usage-based EOQ   666

Net requirements-based EOQ   906

Tables 9.2, 9.3 and 9.4 indicate the relative results of using both versions of the EOQ calculation and part-period balancing.

The relative performance of the three methods, using the example above, can be summarized as in Table 9.5. These results are broadly in line with more scientific studies reported in Vollmann *et al.* (1992). On the other hand Browne *et al.* (1988) infer that the choice of lot-sizing method is largely unimportant, and present examples that indicate the same results from all of the commonly used lot-sizing techniques, although it could be argued that their selection of data was designed to arrive at this conclusion.

So, what is the truth? The answer depends very much on the underlying pattern and trend of demand:

- Where demand is stable the choice of lot-sizing method will more often than not be relatively unimportant. The more continuous the pattern of demand, the more true this will be.
- Where demand is tending upwards or downwards, the more beneficial will it be to use a lot-sizing method that looks to the future rather than to the past. This will be especially true where a sea change in demand has recently

Table 9.2 Usage-based EOQ

	Week no.																			
	11	12	13	14	15	16	17	18	19	20	21	22	23	24	25	26	27	28	29	30
B/F inventory	0	316	570	205	396	562	166	257	460	557	45	313	97	615	342	257	338	428	302	270
Receipts	666	666	0	666	666	0	666	666	666	0	666	0	666	0	0	666	666	666	666	666
Requirements	350	412	365	475	500	396	575	463	569	512	397	216	148	273	85	585	576	792	698	835
C/F inventory	316	570	205	396	562	166	257	460	557	45	313	97	615	342	257	338	428	302	270	101
Carrying cost	34	96	84	65	104	79	46	77	110	65	39	44	77	104	65	64	83	79	62	40
Setup cost	193	193	0	193	193	0	193	193	193	0	193	0	193	0	0	193	193	193	193	193

Total cost 4119

Table 9.3 Net requirements-based EOQ

	Week no.																			
	11	12	13	14	15	16	17	18	19	20	21	22	23	24	25	26	27	28	29	30
B/F inventory	0	556	144	686	211	617	221	553	90	427	822	425	209	61	694	609	24	354	469	677
Receipts	906	0	906	0	906	0	906	0	906	906	0	0	0	906	0	0	906	906	906	906
Requirements	350	412	365	475	500	396	575	463	569	512	397	216	148	273	85	585	576	792	698	835
C/F inventory	556	144	686	211	617	221	553	90	427	822	425	209	61	694	609	24	354	469	677	749
Carrying cost	60	76	90	97	90	91	84	69	56	135	135	68	29	82	141	68	41	89	124	154
Setup cost	193	0	193	0	193	0	193	0	193	193	0	0	0	193	0	0	193	193	193	193

Total cost 3902

Table 9.4　Part-period balancing

										Week no.										
	11	12	13	14	15	16	17	18	19	20	21	22	23	24	25	26	27	28	29	30
B/F inventory	0	412	0	475	0	396	0	463	0	512	0	364	148	0	85	0	576	0	0	835
Receipts	762	0	840	0	896	0	1038	0	1081	0	761	0	0	358	0	1161	0	792	1533	0
Requirements	350	412	365	475	500	396	575	463	569	512	397	216	148	273	85	585	576	792	698	835
C/F inventory	412	0	475	0	396	0	463	0	512	0	364	148	0	85	0	576	0	0	835	0
Carrying cost	45	45	51	51	43	43	50	50	55	55	39	55	16	9	9	62	62	0	90	90
Setup cost	193	0	193	0	193	0	193	0	193	0	193	0	0	193	0	193	0	193	193	0

Total cost　2850

Table 9.5 Relative performance of EOQ and part-period balancing

Method	Total cost	Relative cost
Usage-based EOQ	4111	100
Net requirements-based EOQ	3897	95
Part-period balancing	2848	69

taken place or is forecast to take place over the planning horizon. In these instances the best available evidence suggests that part-period balancing will be the better technique than either of the EOQ methods.

Wight (1984) argues against techniques like part-period balancing on the grounds that they lack transparency. The planner, he says, will always ask 'Why did the computer tell me to do this?' In point of fact part-period balancing can be simulated very quickly and easily using a spreadsheet, and in this way confidence in the use of the technique can be acquired.

It is worth noting in passing that of the other and more scientific techniques for lot sizing normally presented in reference works (e.g. the Wagner–Whitin algorithm or McLaren order moment), the results presented in Vollmann et al. (1992) suggest that their increased performance compared to part-period balancing is minimal in relation to their increased complexity.

Fixed order quantity

With fixed order quantity lot sizing the order quantity is the higher of

- a predetermined fixed order quantity
- net requirements

The fixed order quantity could represent either of:

- a supplier's minimum delivery quantity
- a manually calculated EOQ

Variants of this fixed order quantity technique include options intended to cater for supplier-dictated constraints, especially those relating to fixed pack sizes:

- integral multiples of minimum quantity
- fixed increments above minimum quantity

Fixed order period

In using fixed order periods the order quantity is the net requirements for specific spans of time. With time buckets, the order period may therefore be greater than the span of a bucket—for example, monthly order periods instead of weekly time buckets. In a bucketless system, the fixed order period may be used to consolidate discrete lots, into weekly order quantities for instance.

Non-stock method

This lot-sizing method normally applies to non-standard or special materials, for example in a jobbing business manufacturing to customer specification, where materials will normally only be purchased in line with specific firm customer orders. The determination of lot size is in effect delegated to the materials planner, rather than being calculated by the system itself.

In the majority of cases commercial prudence, aimed at minimizing inventory risk, will dictate that the lot size will normally be lot for lot, and purchase orders will be planned only over the length of the supplier leadtime, and not over the entire planning horizon.

9.2 Purchase-ordering policies

The MRP system results in a series of planned order releases over the extent of the planning horizon. Whether all or only part of these planned order releases is communicated to the supplier depends on the purchase ordering policy. The basic choice of ordering policy is between:

- placing discrete orders for discrete quantities at one time;
- placing a blanket order for delivery in regular scheduled call-off quantities;
- entering into a purchase contract for regular supply, and providing the supplier with updated delivery schedules on a regular basis.

Discrete orders

With discrete orders or call-offs the order quantity may be decided by any of the lot-sizing methods supported by the MRP package. Individual orders are typically released only for the planned receipts for the time periods that would be within the supplier leadtime by the next MRP run.

When given discrete orders the suppliers will normally have to rely on a forecasting and order-point system to plan their own material provisioning. They will be dependent on their record of historical demand, rather than on the visibility of forward demand in their customer's MRP system.

Delivery schedules

With delivery schedules the supplier is given a revised schedule of expected deliveries each time an MRP run takes place. The schedule would cover all or part of the MRP planning horizon. Delivery quantities and frequency will be as decided by the lot-sizing method used in the MRP module.

This method helps the suppliers plan forward, in terms of their own material provisioning and capacity planning, and by doing so helps support a higher level of delivery performance. When issuing delivery schedules it is common practice to subdivide the planning horizon into three time periods:

- the firm schedule
- the tentative schedule
- the planning schedule

The dividing line between these periods is sometimes referred to as a *time fence*.

THE FIRM SCHEDULE

This earliest part of the schedule normally covers the weeks ahead which are within the supplier's manufacturing leadtime. The normal convention is to treat requirements on the firm schedule as authority to deliver. It is also normal to guarantee that firm scheduled requirements for a particular time period will not be changed on subsequent schedules without the supplier's prior agreement.

THE TENTATIVE SCHEDULE

This middle part of the schedule normally covers the remainder of the planning horizon where demand is firm, where requirements derive from firm customer orders on the master schedule. It may alternatively cover a period equal to the supplier's own materials procurement leadtime. A common convention is that tentative requirements are regarded as authority to purchase materials. Tentative requirements may change from one schedule to the next.

THE PLANNING SCHEDULE

This latter part of the schedule covers the remainder of the planning horizon. This is given to the supplier for planning purposes only. There is no commitment. It helps suppliers plan forward capacity and it helps them give forward planning information in turn to their own material suppliers.

THE DIFFERENCE BETWEEN FAIR AND UNFAIR SCHEDULES

A schedule is unfair to the supplier if any of the following conditions prevail:

– Changes are made within his manufacturing leadtime without his prior agreement. The most unfair change of all is one that places him in instant arrears, a new requirement first notified on the schedule only *after* the required date.
– It is not possible to reconcile the previous schedule to the current schedule, for example, because the supplier does not know whether or not particular deliveries have been taken into account, or whether or not there are any rejections from a previous delivery not yet notified to him.

A schedule is fair to the supplier if it generally ensures the following:

– The schedule does not expect the impossible.
– It does not have the effect of passing the buck to the supplier when the planners get it wrong.
– It is supplemented by a list of the most recent receipts from the supplier, plus a list of any receipts not recorded on inventory records, for instance, held in quarantine, or returned to supplier. This enables the supplier to reconcile accurately his previous on-order position with the new position.

9.3 Material yield; scrap and reject rates

In practice both material yield and scrap or reject rates affect the MRP calculations. If either of these is a significant problem, it is necessary to check in detail what provision is made by specific MRP packages.

Material yield

With some raw materials the usable quantity may be less than the unit quantity—for example, where raw materials such as metals and plastics are purchased and stocked in industry-standard dimensions to cater for a variety of specific and smaller dimensions called for by the bills of materials.

In the Birdhomes example, aluminium tube is stocked in four-metre lengths. If the bills of materials called for a variety of different short lengths rather than only one metre and two metres, then the probability of using the whole of each four-metre length would be greatly reduced. If on average the last 400 mm of each tube is not usable, then the scrap will be 10 per cent and the yield will be 90 per cent, and it would then be necessary to multiply planned order quantities by 100/90 to make allowance for this.

In most jobbing businesses the actual yield may vary significantly over time, depending on the mix of work. It is therefore necessary to track the yield factor and, if necessary and possible, to alter the stockholding unit to improve the material yield.

The process of cutting raw materials to size may leave both usable offcuts and scrap, those offcuts too small to be usable. Some MRP software packages may have inventory control modules which support the recording of offcuts.

Scrap or reject rates

Scrap or rejections can occur with both manufactured items and purchased items. This can be expected to be a regularly occurring problem where the basic process capability is either low or has not been established, and this will usually be where the process technology is relatively backward. In these circumstances the scrap or reject rates may vary greatly over time, or from one works order to the next.

Where scrap or rejects occur regularly, provision must be made within the MRP process for this in order to avoid shortages. The basic data source could be the shop-floor data collection module in a closed loop MRPII environment, or the company's quality records in an ISO 9000 environment.

Ways of handling yield and scrap rates

The ways in which both yield and scrap or reject rates can be catered for within MRP systems are as follows:

– A yield percentage parameter, or yield factor, on the parts master record. This would be used within MRP to gross up quantities on the gross requirements schedule from the specified yield percentage to 100 per cent, or from the specified yield factor to 1.0. This could also be used to cater for the scrap or reject rate.
– A multiplier, such as 1.15, which would cause the quantity on the gross requirements schedule to be multiplied by that number. This could be used to cater for both material yield and scrap or reject rates.
– A safety stock to compensate for less than 100 per cent yield or less than 100 per cent quality performance.

Parameters such as these should be regarded as dynamic, requiring recalculation in the light of what is actually happening in the business over time.

9.4 Ordering options or alternatives

Two of the most common ordering options are:

 – make or buy
 – multiple sourcing

How far these are supported will depend on the features of specific software packages.

Make or buy

The item will normally be made in-plant, provided there is sufficient capacity. If there is not sufficient capacity, all or part of the forward requirements may instead be purchased or subcontracted. This decision may be made as a result of a capacity requirements planning run (see Chapter 17), which has identified a short-term capacity overload.

If the software does not specifically provide for a make-or-buy choice, then the material planner may temporarily alter the make-or-buy code to reflect the change in tactics, but this will generally have the effect of altering the sourcing across the whole of the planning horizon, which may not be intended. In practice, many software packages leave the planner to handle resourcing on a manual basis.

Multiple sourcing

Purchasing policy is to split the ordering between two or more suppliers, thus spreading the risk where suppliers' delivery performance or quality performance is unreliable.

The alternative suppliers and the percentage split of order requirements between them would be recorded on the parts master file. If the splitting is done at net requirements level, it gives an answer that arithmetically respects the percentage split, and allows for the possibility of different lot-sizing methods by supplier, for example, if their respective pack sizes are different. If the splitting is done at planned order level, as is most common, it presupposes a common lot-sizing method. With two suppliers, if the lot size is less than the sum of the two suppliers' minimum lot sizes, the entire lot will normally be ordered from the preferred supplier.

If the purchase-ordering module does not support multiple sourcing, then the planner must cater for it manually.

10
Supply chain management

In Chapter 5 supply chain partnership was highlighted as an important manufacturing strategy. In this chapter the relationship as it affects the planning system is considered. In particular, the extension of dependent demand outside the company itself is demonstrated. The chapter then considers the effect of supplier performance on the MRP system, and how to cope with it, and concludes on the question of supplier audits.

10.1 The supply chain

In Figure 10.1 the contrast is drawn very simply between the breadth of the supply chain and the four walls of the factory or company. The wider supply chain is an area where far-reaching and mutually beneficial changes in relationships have taken place over the past decade or so.

Traditional production management systems focused within the four walls, from receipt of materials into the factory, through to despatch of the finished product from the factory. In this world each element in the wider supply chain operated as an independent unit, each seeking to optimize its own performance, and quite often at the expense of other units in the supply chain. No one company can control an entire supply chain, but all organizations are in the end dependent on the success of the total supply chain if all are to attain real benefits.

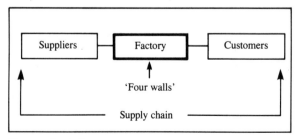

Figure 10.1 The supply chain

Table 10.1 Supplier relationships in the 1990s

Supplier relationships in the 1990s	
will be based on	*and not on*
Partnership	Conflict
Mutual trust	Mutual suspicion
Single sourcing of families of parts	Multiple sourcing of individual parts
Visibility of the future	Ignorance of the future
Sharing information	The mushroom syndrome[†]
Forward schedules	*Ad hoc* orders
Communication by EDI	Communication by post
Supplier quality assurance	Incoming inspection
Inspection by the supplier	100% inspection in goods receiving
High performance	Take it or leave it
Flexibility	Inflexibility
Demand led	Production led

[†] Being kept in the dark and covered with fertilizer.

Just-in-time has focused heavily on supplier relationships, but also more generally on the wider business perspective, which embraces both customers and suppliers. The concept of partnership is becoming accepted as a key to securing high supplier performance. In Table 10.1 the basis of supplier relationships in the 1990s is summarized.

The *integrated vendor* strategy of IBM Greenock is a successful example of supplier relationships founded on partnership. McKenzie (1991) describes how

we require our vendors to have the following capabilities: commercial, financial and technical self sufficiency, quality, CFM [continuous flow manufacturing] expertise, EDI links, design ideas, direct buy and competitive costs. IBM seeks to get agreement on a long-term relationship which entails flexible contracts, family sourcing, partnership pricing and productivity gains. In short, a relationship in which both IBM and the vendor share risks and goals but also share benefits.

As another example, the philosophy of ICL is summed up by Irwin (1993). In ICL's case, the concept of partnership sourcing was enabled by the application of TQM. The company's Vendor Accreditation Programme forms the basis for close collaboration between ICL and selected suppliers, the objective being to enable both ICL and the suppliers to achieve improvements in quality, cost of ownership, and service.

The programme is focused on the 200 of the total of 9000 suppliers who accounted for 80 per cent of the company's annual spend. These became the members of the Accreditation Programme and, in return for long-term commitment to them, ICL expects them to be committed to the ISO 9000 quality standard and to trade via EDI links.

As in the case of IBM, there is the belief that true partnership brings benefits to both parties, that they must be based on mutual confidence and trust, and that there must be financial reward for entering into the partnership. As part of their own contribution to the partnership, ICL undertook a number of improvements, such as greater visibility of relevant planning information, a vendor manager for each accredited vendor, participation in ICL's manufacturing planning process, and access to ICL's training and skills knowledge.

Dependent demand extends beyond the four walls, and with the exception of original equipment manufacturers, dependency of demand is bi-directional—coming from customers, and passing onwards to suppliers. In a logical business environment, the same relationships should therefore exist not only between the company and its suppliers, but also between the company and its customers. This is amplified in section 10.2 below.

Successful supply chain management requires not only effective planning systems, but also effective purchasing systems and effective sales order entry systems; the latter two are at the sharp end of the external relationships.

10.2 External relationships

We noted in Part One that end products were examples of independent demand and that component parts were examples of dependent demand. Earlier in this chapter we noted that for some components there may be a choice between make or buy. From this a simple logic trail leads to the following conclusions:

- Demand will therefore still be dependent even if the component normally made in-company is on occasions purchased rather than manufactured.
- There is no logical distinction between components that may sometimes be purchased and components that are regularly purchased.
- Therefore all purchased components are examples of dependent demand. Demand on suppliers is thus dependent on the demand for the products or parts that appear on their customer's master schedule.
- By extending this reasoning in the opposite direction, it follows that if the company's own manufactured product is used as a component part on its customers' products, then the demand represented on its master production schedule is not truly independent but is instead dependent on the demand for the customers' products.

We should therefore refine our previous definitions of demand:

- Only end products used by a discrete end customer and manufactured by an OEM are examples of independent demand.
- All component parts are examples of dependent demand, and the demand is just as dependent in each of these circumstances:

    the part is used within the four walls;

    the part is supplied to another factory within the company or group to be used there in the manufacturing process;

    the part is supplied to an external customer for the manufacture of that customer's product.

In multiple plant environments MRP is used to coordinate the material requirements planning between plants. The attribute of location on the central parts master file is used to separate out the requirements, location by location, or plant by plant, as the product structure is exploded.

In total supply chain management there is a logical case for coordinated material requirements planning downwards from the OEM manufacturer to all external suppliers of component parts. This is best achieved by providing external suppliers on a regular basis with the forward net requirements schedules generated by the MRP system.

Similarly the company's own planning will be more effective if it is provided with its customers' forward net requirements schedules.

In many cases this exchange of information is now achieved by *electronic data interchange* (EDI) (see Section 10.6). Such sharing of information implies partnership, and partnership also implies single sourcing.

10.3 Supplier performance

Two major aspects of supplier performance impact on MRP systems:

- delivery performance
- quality performance

If either or both of these are less than 100 per cent, then material shortages are likely to occur unless some account is taken during the MRP calculations. In a product-oriented plant a shortage of just one component can bring an entire factory to a standstill. The problem becomes more acute the closer the company itself moves to a JIT environment.

There are several solutions to the problem of poor supplier performance. The most obvious of them are:

- change suppliers, or
- work with the suppliers to help them make improvements.

If these solutions are not possible, then allowance must be made within MRP for the reality of the situation. The alternative solutions are these:

1. Plan to hold a safety stock.
2. Add a safety margin to order quantity.
3. Add a safety margin to the supplier leadtime.

Safety stocks are addressed in Chapter 11, when considering the management of the MRP system. In calculating safety stock or safety margins, the biggest problems are very often the following:

- Getting an objective measurement of the performance. It can be difficult to arrive at the optimum balance between protection and the cost of the protection.
- The possibility of extreme variability in performance over time. This means that calculations of safety stock or safety margins not only require frequent updating, but are more than likely to be either too high or too low for most of the time.

10.4 Measuring supplier performance

Delivery performance can be measured in terms of days' lateness. Quality performance can be measured in terms of percentage rejections. In both cases the source data should be available from within a closed loop MRPII system. If not, delivery lateness can be extracted from closed purchase orders, and quality statistics should be available from quality records in an ISO 9000 environment.

It will be necessary to check whether specific inventory control or purchasing system modules provide for the calculation of supplier performance measures.

The real dilemma is this—if average values of performance are calculated and used, then for half the time there will be excess stock, and for half the time there will be shortages. If shortages are to be avoided completely, the worst-case situation must be provided for, and this will lead to excess stocks for most of the time.

Supplier performance will be dynamic, changing over time for better or for worse, and frequent recalculations are therefore vital.

10.5 Auditing the supplier system

The real answer to unreliable supplier performance is no different to many other ailments—the focus should be on preventative strategies rather than curative ones, and the model already exists in the case of quality performance.

Quality assurance systems depend on initial and periodic audits or assessments of the supplier's quality systems, either by the purchaser or by an external assessment body. This helps a quality manager assess the likelihood of the supplier being able to achieve consistently an acceptable level of quality performance. In a JIT environment the objective will be to achieve zero defects. The practice of quality audits is almost universally acceptable, and has been increasingly adopted since the introduction of ISO 9000.

There is a prima facie case for also carrying out an audit of the supplier's manufacturing systems, but it is less common in practice, particularly on the part of smaller purchasers. A key area for audit will be the use and performance of MRP/MRPII systems or their equivalent.

What is expected of a supplier is very simple—100 per cent good parts delivered on time. The key attributes sought of a supplier are much wider than that:

- competitive price performance
- continuity of supply
- quality performance
- leadtime and delivery performance

and these are the attributes that will be checked out by large customers before engaging in business with a new supplier.

Competitive price performance

The issue of competitive pricing is not directly relevant in the present context, but it should be noted that the competitiveness of today's price has to be viewed in conjunction with what steps the supplier will take to ensure that there is a longer-term reduction in the price. This is likely to accrue from advances in process technology, coupled with a substantial move towards the elimination of waste—in other words, towards a JIT approach. Much of the essence of manufacturing strategy, addressed in Chapter 5, will be of relevance in the suppliers' worlds if longer-term price reductions are to be achieved in the company's striving towards the maintenance of a competitive manufacturing position.

Continuity of supply

The key issue will normally be whether or not this supplier has the underlying financial strength to remain a supplier throughout the foreseeable future. If not, then this supplier quite simply presents too high a risk in terms of future continuity of supply.

The bland figures will be gleaned from the supplier's accounts, and if it is a limited company these will be in the public domain. This financial information in its turn will very largely be a reflection of the supplier's competitive manufacturing and marketing position, and the degree of customer satisfaction with its products, and these are more directly related to the key questions to be addressed during a manufacturing audit.

Quality performance

This is more directly the realm of a quality assurance audit, but a key question will be whether or not there is a quality assurance system accredited to ISO 9000, or its equivalents—BS 5750 or EN 29000. The essential features of this part of the audit will focus on three aspects:

1. Is the supplier's basic process capability established? Or is he dependent on inspecting out the rubbish? A process capability established by means of failure modes and effects analysis (FMEA), followed by statistical process control (SPC) during the manufacturing process, is by far the best means of ensuring product conformance.
2. Are customer complaints recorded? Are in-process quality deviations recorded? Is corrective action always taken in either case? This is the surest means of re-establishing product conformance if things do go wrong.
3. Is there management commitment to the concept of continuous improvement? Nothing in business is static. We either go backwards or forwards; we never stand still. The commitment to continuous improvement is key not only to higher standards in the future, but also to ensuring there is no backsliding from the present position.

Leadtime and delivery performance

These two have been deliberately banded together, for the simple reason that efforts to reduce the manufacturing leadtime are more than likely to result in a higher delivery performance. Long leadtimes are the result of complexity; remove the complexity and there is less that can go wrong and in turn impede delivery performance.

The basic questions that need to be addressed in the context of leadtime and delivery performance are these:

− Does this supplier have the production capacity to supply the quantities we wish to buy? In turn this will lead to the subsidiary question—do they have the measure of their capacity, and do they have a system that shows them how this capacity is loaded in terms of their order book at any point in time? This requires an MRPII system, including capacity requirements planning.

- How important is our business to this supplier? Will we be big enough to wag the tail if necessary, or we will be so small in comparison to other customers that there is a danger of their needs taking precedence over our own? Responsible purchasers also ensure that a supplier never becomes over-dependent on their business; if anything untoward should occur, and orders or schedules were to cease, it is neither right nor fair that the supplier should suffer unduly as a result.
- What is the management culture? Is the managing director interested in our business? Does the managing director and his senior team show that they understand and respect their customers' needs, and regard this as the most important aspect of their business?
- What is their track record in terms of delivery performance? Do they keep records? Can these be believed? Does the track record indicate an improving trend? Do they keep track of this by customer? If they do, then it is worth looking at the record for customers of similar importance to ourselves. It is also good practice to talk to them and see if they will corroborate the supplier's data.
- Do they also track their production efficiency? If that is neither stable nor improving then we are likely to suffer a decrease in delivery performance as a result.
- Do they also track their internal reject rates, and where these are significant, do they ensure that a sufficient order quantity is put into production in order to fulfil our order requirements?
- Do they have a formal scheduling and planning system? Like MRPII, for example? Or is it done on the back of an envelope? A formal system will not only ensure that information is correctly processed, but will also ensure that any forward delivery schedules will be taken into account in their own forward planning.
- How accurate is their data? Apart from ensuring the stability of their planning systems, this will also be relevant in the context of reconciling what their records indicate they have shipped to our own records of what we have received. If these cannot be reconciled we will have ongoing arguments over matters of fact. Also important is just how easily and quickly they are able to ascertain the precise status of every order or scheduled call-off.
- Does their factory operate to the formal system? Or is it controlled by the informal system, the shortage list?
- What levels of control apply to scheduling decisions? Can we be sure that these are objective, and that there is no danger of pressure, in whatever form, from other customers which would displace our own orders in the master schedule?
- Do they have adequate control over their own suppliers? Do they carry out a manufacturing audit of them?

- How flexible is their system? If we have an *in extremis* situation will they be able to respond? How long will it take them to respond?
- What is the present state of their process technology? Is there scope for future reductions in delivery leadtime? Is there a manufacturing strategy that will lead to that? Is the shop floor clean and tidy?
- How far have they followed a JIT approach to the elimination of waste? How many customers insist on JIT deliveries? How is that achieved? By a kanban system, or by holding finished goods stocks?

10.6 Electronic data interchange

With EDI, purchase orders, delivery schedules and forecasts, together with the remainder of the commercial information, such as despatch notes and invoices, normally sent from customer to supplier or vice versa are transmitted electronically, from computer to computer. EDI can be regarded as the sharing of information by the partners in a supply chain partnership.

The benefits of this are two-fold:

1. The information is exchanged more quickly.
2. The information is passed on more accurately, because data is being entered into a system at source, and not having to be re-entered by the recipient.

The initial EDI standards were industry or country specific, with their own unique communication protocols, and examples included:

- EAN–COM in the distribution and retail industries;
- ODETTE in the automotive industry;
- CEFIC in the chemical industry;
- EDIFICE in the electronics and computer industries;
- RINET in the insurance industry.

By 1993 one EDI network provider, International Network Services, had claimed 55 per cent of the UK market and 35 per cent of the European market (*Logistics Today*, 1993), with over six million documents per month being exchanged through three major EDI networks:

1. TRADANET: for retailing, distribution, health, pharmaceuticals and international trade; participants in this network include companies such as Tesco and Boots.
2. BROKERNET: for insurance.
3. FLEETNET: for fleet leasing management.

There is now an international standard—EDIFACT—which is still not universally used, while in Europe EDI standards are becoming coordinated by the European Community.

It is still essential to ascertain which EDI standard is being used by one's trading partners, and for smaller manufacturers the decision is often imposed by a large customer in the supply chain.

EDI software is fast becoming an accepted addition to MRP systems, and the state-of-the-art systems will enable translation to or from most of the common extant standards. This is often referred to as a *value-added network* (VAN).

11
The management of MRP

11.1 Management parameters

In the management of an MRP system the key parameters at a technical level are:

- the choice between a bucketless or time-bucketed system;
- the choice between regenerative or net change mode;
- the frequency of replanning;
- the planning horizon.

The difference between a time-bucketed system and a bucketless system has been covered in Chapter 8. A bucketless system is the state-of-the-art alternative in the 1990s. The other key parameters listed above are dealt with now. After that this chapter then addresses other aspects of importance in the management of MRP:

- the management aids available to the planner
- safety stocks
- inventory management with an MRP system
- stability
- planning leadtimes

11.2 Regenerative mode and net change mode

A fundamental difference in MRP systems engineering is between the two modes of carrying out the MRP process. These modes are:

- regenerative mode
- net change mode

Regenerative mode

Regenerative mode begins with the latest version of the MPS, and totally re-explodes it to net requirements level. This is typically a batch processing function, which normally requires extensive data processing time. It is therefore most usually run on a weekly or monthly frequency. Regenerative mode was very often the only choice available with the early generations of computers.

Net change mode

Net change mode has a material requirements plan which is continuously stored and available within the system. In net change mode MRP reacts on-line to all events, such as changes to MPS, changes to inventory, changes to bills of materials, order receipt, etc.

The net change system mechanism distinguishes between planned and unplanned events:

- For all planned events, MRP updates the status, but does not trigger replanning because the original materials plan is still valid.
- For unplanned events, MRP replans by calculating the net changes, and exploding only the net changes, giving as a result the net changes at net material requirements level. This can be done either on-line or in overnight batch processing mode.

Net change mode is more reactive than regenerative mode, but any errors are self-perpetuating. If net change mode is used as the norm, complete regeneration should be carried out periodically to purge the system of any errors that may have accumulated.

The state-of-the-art MRP system is a bucketless net change system with periodic regeneration.

11.3 The planning horizon

In MRP the planning horizon is the span of time from now to the future point beyond which materials plans will not be generated. It should be the longer of:

- cumulative manufacturing leadtime
- firm demand coverage on the master schedule

The longer the planning horizon is, the more time there is to ensure that both capacity and material requirements can be satisfied, but at the same time the more difficult it becomes to make reasonable estimates of demand towards the latter part of the planning horizon.

11.4 Replanning frequency

The time between MRP replanning runs will be an addition to the leadtime. For example, if replanning is carried out only on a monthly basis, and if a new sales order is added to the master schedule immediately after a replanning run, then a full month will elapse before any account is taken of this in the planning process. In this worst-case example, there is therefore a system leadtime of one month, and this becomes a *de facto*, albeit unplanned, addition to the cumulative manufacturing leadtime.

The most typical replanning frequency is weekly. Little and Jarvis (1992) found that 60 per cent of all users operated weekly replanning. For 25 per cent the replanning frequency was daily, for nine per cent twice weekly, and only six per cent replanned monthly. A net change system will be supportive of changes that occur between regenerative planning runs, and may account for a proportion of the users replanning daily. Where data volumes are high the amount of computer time needed may be a factor determining frequency of replanning in a regenerative system.

11.5 Top–down planning and bottom–up replanning

The MRP system in operation will be a combination of

1. *Top–down planning*: in which the system itself carries out the planning.
2. *Bottom–up replanning*: in which the materials planner may make reactive decisions to override the system.

Top–down planning

The MRP system assumes it is always possible, and tells the planner what should be done, rather than what can be done. It expects the materials planner to react and resolve conflict. It typically provides a set of warning or exception messages, requiring action, which the materials planner may confirm on-line in order to allow the ordering system to proceed automatically; otherwise the planner will initiate the action, and confirm his feedback to the system later.

In many MRP systems the catalogue of exception messages is lengthy and confusing. They can all be classified into one of six basic categories, and in its simplest form these six will comprise the system's list of exceptions:

– order
– cancel
– increase
– decrease
– defer
– expedite

Of these the most problematical is expedite, which will refer primarily to:

– orders that should have been received, but have not;
– orders already placed, but that are now required earlier;
– new orders that are needed in less than the planning leadtime.

In the case of new orders to be released, the system may make provision for automatic release of orders or delivery schedules, either on a global basis, or selectively by location, by supplier or by product family.

Bottom–up replanning

The request to expedite requires decision making on the part of the planner, and normally involves resolving conflict of priorities. The tools available to the planner in this task are:

- pegging
- firm planned orders

Pegging

Pegging is the use of the where-used technique, described in Chapter 7, to peg, or cross-refer, a planned order to the higher-level requirement(s) generating the order. This allows the planner to identify the higher-level impact of potential shortages, for example parts which the top–down system planning tagged as expedite.

With lot-for-lot sizing and a bucketless system, it is feasible to use full or multi-level pegging to identify the highest-level requirement (for example, a master schedule order) generating the order.

Otherwise it is normal for the planner to use single-level pegging, and trace upwards to all higher-level requirements generating the order.

Firm planned orders

The firm planned order is the method available to the planner to override the system's action in top–down planning. It allows the planner to override lot size or leadtime, normally by specifying a fixed quantity and planned receipt date.

A firm planned order can therefore be used by the planner to communicate the action he has taken in order to maintain master schedule due date. He may, for example:

- increase a previous planned order quantity, if the works or supplier are able to run on;
- compress the supplier or manufacturing leadtime of a component, if it can be supplied on a shorter than normal leadtime;
- compress the manufacturing leadtime of the subassembly or product using the component, so that a delay in availability will be compensated for during the manufacturing or assembly process. This will normally only be possible if there are queue or move times which can be compressed.

A requirement entered by the planner as a firm planned order will not subsequently be altered by an MRP time-phased explosion or lot-sizing calculation.

11.6 Safety stocks

The use of safety stocks should be viewed as insurance against the unexpected or unplanned, for example:

- unexpected changes in demand at master schedule level;
- unplanned variations in supply of component parts, whether purchased or manufactured. This would include failures of either delivery performance or quality performance.

Safety stocks are accepted by classical MRP theory. Orlicky (1975) advocated their use in the following circumstances:

- safety stock of independent demand items, as a protection against forecast error;
- safety stock or safety leadtime for dependent demand items, as a protection against unreliable suppliers.

Safety stock may be specified item by item on the parts master file. If a safety stock is specified, MRP will deduct the safety stock from the inventory level during the netting process. In other words, MRP will always plan to leave safety stocks intact.

There are typically three ways in which a safety stock may be specified by the planner to MRP:

1. A fixed quantity.
2. A fixed number of periods' requirements.
3. A safety time to be added to the planning leadtime.

In addition there is a further method, the calculation of a safety stock to achieve a specified level of service, taking account of the variability of demand. This is normally generated from independent demand by a demand forecasting system, and has theoretical validity *only* in the case of independent demand items.

In most instances safety stock for dependent demand items is calculated empirically (rather than scientifically) by the materials planner, for instance, to cover a percentage of the likely demand over the leadtime of an item. The availability within a software package of quantitative measurements of delivery and quality performance may make possible a more defensible calculation than this.

The most dangerous feature in an MRP package is one that provides for the calculation of safety stock of dependent demand items based on their historical usage. There are examples of packages providing this facility. These exhibit a fundamental misunderstanding of the distinction between dependent and independent demand, and are likely to result in excess stock for most of the time.

Safety stock calculation

The following is an example of a calculation of safety stock to achieve a specified service level. Let us assume that the most recent 12 periods' demand was as follows:

$$437 \quad 255 \quad 259 \quad 482 \quad 159 \quad 405$$

$$136 \quad 435 \quad 69 \quad 109 \quad 131 \quad 154$$

Using a simple mathematical pocket calculator, the following data may be established:

$$\text{Mean demand} = 253$$

$$\text{Standard deviation} = 149$$

The safety stock to achieve a range of service levels is shown below:

Service level	Safety stock	Calculation
100%	Infinite	
99.9%	447	3 × standard deviation
97.5%	298	2 × standard deviation
80%	149	1 × standard deviation
50%	0	

The adverse consequences of safety stocks are:

− Safety stock of a higher-level item will generate additional requirements for lower-level items.
− Safety stocks will increase inventory costs.
− Safety stocks may be used to disguise errors in planning or shortcomings in performance, and thus divert attention from solving these problems.

Surveys indicate that in practice:

1. Twenty per cent of MRP users have safety stock at all levels in the product structure; the inference of this is that both the shop floor and external suppliers are failing to provide an acceptable delivery and quality performance.

2. Forty per cent have safety stocks only at the lowest-level items; this can be a justifiable protection against poor supplier delivery performance or poor supplier quality performance.
3. Forty per cent have safety stocks only at finished product level; the justification for this may be either as a protection against unreliable forecasts or, in a make-to-stock environment, to cater for variability in the demand pattern.

11.7 Inventory management

MRP is concerned with managing the time-phased flow of materials, and not the level of inventory. Inventory levels in an MRP system will be determined primarily by:

- the lot-sizing rules in operation;
- safety stock;
- the span of time buckets and the frequency of replanning.

The inventory management module of MRP typically assists the planner in the control of inventory levels by providing the following information:

- ABC analyses—to help direct management attention more frequently to the areas of inventory where the greatest amount of money is tied up;
- excess inventory analyses;
- stockturn analyses—to provide a measure of inventory management performance.

11.8 Stability

An MRP system will be relatively stable where the firm demand horizon is longer than the *cumulative manufacturing leadtime* (CMLT). It will be fundamentally unstable if the firm demand horizon is shorter than the CMLT. This will be typical where there are externally purchased parts on long leadtimes.

Figure 11.1 illustrates in very crude terms how stability is determined by the *relationship* between demand visibility and the flexibility of procurement or manufacture, and not by either of these factors on its own.

The techniques for coping with inherent instability are:

- a contingency plan (or hedge) in the master schedule;
- safety stocks of critical long leadtime components.

11.9 Planning leadtimes

Actual manufacturing leadtimes comprise the following elements:

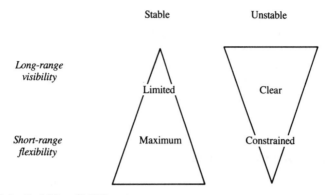

Figure 11.1   Stability of MRP systems

1. Queue time, which is independent of batch size.
2. Setup time, also independent of batch size.
3. Manufacturing time, which *is* dependent on batch size.
4. Move time, again independent of batch size.

The textbook MRP solution makes the following assumptions:

– queue and setup times are high in relation to manufacturing times;
– therefore the planning leadtime for an item is fixed, regardless of batch size.

In many manufacturing environments these assumptions are not true, especially if manufacturing strategy has been directed towards minimizing queue and setup times, in a JIT environment, for example. Manufacturing leadtimes will vary according to batch size, in which case the time phasing of requirements within MRP will be incorrect.

There are simple ways in which MRP can cope with leadtimes that are variable depending on batch size, and an increasing number of packages support this.

Some MRP systems allow planning leadtime to be either fixed or variable. It is necessary to check the specification of specific software packages. Depending on the software, the variable leadtimes may be calculated in either of these ways:

– By the user specifying the leadtime on the parts master record as two components:
    fixed (queue and/or setup)
    variable (manufacturing time per unit quantity).
Where n is the batch size, the MRP system calculation of leadtime will therefore be
    fixed + (n × variable)

- The other way of deriving variable planning leadtimes is by the MRP system extracting the detailed manufacturing operations data from the MRPII capacity requirements planning database, and summing the capacity planning calculations operation by operation to give the total batch manufacturing leadtime.

Some software packages may include a detailed production scheduling module, in which scheduling to finite production capacity is carried out. Without exception such modules will recognize the variability of leadtime with batch size. During the scheduling process a planned start date of a batch or order is calculated. This planned start date becomes the due date used by MRP at gross requirements planning level, rather than the date calculated by the normal time-phasing method using the planning leadtime.

12
System drivers

In the textbook system, MRP is driven by the master production schedule (MPS), and this is explained in detail in Chapter 16.

Many software packages will allow alternative drivers of MRP, and these include the following:

- *The sales order file*: this may be used directly to drive MRP, or it may be used indirectly by means of a process of releasing sales orders onto a works order file.
- *The works order file*: this may comprise orders that have been scheduled, with planned start dates calculated by a production scheduling module, or it may be unscheduled, in which case the orders retain their original due dates.
- *The production plan*: this will be produced by the production planning module (see Chapter 15), and will consist of planned production quantities over future periods of time. This may be used as the driver of MRP if rate-based scheduling is being used.

The alternative order-based system drivers are depicted in Figure 12.1.

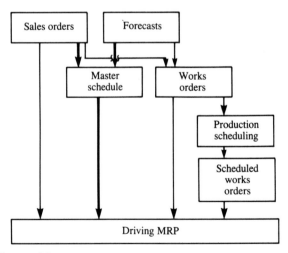

Figure 12.1   System drivers

These alternatives to the master schedule may be more appropriate in a number of manufacturing environments:

– where rate-based scheduling is feasible, and has been adopted;
– a make-to-order environment;
– a highly customized jobbing environment;
– any environment where the benefits of top-level-only production smoothing do not justify the cost of the master production scheduling software module.

This aspect is discussed more fully in Part Three, Chapter 16, and for the moment it is sufficient to conclude that there are four alternative system drivers in an MRP system:

– the MPS
– a rate-based production plan
– sales orders
– works orders

This is contrary to what is prescribed in the definitive version of MRPII given by Wight (1984), where the MPS is accorded an importance that may not always be appropriate.

PART THREE
PRODUCTION
MANAGEMENT
SYSTEMS

Chapter 13 introduces the subject of production management systems. The textbook MRPII standard system is covered in Chapters 14 to 20, and the abbreviated or part-standard system in Chapters 16 to 20. The fit with JIT is dealt with in Chapter 21, and the make-to-order variant in Chapter 22. Chapter 23 then describes distribution resource planning (DRP), while distributed MRPII (DMRP) is the subject of Chapter 24. Part Three then concludes by examining in Chapter 25 the interfaces with costing and accounting systems.

13
Overview of MRPII

This chapter serves as an introduction to the subject of production management systems. To recap—we accept MRPII as a non-prescriptive framework for the production management system. We therefore begin by examining how MRPII evolved, and we then note its principal feature—that of a closed loop system. We will then define the scope of MRPII and establish a generalized overview of MRPII's functionality. After that the most common variants of the general framework are defined; these include the MRPII standard system, along with a number of alternative solutions better adapted to specific manufacturing environments. This chapter concludes with a pathway to the remainder of Part Three, and this is keyed to the different variants of the MRPII framework.

13.1 The evolution from MRP to MRPII

In looking at MRP in Part Two we have examined in depth a materials planning module or subsystem, planning the requirements for both make and buy items. This planning module is driven by a master production schedule or one of the alternative system drivers noted in Chapter 12, and in its turn it drives a purchase-ordering system module.

In simplistic terms MRPII is an integrated extension from MRP which adds the following major functions to the system:

- *Capacity planning*: this is the balancing of workload with capacity.
- *Production activity control*: the controlled release of works orders to production.

13.2 A closed loop system

A major feature of MRPII is that it is a closed loop system, and the two major features of a closed loop system are:

- the feedback of events, both planned and unplanned, to maintain the currency of information status;
- the integration of the different system modules.

The key feedback or integration loops within MRPII are:

- the receipt of supplier orders into inventory;
- the completion of works orders into inventory or despatch. This link may be provided by a shop-floor data collection (SFDC) module.

Most MRPII software also provides for the following additional systems integration:

- an interface between a sales order processing module and the MPS module;
- the generation of sales analyses from the database generated by the sales order processing module, and the linking of this sales analysis data into a demand forecasting module;
- the linking of the forecasts generated into the MPS module, to help drive the master schedule;
- the generation of actual or standard costs, and linking these into the financial systems.

Many MRPII software packages will also provide some further degree of systems integration, and three are worthy of mention:

- an interface between a CAD system and the bill of materials module;
- an EDI module, enabling translation of data into or from the protocol of an EDI network within the company's supply chain;
- a distribution resource planning (DRP) subsystem, linking a downstream-integrated distribution network with the overall MRPII planning system.

Two significant loops are not closed effectively within MRPII:

- the impact of material unavailability on capacity planning and production scheduling;
- the impact of capacity constraints on detailed materials requirements planning.

The failure to close these two loops stems primarily from the reasoning of the authors of the MRPII standard system. In the name of transparency the system was to be a decision-support tool, not a decision-making tool. The job of the system is to tell planners what should happen, and to provide them with the decision-support information that allows them to resolve conflict; it is not for the system to make the decisions.

13.3 The scope of MRPII

The scope of MRPII in terms of both system modules and closed loops is in practice heavily dependent on specific software.

The MRPII standard system was formulated in the late 1970s and achieved widespread publicity in the early 1980s, but it is based on a systems concept whose origins date from the late 1960s. It preceded the widespread adoption of JIT and had later to be revised with the incorporation of a repetitive manufacturing module to overcome a major misfit with JIT.

MRPII's higher-level planning functions were conceived before the advent of spreadsheets. It could reasonably be argued that Lotus 1–2–3 made MRPII redundant above the level of master production scheduling in many companies by offering a more powerful and flexible planning tool.

The state of the art in the 1990s is therefore represented by the wide choice of available MRPII software, and not by the MRPII standard system. That software has developed over time to meet the real needs of users in many different manufacturing environments, rather than the specific environment in which MRPII evolved and which it primarily addressed.

For practical purposes this book therefore defines MRPII in terms of what is achieved by that wide choice of available software, and not in terms of what is prescribed by the textbooks. Many software packages are, or claim to be, based on the MRPII standard system. They vary considerably in terms of the support given to the user at or above master production scheduling level. Other packages address the principles and objectives of MRPII, but allow variations or non-standard approaches, particularly in the area of production scheduling.

Both at execution level and in terms of integration with financial and commercial subsystems there is considerable divergence between software packages. The MRPII standard system defined clearly and comprehensively only the planning method; it was not a blueprint for an integrated management information system.

13.4 Generalized overview of MRPII functional levels

A generalized overview of MRPII, its functional levels and its principal system modules is given in Figure 13.1. A full explanation of each module is given in the remainder of Part Three.

The major variations to that generalized overview are as follows:

– The presence or absence of system modules at the highest level of tactical planning, namely forecasting, and longer-term production planning and resource planning.
– The presence or absence of business planning support tools, based on fourth-generation language (4GL) software accessing the MRPII database, to assist business managers in strategic planning or highest-level tactical planning.
– The presence or absence of a distribution resource planning (DRP) module

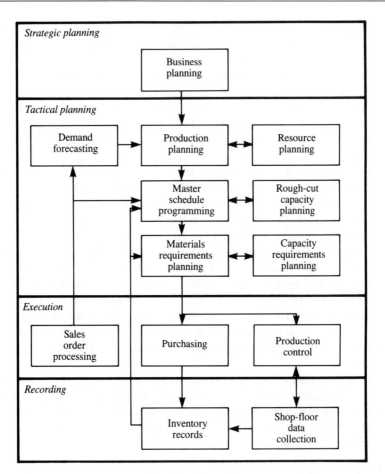

Figure 13.1 MRPII system overview (based on IBM MAAPICS/DB Manufacturing Resource Planning System)

to act as a system driver where end-product inventories are wholly or partly held downstream in an integrated physical distribution system.

- What drives the MPS, and the degree to which the system assists in the planning or smoothing of production at this level.
- The degree of interaction between the MPS and rough cut capacity planning modules.
- Non-standard solutions catering for make-to-order and jobbing shop environments, in which detailed production scheduling takes place and may in its turn drive material requirements planning.
- The presence or absence of a repetitive manufacturing module, which allows MRPII planning to be coordinated with JIT methods at execution level.

- Whether or not ordering and production control modules generate turn-around documents for use in the feedback loops to minimize data error.
- The extent to which inventory modules support lot or batch traceability, especially in the context of ISO 9000 quality assurance system require-ments.
- The extent to which supplier and manufacturing delivery and quality per-formance is captured and made available for finetuning the key parameters of safety stock or safety leadtime.

13.5 The most common variants

It is possible to recognize a number of generic variants on the general theme:

- the full textbook MRPII standard system
- a part-standard MRPII system
- the fit with JIT
- the make-to-order non-standard system
- integrated DRP
- distributed MRP (DMRP)

The standard system

Figure 13.1 depicts the modular structure of the standard system. The pro-portion of software packages which conforms to this model varies according to the IT platform, and is addressed in detail in Chapter 27. It remains the standard system on IBM mid-range platforms, but is far from being the *de facto* standard on open system platforms.

Equally significant is that not all users of packages conforming to the full standard system use all of the system modules. Both Burcher (1991) and Little and Jarvis (1992) surveyed the usage by module. Material requirements planning tops the charts at over 90 per cent of all users. Next comes master production scheduling at 80 per cent. Capacity planning modules are only used in 50–60 per cent of installations, about the same as production activity control, and shop-floor data collection has only a 40 per cent adherence.

The MRPII part-standard system

This is the form of MRPII that is supported by the largest number of soft-ware packages, and is an abbreviated form of the textbook system which gen-erally omits the higher level planning modules. In structure it will resemble Figure 13.2. Some of these packages may include:

- business planning support tools with access to the MRPII database;

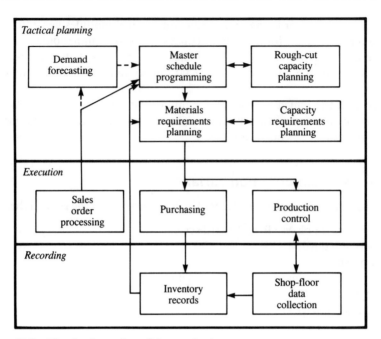

Figure 13.2 The simple version of the standard system

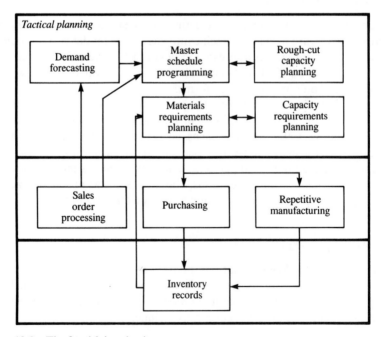

Figure 13.3 The fit with just-in-time

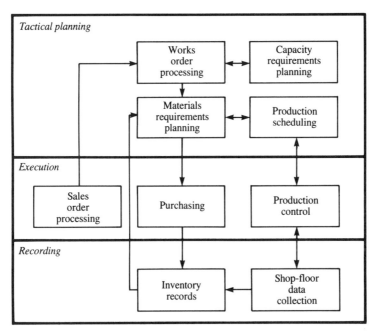

Figure 13.4   The make-to-order hybrid

– a demand forecasting module, which may or may not interface with the master schedule.

This abbreviated form of the MRPII standard system will be appropriate in most manufacturing environments except for assemble-to-order, where there may be a need for higher-level planning at product group or product family level.

The fit with JIT

This is the form of MRPII that interfaces with JIT production methods, and is depicted in Figure 13.3. The many variations or adaptations in practice will be noted in Chapter 21.

The make-to-order non-standard system

Strictly speaking, this model is not textbook MRPII but a non-standard system. It is just as valid an adaptation to a specific type of manufacturing environment as the repetitive manufacturing module of MRPII. There is therefore a sound case for regarding it as an alternative to the textbook MRPII standard system. Figure 13.4 illustrates a typical non-standard system.

14
Demand forecasting

This chapter begins by examining the use that is made of forecasts of demand in an MRPII system. We will then look more closely at the different types of demand patterns, and the forecasting techniques that are used. Finally, we will set forecasting in perspective by challenging the circumstances in which it is a valid systems tool.

14.1 Forecasts

In manufacturing planning systems, forecasts are used to allow planning over a forward horizon which spans a time period beyond the limit of firm customer orders. Forecasting is confined to independent demand items. Requirements for dependent demand components to support the forecast will be generated automatically by MRP once the forecast is incorporated in the master schedule.

A forecast will be expressed in terms of quantities of a product over future periods of time. *Demand forecasting systems* are based on an analysis of historical demand. In MRPII systems the source of historical demand is typically sales analysis data created as a by-product of sales order entry system modules.

In a demand forecasting system there are two important time dimensions, typically set by user-given system parameters:

– the number of past periods of historical demand to be used in forecasting future demand;
– the time buckets on which the future forecast is to be based. The span of the time buckets may vary over the forecast horizon—for example, weeks or months over the short to medium term, and months or quarters towards the latter part of the forecasting horizon.

An important option may include forecasting at product group or product family level, rather than at individual item or part number level. This is important in an assemble-to-order environment, where there are feature-dependent standard products, and where the large number of specific configurations requires some form of synthesis in order to be meaningful both for forecasting and longer-term planning purposes. In this case, forecasting should provide the percentage split or mix of the various features or options of the product specification; this split is the planning bill of materials, and we shall see the usefulness of this when looking at master production scheduling in Chapter 16.

Where there is an integrated distribution system, forecasting should begin at individual warehouse level, and be consolidated upwards or backwards through the distribution pipeline to give the forecast at manufacturing plant level. Alternatively this may fall within the scope of a DRP system module.

At component part level, forecasts may also be made of service or spares requirements.

Where finished product stocks are held, the forecasting module should also recommend safety stocks to give protection against variability in demand. It may also recommend re-order points and re-order quantities in the case of distributed inventories. Re-order point would be relevant only if distributed inventories were controlled by an order-point system rather than a DRP system.

14.2 Demand patterns

The pattern of order arrival or quantities ordered over time will display varying mixtures of two attributes:

– trends
– randomness

There are four major types of trends:

1. Seasonal trends, which are related to the calendar.
2. Cyclical trends, related to changes in market size.
3. Business trends, related to changes in market share.
4. Product life cycle, reflecting the stages in the product life from its introduction and subsequent growth, through to its maturity, and finally on to its decline and eventual withdrawal.

The typical characteristics of these four trends are summarized in Table 14.1. The awkward questions that can be asked are these:

Table 14.1   Characteristics of trends

Trend	Time amplitude	Typical driving forces
Seasonal	12 months, fixed	Holidays; weather; financial periods
Cyclical	3–5 years, variable	National economies; political change
Business	1–5 years, variable	Marketing; competition; performance
Product life	1–5 years, shortening	Product substitution

- Which of these trends can you predict from analysis of historical demand?
- How many past cycles of data do you need to make a forecast?

These are very pertinent questions to be considered when deciding whether or not to use forecasts to drive company planning systems. The answer is that normally only seasonal trends can be predicted with any degree of accuracy from historical sales data. The remaining trends are notoriously difficult to predict, even by experts, and tend to be the most important trends influencing the future level of sales demand.

14.3 Forecasting techniques

A number of sophisticated forecasting techniques have been developed in order to cater for differing underlying patterns of demand. The most common of these are based on a combination of *time series analysis* and *exponential smoothing*.

Some forecasting modules will incorporate a choice of different forecasting techniques, and there may also be provision for the user to insert his own specific forecasting technique. Where a choice of method is offered, many systems will select the one with the best fit to the underlying pattern of demand. This is done by taking each method in turn and using more distant demand history to forecast the more recent past periods, and then comparing the forecast made to the actual demand in those periods. The method that gave the most accurate forecast in those more recent periods will then be selected. This is sometimes referred to as *focus forecasting*.

Most forecasting techniques are sensitive to weightings or coefficients used in the smoothing formulae. Most forecasting systems will therefore have an error tracking mechanism which allows for correction of these weightings or coefficients based on comparisons of forecast and actual results.

Seasonal trends are fairly readily detectable by time series analysis, provided sufficient historical data exists. Future forecasting will typically be based on a forecast of the trend in annual demand, followed by the profiling of forecast annual demand around the detected seasonal pattern.

Other trends will normally not be predictable from the typical time history span of most databases. Most forecasting techniques will therefore tend to forecast that the current trend will continue indefinitely, unless there is provision for the introduction of external forecasts of the criteria driving these trends.

Some systems may allow a product life cycle template to be fitted to the historical demand pattern. A major problem is that product life cycles are continually shortening, and furthermore that the early stages of the product life cycle may be interrupted by a downward cyclical trend, as happened in 1980 and 1990. It was quite fashionable in the UK in the mid 1980s to assume that cyclical recessions had disappeared from the economic agenda; the events of 1990–92 were unforeseen by many who had not experienced the cyclical ups and downs more prevalent throughout the period from 1951 to 1979.

Discontinuous randomness in demand patterns will normally be smoothed by forecasting techniques into a continuous average forecast demand. It must not be assumed that the ensuing order-arrival pattern will be similarly continuous; it is more than likely to be what Orlicky (1975) described as lumpy.

Most packages allow user overrides to the forecast, and the system will track the accuracy of these overrides. Manual overrides could be used to make due allowance for the expected future pattern of any of the cyclical trends not forecastable by the technique in use.

14.4 Forecasting in practice

Depending on the software package, an MRPII forecasting module may interrelate to other system modules in several ways:

- The forecast may be automatically inserted on the master schedule.
- The forecast may be processed by a production planning module prior to insertion on the master schedule.
- There may be no automatic link to the master schedule. In other words it is a standalone tool for business planning purposes.

State-of-the-art spreadsheets offer forecasting tools just as powerful as those offered by MRPII software. Of the two, spreadsheets are by far the more

Table 14.2   Potential accuracy of forecasts

End customer	Domestic consumer	Industrial consumer
Customer base	Large	Small
Product type	F.m.c.g.[†]	Capital goods
Production	For POS inventories	Make to order
Selling	Multiple retail POS	Ex-factory
Leadtime	Off-shelf	Long
Sales volume	High	Low
Driven by	Recurring need	Available funds
Market price	Low	High
Order frequency	Regular	Infrequent
Order interval	Short	Long
Forecast accuracy	High	Poor
Forecast validity	Medium-term	Very short-term
Forecast will be replaced by		Sales plan, based on marketing information

[†] Fast-moving consumer goods.

flexible. With the advent of open systems the transfer of data between MRPII systems and spreadsheets is achieved quite easily.

Product life cycles are becoming shorter. This makes forecasting forward from historical data increasingly inaccurate. Inaccuracy of forecasts is cited as one of the major reasons for poor performance of many installed MRPII systems. Where the nature of future demand is not known, there will be no valid basis for a future forecast. Luscombe (1993) views this problem in a different light, and argues that 'unforecastability is not a technical problem, it is a warning sign that the product is not viable'.

The potential accuracy and usefulness of forecasts based on historical demand patterns will therefore depend on the market environment. The extremes are summarized in Table 14.2. Towards the right-hand extreme, manually generated forecasts, or sales plans based on marketing information, tend to replace forecasts generated by demand forecasting modules of MRPII. The sales plan will normally be entered on the master schedule in place of a forecast.

15
Production planning

The purpose of the production planning module is to generate top-level production plans, based on groups or families of products. It is logically equivalent to a master schedule by product family, but based solely upon forecasts, and is sometimes described as *first-cut scheduling* or *rough-cut master scheduling*.

Production planning is based on a combination of two sets of data:

1. Demand forecasts, which are derived from historical sales analysis data by a demand forecasting module.
2. Production targets by product family, which derive from the company's top-level business plan.

The resulting production plan is expressed as quantities over future time buckets, rather than the planned orders associated with master production scheduling. The production plan will be used in master production scheduling as the forecast element in the generation of planned orders. Where rate-based scheduling is being used, the production plan may be passed directly to MRP, thus bypassing the process of master production scheduling.

The key functions of production planning are shown in Figure 15.1. These key functions are as follows:

- to consolidate demand forecasts by product family;
- to generate planning bills at product family level (the concept and use of planning bills is described in detail in Chapter 16);
- to expand production targets from product family level to item level using planning bills;
- to smooth the resulting production targets over successive time periods;
- to test these smoothed production targets for feasibility against the planned resources;
- to pass these smoothed and feasible production plans at item level to the master production scheduling module. This may also be the source of production rate if rate-based scheduling is to be used.

Very few software packages include this module, and in some of these it is a standalone module rather than a module integrated with master production scheduling.

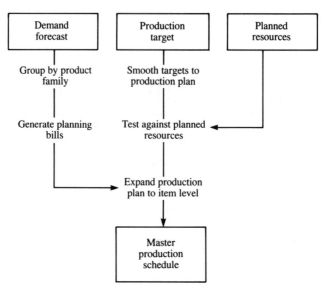

Figure 15.1 Production planning

The principal use of the production planning module is in an assemble-to-order environment, where it may be used to plan product-oriented production lines. It has potential use in other manufacturing environments where there are recognizable production units or work centres associated with a set of discrete products or part numbers.

Production planning is essentially an interactive decision support tool, rather than a decision-making technique, and it will typically be supported interactively by either the resource planning or rough-cut capacity planning module.

Wight (1984) renamed this module as *sales and operations planning*, and this appears to have been in an attempt to focus attention at the time to the sorely needed synergy between marketing and manufacturing. Such synergy has been identified in Chapter 5 as a key element of manufacturing strategy. Creating real synergy between marketing and manufacturing results from a conscious management culture, and not a planning tool, and for the most part software suppliers continue to refer to this module as production planning. In many companies, other than those in an assemble-to-order environment, the same functions may be carried out with much greater flexibility using spreadsheets.

16
Master production scheduling

This chapter begins by putting master production scheduling in perspective for the reader. After that the master production schedule is described in greater detail, the balancing of demand components of the schedule with the supply components is examined, and this leads to the consideration of the MPS analysis itself. The similarity of logic between MRP and MPS is noted, as are the concepts unique to MPS, such as the available-to-promise calculation and time fences. What is very significant, and often confusing, is the wide variation in the treatment of master production scheduling from one software package to another. We will note the major differences, and then place these in perspective by defining the generic options that exist. Then we will look in more detail at those features of master production scheduling which are both necessary and specific to an assemble-to-order environment. After that we will consider rate-based master scheduling. This chapter concludes with a case study of a successful MRPII implementation which is founded solely on the functionality described thus far.

In an order-based scheduling environment, the process of master production scheduling involves the planning manager in one of the key decision-making functions in the entire manufacturing planning system, the preparation of a schedule which has validity for the more detailed tasks of materials planning and capacity planning. The concept of master production scheduling, as described in this chapter, will be modified and may be unnecessary if rate-based scheduling has been adopted, and in a jobbing type of environment where there is limited forward visibility of demand, the process of master production scheduling may not be appropriate.

The process of master production scheduling is driven by independent demand. In its scope it applies to all independent demand items, and they will be designated thus, or in some other manner, on the parts master file. The outcome of master production scheduling is the generation of the MPS, and this has the following major significance:

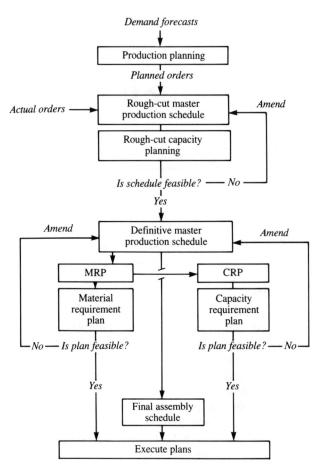

Figure 16.1 The keystone role of MPS

- It balances demand and supply. This is almost always a fine balance between the needs of the market and the company's production capability.
- It is the keystone of the MRPII system.
- It drives all lower-level planning systems including MRP.

That keystone role of MPS is illustrated in flowchart form in Figure 16.1:

- MPS is the first module in the overall system hierarchy to which real customer orders are introduced, and one of its priorities is conditioning all subsequent planning to ensure that the due dates of these customer orders are observed. In some instances MPS may itself be the direct source of the final assembly schedules which trigger production at finished product level.

– In the event that the lower-level materials requirement and capacity
requirement plans, generated by MRP and CRP, prove not to be feasible
and not themselves capable of modification by the planner, then the only
recourse is modification of the MPS itself. In this sense it represents the
heart of the system.

The master production scheduling software may have special features to
cater for the unique requirements of an assemble-to-order environment or for
seasonal stock build.

16.1 The master production schedule

The MPS is the result of master production scheduling. It is a set of planned
orders to satisfy demand. These planned orders are logically equivalent to the
firm planned orders described in Chapter 11, when we examined how the
planner manages MRP.

The MPS is normally tested against planned production resources. This is
the function of rough-cut capacity planning (RCCP), which is described in
Chapter 18. The MPS is then approved or modified by the planning manager
before being released to MRP for detailed planning.

Wight (1984) repeatedly stresses the importance of a valid schedule.
Without a valid schedule the formal system would break down and the factory would revert to being controlled by the informal system, or shortage list.
The most common cause of an invalid schedule is an overloaded schedule,
and its by-products are these:

– Customer delivery dates are not met, or there is a shortfall on the quantity
delivered.
– Most works orders become overdue.
– Orders are completed in a panic in the last week of the month. A common
feature of many poorly planned manufacturing operations is that over 40
per cent of all works orders are completed in the last five working days of
each accounting period. In businesses like these the push system is imperfect; the ultimate driver is a pull mechanism, the need to make up the shortfall on despatches against plan before the data cut-off date of the current
accounting period.
– Certain work centres are overloaded. In a make-to-order environment
these may, to the consternation of the planner, differ from month to
month. The bottleneck may move around the factory, reflecting the variation in product mix from one period to another, thus apparently defying
medium-term corrective measures.

16.2 Demand components and supply components

The MPS is the result of balancing two sets of potentially conflicting data:

– demand components
– supply components

Demand components

The demand components of the MPS are:

– forecasts
– customer orders
– service or spares orders
– safety stocks

Supply components

The supply components of the MPS are:

– the available inventory
– scheduled receipts from production or from suppliers
– planned orders

16.3 The MPS analysis

Table 16.1 shows a typical presentation of the MPS analysis. The arithmetic logic is virtually identical to that of the MRP analysis described in Chapter 8. The meaning of these various elements in the MPS analysis is as follows.

Forecast

This is the forecast of demand over future time periods, typically provided automatically by a demand forecasting module. Some systems may provide for separate system-generated and manually entered forecasts, in which case the manual forecast, if present, will normally override the system forecast. This is a means of allowing management to override, over all or part of the planning horizon, the forecasts generated by the demand forecasting module.

Table 16.1 MPS analysis

	0	1	2	3	4	5	6	7	8	9	10	11	12	13	14	15	16
								Week no.									
Part no. A123																	
Forecast		30	30	30	35	35	40	40	40	40	40	45	45	45	50	50	50
Customer orders		28	34	26	22	18	9	0	5	0	0	0	0	0	0	0	0
Total demand		28	34	30	35	35	40	40	40	40	40	45	45	45	50	50	50
Planned orders		35	35	35	40	40	40	40	40	40	40	45	45	45	50	50	50
Initial inventory	25																	
Projected inventory		32	1	5	5	5	0	0	0	0	0	0	0	0	0	0	0
Net requirements		0	0	0	0	0	0	40	40	40	40	45	45	45	50	50	50
Available to promise		32	1	9	18	22	31	0	0	0	0	0	0	0	0	0	0
Cumulative ATP		32	33	42	60	82	113	113	108	108	108	108	108	108	108	108	108

Customer orders

That is, the quantities and required dates represented by firm customer orders. This data will normally be updated by, or will be extracted from, the sales order entry system. In a closed loop system this will take place automatically, either on-line, or at predetermined intervals.

Total demand

This is typically a user-specified option which allows the process of master scheduling to be driven by one of the following:

- the forecast plus customer orders
- the greater of forecast or customer orders
- the forecast only
- customer orders only

This option may be specified separately for different parts of the planning horizon: for example, customer orders only in a frozen demand zone, and the greater of forecast or customer orders across the rest of the planning horizon.

Planned orders

These are the orders recommended by MPS, or planned by the planner, as a result of all previous MPS runs. MPS will plan orders using lot-sizing techniques similar to those available in MRP (see Chapter 9). Some software packages recommend planned orders which must then be firmed up by the planner into firm planned orders, the default option being in most cases acceptance of the system's recommendation. Firm planned orders will never subsequently be changed by the MPS system. In some systems, the term master production schedule is used to denote planned orders, and there is no distinction between planned orders and firm planned orders. In general, however, order status may be a progression through these three stages:

1. Planned order
2. Firm planned order
3. Live order—one already released to production

The distinction between planned orders and firm planned orders is most significant in an assemble-to-order environment, and this will be explained in more detail later in this chapter.

Initial inventory

This is the physical inventory of this item, less any inventory allocated against sales orders released but not picked, and less any safety stock specified on the parts master record. Some packages may alternatively show safety stock as a separate item of demand on the MPS analysis, thus allowing it to be varied over future time periods depending on the prevailing level of demand, or as a means of enabling advance stock build to cater for a seasonal pattern of demand.

Projected inventory

This is the end-of-period inventory, equal to initial or previous period closing inventory, plus *firm* planned orders, less total demand.

Net requirements

This is the quantity required to be received and planned in order to achieve zero inventory at the end of the period. In most systems the planned order quantity will then be determined by the lot-sizing rules in use, as in MRP.

Available to promise (ATP)

That is, the quantity available to satisfy new customer orders not yet received. This is often shown as the cumulative quantity in each period. The calculation is initial or previous period closing inventory, plus firm planned orders, less actual customer orders.

Cumulative ATP is the key to availability in an order promise situation. The key is using tomorrow's receipts to cover tomorrow's demand, and retaining today's inventory as long as possible to provide cover for a new order which may be received and which can *not* be covered by planned receipts at a future date.

The reader is invited at this point to work through the MRP analysis exercise in Appendix B3.

16.4 Comparison of MPS and MRP

The basic netting arithmetic of MPS and MRP is virtually identical. In many software packages MRP and MPS are closely integrated to avoid duplication of both data and system logic. In such systems MPS is in fact a top-level pass of the MRP system, and a common display format will be used for both the MPS analysis and the MRP net requirements analysis. This may show demand split separately between its major components:

- independent demand, including spares requirements;
- dependent demand at component part level, generated via the bills of material explosion from higher-level independent demand.

The following concepts apply in MPS just as they do in MRP:

- the choice between a time-bucketed or a bucketless system;
- variable time buckets across the planning horizon;
- the choice between a net change or a regenerative system;
- pegging, to allow backtracking from planned orders to the highest-level source demand;
- firm planned orders;
- lot sizing;
- order release.

Lot sizing has been addressed in Chapter 9, and the remainder of these concepts were dealt with in Chapter 11.

16.5 Time fences

The concepts of *time fences* and *horizon* apply primarily to MPS, but by virtue of their application to MPS they will also indirectly constrain MRP. The typical MPS system will have three time fences, which are illustrated in Figure 16.2:

1. The demand time fence delimits the early periods into a frozen zone so as to ensure the stability of plans within critical leadtimes. Only intervention

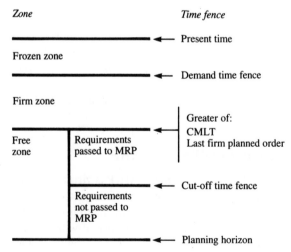

Figure 16.2 Time fences

by the planner can make changes within this frozen zone. Planned orders within this time fence therefore always have the status of firm planned orders.

2. The greater of cumulative manufacturing leadtime or the latest firm planned order divides the remainder of the planning horizon between a firm zone and a free zone. Firm planned orders will normally exist beyond the cumulative manufacturing leadtime only in an assemble-to-order environment. The main significance implicit in the recognition of the firm zone is that increases to the MPS within the cumulative manufacturing leadtime will have repercussions on the feasibility of plans at MRP level.

3. Cut-off time fence delimits the forward extent of the detailed planning horizon. Requirements beyond this point will not be passed to MRP. In many instances this time fence may also be the cumulative manufacturing leadtime, especially in a make-to-order environment.

Wight (1984) very aptly describes these three zones as being *frozen*, *slushy* and *liquid*.

Levels of authority

Alongside these frozen, slushy and liquid zones, and their associated time fences, is a concept vital for the proper management of the MRPII system— levels of decision-making authority appropriate to the greatly different constraints which apply within these different zones.

Within the liquid zone, authority can be delegated entirely to the planner. Within the limits of the overall production plan, there are no changes that cannot in theory be accommodated within the future plans.

By the time the slushy zone is entered, the majority of changes at MPS level will begin to have a major impact on production or procurement plans for some, but not all, of the component parts. Because of this the appropriate decision-making authority is not the planner, but the senior manager responsible for the whole manufacturing operations.

Within the firm zone, changes to the MPS are, in theory, impossible to cater for, unless additional short-term additions to the production or procurement capacity can be found, or unless critical leadtimes can be compressed. Failing that, an addition to the schedule can be accommodated only at the expense of putting another order into arrears. The implications of decisions like these should be made by top-level management, the level above both marketing and manufacturing functional management, where an assessment of the consequences, both of the disruption to production or procurement plans and loss of opportunity by refusing the change, can be weighed objectively.

Here lies the nub of the historic contention between manufacturing and marketing—allow the planner to refuse to accept changes within the critical leadtime and the system is seen to fail to respond to customer expectation; on the other hand, allow marketing solely to decide whether to accept changes to the schedule, and the result may well be to throw the entire order book into an arrears position. The objective view of top management, taking due account of all the potential repercussions, is critical to the decision-making process within the frozen zone, and in turn to an acceptance by both planners and salesmen that the system is impartial.

16.6 Variations between MRPII software packages

The principal variations in currently available software packages are as follows:

1. In some packages there may be provision only for MPS maintenance, the basic data entry and updating of the MPS, as distinct from a planning tool assisting in the balancing of supply and demand.
2. In some systems there may be a distinction between planned orders and firm planned orders. The system may recommend planned orders, while the planner confirms as firm planned orders those planned or recommended orders close to the critical leadtime.
3. In some systems, there may be provision for actual customer orders to consume the forecast. In this case receipt of a customer order will lead to a decrease in the balance of the forecast, and the customer order will normally lead to the generation of a corresponding firm planned order. This will be most common in a bucketless system oriented to an assemble-to-order environment.
4. Some systems may contain simple algorithms for smoothing production plans at MPS level. In this case the system will recommend planned orders, using variations in planned inventory to achieve a level set of planned orders. This is most common in systems that have been developed to cater for rate-based scheduling or for a seasonal pattern of demand, where company policy may be to spread production evenly over a year, and to build up inventory in advance of seasonal peaks. In this case, it is common for the logic to recognize the planned inventory build-up as a form of safety stock and to exclude it from the available-to-promise calculation.
5. Some systems may have special provision for feature dependency in the product specification. This will be most applicable in the assemble-to-order or make-to-stock environments.

16.7 The master production scheduling options

The wide variation in software functionality at MPS level stems from the early days of MRP. The definitive work on MRP (Orlicky 1975) defined a processing logic which was already established in practice. The very nature of MRP logic led to a standard with relatively minor variations, but the same was not true of master production scheduling, and Orlicky's work merely accepted the status quo, which by that time spanned considerable variations in practice.

Orlicky noted that master production schedules can imply any of the following:

- gross requirements
- a production plan
- planned order releases

Gross requirements option

In this case the MPS represents a set of gross requirements, which will subsequently be netted against inventory by MRP. In this situation actual orders released for production will fall short of the MPS in the short-term horizon by the amount of any inventory of MPS items. Orlicky believed this to be inconsistent with the definition master *production* schedule.

Production plan option

With this option the MPS is a production plan, which actually represents what is going to be manufactured. In this case the netting of demand against inventory must be done during the preparation of the MPS. Orlicky recommended this as the most logical approach.

In this case the only difference between MPS and MRP lies in the representation of demand, and there is a prima facie case for simply treating MPS as a top-level pass of MRP. This is the approach adopted by many software packages, and is both logically adequate and the simplest to understand for all manufacturing environments except assemble-to-order. Taking this approach means that MRP will plan works orders for final assembly or top-level production without complication, just as it will do for all of the lower-level manufactured components.

Planned order release option

In this option the MPS represents a set of planned order releases, in which case MRP will not plan to release to production the top-level product, but only its immediate component parts or subassemblies. Orlicky associated this approach with feature-dependent products in an assemble-to-order environment. In this case both the basic product and all of its optional features appear at the highest level in both the bills of materials and the MPS.

MRP is therefore not concerned with the planning of final assembly orders. This is done instead by a final assembly scheduling routine, using special manufacturing bills of materials. In many assemble-to-order environments, rate-based scheduling is now used, and the final assembly schedule may be derived directly from the sales order file.

Much of the complexity of MRPII revolves around the complexities of assembly to order, the environment in which MRPII was conceived. Much of the complexity of assembly to order has since been eliminated by logical advances in product design, such as *design for manufacture* (DFM) or *design for manufacture and assembly* (DFMA), which now make the treatment of feature dependency much simpler in terms of MPS.

In terms of the 1990s state-of-the-art application of master production scheduling, the following recommendations are offered:

1. The production plan option should be regarded as the norm or standard. In that case there is a prima facie case for selecting software that *combines* the MPS and MRP logic into a single module, rather than paying for two separate modules, and introducing unnecessary complexity, just to conform more closely to the MRPII standard system.
2. The planned order release option should be regarded as the variant applicable to an assemble-to-order manufacturing environment. In this case MRP will not plan final assembly orders, nor will MRPII's production control module release them to the works. Exactly *how* this is achieved will depend on specific software packages. In the case of high-volume or repetitive assembly to order this will normally be achieved by the repetitive manufacturing module of MRPII, and it will quite often be driven directly by the sales order database.

In the case of low-volume assembly to order, and where the combination of end-product configurations is much more limited, the best solution is instead to invoke design-to-order options in the bills of materials. This creates a unique bill of material for the customized product, combining the bills of materials of both the basic product and all its optional features. The application of the production plan option will then lead, without problem, to the planning and release of final assembly orders by MRP.

16.8 MPS and assembly to order

The typical environment of feature-dependent products is assembly to order. There is a limited range of standard OEM products which are heavily

Table 16.2 Birdhomes' historical demand

| | | | | Period | | | | |
	1	2	3	4	5	6	7	Total
A123	22	6	18	0	30	2	12	90
A124	11	24	3	21	3	11	15	88
A125	12	0	15	15	10	27	0	79
A126	2	0	0	5	1	3	0	11
A127	0	15	9	7	2	5	18	56
A128	3	5	5	2	4	2	5	26

customized. This is given special attention in MRPII systems because it is the manufacturing environment in which MRPII evolved.

By way of example, suppose that the historical demand for the Birdhomes' end products (see Table 7.1) was as given in Table 16.2. We will not attempt to predict the result of demand forecasting at item level with a set of numbers such as these.

Suppose that we had instead configured these six products as a standard product (A122) plus feature options of roof (mandatory) and stalk (optional). The concept of feature-dependent bills of materials has already been addressed in Chapter 7. That demand pattern expressed in Table 16.2 would instead be expressed as follows:

| | | | | Period | | | | |
	1	2	3	4	5	6	7	Forecast
A122	50	50	50	50	50	50	50	50

And with that set of numbers our demand forecasting system is almost certain to forecast demand of 50 units in each forward-planning period. At this point we should recap on the features associated with the Birdhomes' part numbers in Table 16.2, and the following summary may be cross-checked against the parts master file (Table 7.1):

Part no.	Roof	Stalk
A123	Red	None
A124	Green	None
A125	Red	Short
A126	Red	Long
A127	Green	Short
A128	Green	Long

The total demand, and the percentage occurrence of the various features, over those periods given in Table 16.2 was as follows:

Red roof	180	51.4%
Green roof	170	48.6%
No stalk	178	50.8%
Short stalk	135	38.6%
Long stalk	37	10.6%

A set of planning bills would then be generated, showing the likely combination of optional features on the bird homes. In the case of part number A122, the resulting planning bill is shown in Table 16.3. Depending on the software package, the provision for generating this planning bill might be in master production scheduling, demand forecasting, or production planning, but in all cases the source data will be the same—historical sales analysis.

What happens within the MPS logic is this. Our forecast for part number A122 for period n is 50 units, and we have no customer orders for this period. The MPS system will now generate the following orders:

– a planned order for 50 units of A122 for period n;
– planned orders for period n for the features according to the percentage mix indicated on the planning bill, namely:

B235	26 units
B236	24 units
B237	19 units
B238	5 units

Suppose we now receive 15 customer orders each for one bird home, and according to each customer's unique specification. These orders are entered into the sales order entry system, which checks the validity of the combination of optional features, and makes the order details available to MPS. What MPS will now do is this:

– It will generate 15 firm planned orders, one for each customer order and configured according to the actual order specification.
– It will make each order consume the forecast. The unconsumed forecast

Table 16.3 Planning bill of materials—Part no. A122

Part no.	Feature	Mix
A122	B235	51.4%
	B236	48.6%
	B237	38.6%
	B238	10.6%

for period *n* will now be reduced to 35. Because the forecast has been partially consumed, the planned orders will be regenerated, and the new planned order will be for 35 units for period *n*. The planned orders for the features will again be generated according to the planning bill, but relative only to the unconsumed forecast quantity of 35 units:

B235	18 units
B236	17 units
B237	14 units
B238	4 units

Case study   Quantel Ltd, Newbury, Berks

Quantel is world leader in the digital imaging technology used in the manufacture of advanced video graphics and editing systems. The company is part of the Carlton Communications group and has an annual turnover in excess of £50 million. The characteristics of Quantel's manufacturing environment are these:

- high technology products driven by in-company research and development;
- a high level of product innovation, leading to frequent engineering change;
- low volume batch production, with highly customized product specifications, often comprising 2000 or more component parts;
- a dependency on imported electronic components, many of which have delivery leadtimes of up to a year.

In 1988 Quantel installed ASK Computer System's MANMAN system, and this replaced an earlier system which had not performed to the company's satisfaction. Seven modules of MANMAN are installed on DEC-VAX hardware, and provide a fully integrated manufacturing planning and management information system. At the core of the system is the /MFG manufacturing management module, which is generically in keeping with the MRPII standard system at and below the level of master production scheduling, and will support a user seeking MRPII class A registration (see Chapter 29).

Quantel's objectives at the time the MANMAN system was installed were twofold:

1. To gain increased control over the manufacturing activity, especially in the context of lengthy supplier leadtimes and frequent engineering change.
2. To support the future introduction of a JIT environment.

For Quantel part of the key to gaining greater control over their manufacturing process lay in the conceptual change away from a wholly make-to-order environment and towards an assemble-to-order environment. Identifying the common subassemblies made forecasting and planning of these more reliable than before. Customer-optional features are now treated by /MFG using the MRPII standard system's concept of planning bills of materials, described in Chapter 7. The effect is to allow planning of these optional features to be related to a percentage of the forecast demand for their respective end product. The way in which this is handled by master production scheduling has been described earlier in this chapter (pages 138–140).

The advantage of this approach is one that will be applicable to many potential businesses manufacturing original equipment which is heavily customized. The benefits of treating the product as assemble to order are threefold:

1. There is less duplication in both bills of materials and production routings, as a result of identifying common subassemblies. This will in turn lead to a higher degree of data integrity. In Quantel's case, data integrity is further assured by the use of EDM technology (see Chapter 5), which links its CAD system directly to the manufacturing management module of MANMAN. In the case of a printed circuit board containing 600 to 1000 components the saving in manual verification effort is an added benefit.

2. The planning of material requirements for common subassemblies within a product family becomes more transparent. There is clearly visible pegging to the demand forecast at subassembly level, and therefore greater stability. This is in contrast to a make-to-order environment, where any semblance of rational planning would require constant juggling by the planner with a large number of end-product part numbers within the forecast element of the MPS. In many instances the time and cost of product redesign to facilitate common subassemblies would be a highly cost-effective strategy.

3. The planning of customer options becomes handled by an inbuilt feature of MRPII, rather than by the planner having to take account of this manually on the MPS.

In Quantel's case the resulting benefits which accrued from the adoption of these concepts within MANMAN were as follows:

- Inventory was reduced by 30 per cent in total value over a period when sales growth was 25 per cent. As a result the inventory value per £ of sales decreased by 45 per cent.
- Manufacturing leadtime for the most complex product was halved, from 16 weeks to just 8 weeks.

16.9 Rate-based master production scheduling

The core concept of master production scheduling as described thus far is the balancing of supply and demand in such a way that the production plan varies over time according to the level of demand. Rate-based scheduling, on the other hand, implies the smoothing of demand over time to result in a level production plan.

The basic technique for rate-based master production scheduling is described by Woodhead (1992). The objective is to plan final production or final assembly based on a standard production rate in each time period. The three steps in this logic are as follows:

1. Determine target closing stocks. This may be done by product or by product family. Woodhead advocates varying the level of target closing stock by ABC usage-value classification.

2. Define a frozen time period. This is equivalent to a time fence, within which the production rate will not be changed on subsequent revisions to the MPS.
3. Calculate a new production rate to achieve both the total demand over the scheduling horizon and the target closing stock.

The arithmetic is simple:

– Supply = total demand within the schedule horizon plus a stock balancing quantity.
– Stock balancing quantity = target closing stock minus opening stock.
– Production rate = supply divided by discrete time periods, such as hours, shifts, days, etc.

Where there is a frozen time period, the new rate will be the balancing item in the following equation:

$$\text{Supply} = \text{old rate} \times \text{firm days} + \text{new rate} \times \text{remaining days}$$

The results of this rate-based master production scheduling will be used to drive MRP.

Woodhead notes that lumpy demand and low volumes of demand are the main limitations to the adoption of rate-based scheduling. He also notes that the basic calculations may easily be handled by spreadsheet provided the volume of products and orders is not too high. If that is so, the MPS module of the MRPII system becomes unnecessary unless the specific features applicable to a configure-to-order product are required, in which case the logic outlined by Woodhead could equally well be performed on spreadsheet as a replacement for the production planning module described in Chapter 15.

Thus far we have been concerned primarily with establishing only a uniform *rate* of production. If we recap from earlier in this chapter, order-based master production scheduling effectively results in a production plan comprising actual customer orders for each time period. With rate-based scheduling there are two methods of generating the detailed production schedule:

1. The repetitive manufacturing module of the MRPII system may generate a final assembly schedule to match the predetermined rate of production by extracting orders from the sales order database in a specified order priority sequence. This will normally be suitable for products other than configure-to-order products.
2. In the case of configure-to-order products, the MPS module may contain smoothing logic which establishes a uniform rate of production. If it does not, then there will be a need for the production planning module (see Chapter 15) or a spreadsheet equivalent. In either event, the vital element performed by master production scheduling will be that of consuming the

forecast—replacing forecast orders generated from planning bills of materials by the specific order configurations associated with actual customer orders received. The final assembly schedule will then normally be derived directly from the MPS, and the fine-tuning undertaken by the repetitive manufacturing module may be concerned with calculating an optimum daily product mix cycle and fitting the schedule around this cycle.

16.10 The MPS management process

Just as the MPS module of MRPII is the cornerstone of the overall planning system, so is the management of MPS of critical importance to the system's operation. The management process involved is a quite specific one.

Wight (1984) asserts that we cannot have MPS without also having a master scheduling policy, and he summarizes that policy under six headings:

- *What it is*: according to Wight the master scheduling policy is a trade-off between customer service, inventory turn and plant efficiency, a trade-off between what is desirable and what is feasible. In this policy no past due orders may be allowed, and above all the resulting schedule must be achievable. It must be a production plan and not a sales forecast.
- *Forecasts*: the policy must address who will forecast, what forecasting techniques will be used, and how forecast accuracy will be measured. The ultimate responsibility for forecasting lies with the marketing function of the company.
- *Making the master schedule*: the policy must deal with who does it, who approves it, the rules for rescheduling orders, the planning horizon and the size of time buckets to be used.
- *Communication*: this includes manufacturing and purchasing feedback to both planners and master schedulers. Wight emphasizes the need for replanning *before* and not *after* problems occur. The frequency of planning meetings must be decided, and a formalized system of communication set up.
- *Promises and schedule changes*: the use of time fences to delineate differing levels of authority (see page 135) has to be considered. Wight advises a policy of manufacturing signing off on changes that move the schedule in, and marketing signing off on changes that move the schedule out. He also recommends a defined response time for interdepartmental communications of this type.
- *Controls on the master schedule*: the master schedule is the *de facto* production plan, and that must also be the same as the business plan. According to Wight the shortage list is a control on the master schedule quantity; if the schedule is valid then there will not be a shortage list. The performance according to the master schedule must be measured, and only top management may change the company's established master scheduling policy.

On the question of performance, Luscombe (1993) goes further than even Wight, and asserts that adherence to the schedule is the *only* performance measurement that matters, although this degree of insistence gives the impression that the prime business objective is to make MRPII work, rather than to achieve more fundamental business benefits.

The most important facets of the MPS management process are treated authoritatively in Vollman *et al.* (1992):

– A realistic master schedule requires stability.
– The master schedule must never be overstated.
– If an addition is requested, then the correct response is to ask what can be reduced, otherwise the production plan and resources must be changed in order to increase capacity.

Vollman *et al.* emphasize the management concept of integrated planning. The production plan is seen as the key link between top management and manufacturing, and is the framework within which the MPS is developed. The production plan must be stated in understandable aggregate terms, and a plan based on between 5 and 15 product groups is recommended. Inherent in this planning process is the trade-off between sales, manufacturing, inventory and arrears, and this is described as 'game planning'.

Three critical linkages are defined by Vollman *et al.* as part of the company 'game planning':

1. Master production scheduling, which is the disaggregation of the production plan, from the level of product groups to the level of discrete final part numbers, or features and options. This is the key linkage.
2. Demand management, which links order entry, order promising, physical distribution and forecasting into the scheduling process.
3. Resource planning—the longer-range planning of facilities. Top management must commit to this game planning process, and they must force the resolution of interfunctional trade-offs before approving plans at each level in the planning process. The most obvious trade-off is that between marketing and manufacturing.

Adherence to the schedule is also seen as critical by Vollman *et al.* Over-selling is seen as being as bad as under-selling, because it will nevertheless result in a mismatch between the manufacturing operation, financial plans, and inventory plans.

This conventional view of the master scheduling management process is one that may legitimately be challenged in the 1990s. The fundamentals of the process have their roots in an era when the manufacturing process was complex, and leadtimes were typically lengthy. Complexity and inflexibility of the manufacturing process bred the need for plans to be cast in the tablets relatively far in advance of production.

The concept of being able to accept an addition to the schedule only if it is matched by a corresponding reduction is at odds with manufacturing strategies aimed at greater responsiveness. Shorter manufacturing leadtimes overcome the need for schedules to be firmed up so far in advance of production, and the example of Japanese companies in particular demonstrates that the provision of capacity slightly in excess of forecast enables additions to the schedule to be incorporated, with spin-off benefits in terms of competitiveness of customer service; any unused capacity in terms of workforce provision is quite typically used for completion of employee training plans.

Case study   Boss Trucks Ltd, Leighton Buzzard

With 780 employees in the UK, including 330 in the manufacturing division, Boss Trucks is a leading manufacturer of fork trucks. Its manufacturing environment is assembly to order. The product range comprises 15 basic model series, each with an extensive series of customer options. These options include tonnage, power unit, mast height, attachments, tyre rating, type of forks, mast features, load-sensing indicators, cabs or load guards, lighting, and exhaust conditioning. As an indication, there are 54 different exhaust conditioning options, and the net result is the possibility of several thousand variants of each of the 15 basic model series.

These product configurations result in no less than 70 000 live parts on the parts master file, which extends to a total of around 250 000 parts when spares components for earlier models are taken into account. A typical month's material procurement schedule comprises about 11 000 parts, many of them in small quantities.

Production at the Leighton Buzzard plant is carried out on assembly lines. Hoses and pipes and a range of about 90 machined components are manufactured in-company. All other components are externally sourced.

The in-company component manufacturing units are treated as semi-autonomous units. The central MRP system schedules their incoming raw material supplies and their production assembly schedules. The internal production control in these units is divorced from the central system, and left in the hands of the production supervisors. This is similar in concept to the principle of distributed MRP, described later in Chapter 24, except that the bills of materials and inbound material scheduling is not distributed to the component manufacturing units.

The manufacturing planning system in use at Boss Trucks is the IBM COPICS package, and is run on an IBM ES9000 mainframe. The modules used to control manufacturing and materials planning comprise:

- bills of materials
- master production scheduling
- MRP
- purchasing

The reader will at this point note the absence of any of the capacity planning modules illustrated in Figure 13.1. At Boss Trucks, a flexible multi-skilled workforce enables short-term variations to capacity to be accommodated without using any of the capacity planning modules described later in Chapters 17 and 18. In Chapter 21, we will note that Wilson (1993) described this as also being a characteristic of a JIT environment. Boss Trucks operate a *push* philosophy, but the common link with the JIT example is the flexibility of the workforce.

Forecasting at Boss Trucks is carried out within the context of the company's annual budget, and is typically based on recent historical demand, modified in the light of known market conditions. With only 15 basic model series this does not necessitate computerized demand forecasting techniques. Every two months a sales analysis of the mix of features and options is carried out, and forms the basis for the generation of planning bills of materials (see section 16.8).

Master production scheduling follows the assemble-to-order model described in section 16.8. The demand side of each model series MPS analysis is represented by actual orders and forecast. The configuration of forecast orders is generated from planning bills of materials and, as actual orders with specific customer configurations are received, the forecast is consumed, as explained in section 16.8. MPS has access to individual works orders which are fully specified, and these in turn drive the materials planning module.

The planning horizon at Boss Trucks is a rolling 12-month period. There is a complete regeneration once a month, with a net change run twice monthly. The system operates in weekly time buckets for the first 8 weeks, then in fortnightly buckets for a further 13 weeks, after which the time buckets are months. The system does not have inbuilt supplier leadtimes for calculating planned order releases. Instead, suppliers are given forward schedules covering a three-month forward period. Apart from an exceptional case where the supplier leadtime is 14 weeks, the great majority of supplier leadtimes are considerably shorter than the horizon of the forward schedules. Except in the time periods in the very immediate future, the principle is *procure to forecast*, and delivery schedules will change as the forecast is consumed by actual customer order configurations.

The MPS module produces the assembly line schedules in terms of specific trucks by works order number. Depending on the assembly line this schedule is specific either by day or by week. The schedule specifies three dates:

1. Material due date—this is between zero and five days prior to order start date, a reflection of the weekly time bucket used on the supplier delivery schedule.
2. Chassis down date—the effective order start date.
3. Order completion date.

The additional information provided by MPS to final assembly supervisors comprises:

- *Build sheet*: this lists all the top-level part numbers relevant to each specific works order. This includes the basic model and all of the customer options.
- *Engineering change status list*: highlighting engineering changes due to be implemented over the short-term horizon.
- *Parts lists*: for each of the top-level part numbers. Master copies of these are retained on the assembly line, and their replacement is generated only periodically.

Parts for assembly are picked and issued to the assembly track in batches of two or three trucks at a time, using the parts lists as the data source. The parts list serves as a feedback document between pick and issue, as a result of which stock status is changed from a stores location to work-in-progress (WIP). There is no subsequent recording of stock movement; WIP inventory records are down-dated by backflushing. This is triggered by the final acceptance certificate, which is issued once the truck is completed and tested. Bulk issue parts are handled separately. As an aid to inventory accuracy, inventory cycle counts are directed at part numbers which appear on forward requirement schedules.

Although the COPICS system has been in use at Boss Trucks for several years, the improvements in performance over a 20-month period since the beginning of 1991 have been dramatic:

– Total inventory is down 50 per cent during a period when sales and production remained approximately constant, and stockturn has improved from four times a year to eight times a year.
– Manufacturing inventory is down by almost 40 per cent.
– The biggest reduction is in finished inventory which has reduced to about 15 per cent of its previous level. In part this is a reflection of a reduction in manufacturing leadtime, which has reduced by between 30 per cent and 50 per cent depending on the assembly track. The shorter assembly leadtime has in effect dramatically reduced the number of forecast orders on the assembly schedule.

The key to these improvements at Boss Trucks lay in the way the MRP system was used. For some time after the installation of the COPICS system, what Wight (1984) described as the informal system—the shortage list—still controlled production, and the root of this lay in an overstated MPS, in which the features and options incorporated in the forecast element seldom matched those of customer orders accepted on short delivery promises.

The result was that production schedules and supplier delivery schedules had little validity. Each shortfall compared to forecast resulted in supplier schedules being cut back, with the result that suppliers no longer believed in them, and in many cases disregarded them. The variation between the forecast product mix and the actual customer-order configurations resulted at one point in over 2500 parts in arrears. Expediting arrears became the norm, but often resulted in suppliers delivering what had been produced in accordance with the original over-optimistic schedules, with a resulting increase in manufacturing inventory. Eliminating these arrears was the key to reducing the assembly leadtimes.

In summary, simple but sensible forecasting was the crucial element in bringing Boss Trucks' system to the state of stability which has resulted in the performance levels noted above.

17
Capacity requirements planning

In this chapter we begin by relating the different levels of capacity planning to their corresponding levels of production or materials planning. We then examine in greater detail the two sides of the capacity planning equation—workload and resources, and this is followed by a detailed explanation of the CRP process itself, using a worked example in the process. The optional features a potential user may encounter are noted, and then we consider the respective bases for scheduling within MRP and CRP. The chapter concludes by summarizing the content of the CRP database.

To manufacture products requires both production materials and production capacity, and the provision of these is the job of the planner. Within MRPII the planner is assisted in the task of executing the MPS by two other system modules:

1. Material requirements planning (MRP), which helps plan material requirements, including the requirements of items to be manufactured. This has been described in Part One.
2. Capacity requirements planning (CRP), which helps plan capacity requirements, the subject of this chapter.

Both the MPS and the MRP modules of MRPII help the planner to balance component or material supply and demand. The capacity planning modules help the planner to balance workload and capacity, or in other words, to balance the demand for manufacturing capacity and the supply of that capacity.

The capacity planning modules of MRPII are decision-support tools. They give the planner information, but do not make decisions for him, and they give the planner differing levels of support at different levels in the planning hierarchy. These different levels of capacity planning are linked with the appropriate planning module within a hierarchical system structure.

17.1 Capacity planning levels

There are three levels in the capacity planning hierarchy. Figure 17.1 shows their positions in the hierarchy, and the main materials planning modules to

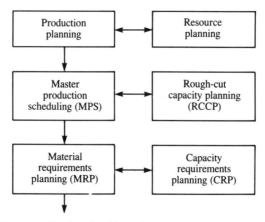

Figure 17.1   The capacity planning hierarchy

which they are linked. These modules differ in the level of detail they encompass.

CRP

CRP itself is concerned with requirements at the lowest level of detail: production operation by production operation, and work centre by work centre. Its main purpose is to test that sufficient capacity exists to achieve the detailed works orders planned by MRP.

Rough-cut capacity planning (RCCP)

RCCP focuses only on aggregate resources or key or bottleneck work departments. Its main purpose is to test the feasibility of the master production schedule. Some software provides fairly sophisticated means of interaction between the planner, the master production schedule and the capacity plans.

Resource planning

This takes place at a similar level of detail to the rough-cut. Its main purpose is to provide a statement of resources needed for achievement of the highest-level production plan, normally at product family level. Resource planning and production planning modules are often not included in MRPII software, and many companies today use spreadsheets at this level of planning.

Burcher (1991) noted that capacity planning modules were used by just over half of the MRPII users surveyed. The average planning horizons ranged from 20 months in the case of resource planning, to 33 weeks for RCCP and only 23 weeks for CRP. The survey indicated that both resource planning and RCCP typically were based on monthly time buckets, but that CRP was usually based on weekly buckets. Two thirds of companies use spreadsheets for resource planning and over half of them also use spreadsheets for RCCP, but just over a quarter do so for CRP where the volume of data to be handled is significantly greater. Burcher also reported that of the three capacity planning modules RCCP is the most widely used, and the most successful. Resource planning is used with equal frequency at the levels of plant, department and work centre, but both RCCP and CRP are typically focused at the level of individual work centres.

17.2 Workload and standard times

Workload can be defined as the units of time of the resources needed to carry out the discrete production operations of an order or set of orders. These resources may be either machines or labour. Workload may comprise two distinct elements:

– setup time
– run time

Setup time

This is usually a fixed time per batch, for example, to set the tools or jigs used in the manufacturing operation. In many instances setup time might be zero.

Run time

This is the actual production time required per unit of the product or component part. A frequently used alternative is to allow this to be expressed as production quantity per unit of time, for example 500 per hour.

Two elementary points must be noted:

1. Total run time is variable depending upon the production batch size, and it follows that total operation time is therefore also variable depending on the production batch size.
2. Unless the setup time is zero, this element will be incurred for every works order, and the workload represented by a set of works orders will therefore be dependent on the lot-sizing technique used in the MRP system.

The total operation time per batch is calculated as follows:

$$\text{setup time} + (n \times \text{run time})$$

where n = batch quantity. Where production comprises more than one operation, the total production time required will be the sum of the discrete operation times.

For example, the Birdhomes' production used in previous examples (see Chapter 7) is organized into four production departments:

- *Assembly*: in this department three operations are carried out:
    the gluing together of the sides, front and house base;
    the assembly of the roof to the house subassembly;
    the assembly of the stalk subassemblies to the house.
- *Paint shop*: where the roof painting is done.
- *Welding shop*: where the stalk is welded to the ground base.
- *Cutting shop*: where the aluminium tube is cut into short lengths or long lengths.

After gluing, painting and welding, the parts or subassemblies have to be left to cure for a time before they can be used in the next operation.

The list of Birdhomes' operations and times by part number could be as given in Table 17.1.

In many companies both the setup times and the run times will be standard times established by using engineering time standards. This is historically the job of an industrial engineer or work measurement engineer. Software packages are now available which will calculate synthetic standard times for certain types of production operations, including metalworking, machine tool operations and printed circuit board (pcb) assembly.

Table 17.1   Birdhomes' operations and standard times

Part no.	Dept.	Setup (mins)	Run (mins)	Move (days)	Operation
A123	A	15	4	0	Assemble red roof to house sub assembly
A124	A	15	4	0	Assemble green roof to house sub assembly
A125	A	0	2	0	Assemble short stalk to red house unit
A126	A	0	2	0	Assemble long stalk to red house unit
A127	A	0	2	0	Assemble short stalk to green house unit
A128	A	0	2	0	Assemble long stalk to green house unit
B234	A	45	12	4	Glue sides and front to house base
B235	P	60	6	2	Paint roof red
B236	P	60	6	2	Paint roof green
B237	W	25	4	1	Weld short stalk to ground base
B238	W	25	4	1	Weld long stalk to ground base
C349	C	10	2	0	Cut short stalk from 4 metre tube
C350	C	10	2	0	Cut long stalk from 4 metre tube

Move time

In the Birdhomes example, move time has been used to cater for the curing time following gluing, painting and welding. Move time could also be used to allow for transit time between operations, or to define the total time required in the case of an operation subcontracted to an external subcontractor.

There are two attributes of workload: how much capacity is needed? And when is it needed?

HOW MUCH CAPACITY IS NEEDED?

This is arrived at by the multiplication of two elements:

- *The batch quantity*: the quantity already calculated on the MRP schedule of planned orders.
- *The standard times*: for example, the times given on the Birdhomes list of operations in Table 17.1.

WHEN IS THE CAPACITY NEEDED?

This also depends on two elements:

- *The date required*: the required date or time bucket shown on the MRP schedule of planned orders.
- *The time offsets, or time phasing*: in the Birdhomes example there are two factors to be taken into account:

    because our example was expressed using time buckets, the production of a requirement for bucket n must be completed by the end of bucket $n - 1$. In a bucketless system, the net requirements would have discrete dates, and production must be completed by the previous day;

    move time—actual production must be offset or advanced from the required completion time by an amount of time equal to the specified move time.

In the Birdhomes example, each part is manufactured in a single operation. In real life there will more usually be more than one operation. In that case the production of any operation must be offset by the cumulative time needed for all subsequent operations.

17.3 Capacity and resources

Whereas workload is the units of time of a resource *needed* to execute all or part of a production plan, capacity is the units of time of a resource *available* to carry out all of the production operations requiring that resource.

In the Birdhomes example there were four resources:

- assembly
- paint shop
- welding shop
- cutting shop

These resources may be constrained by either of the following factors:

- the number of machines available;
- the number of labour operatives available.

In the Birdhomes example it is likely that both the paint shop and the welding shop will be machine-constrained. Additions to capacity will require additional capital equipment, and the provision of that will be constrained both by the capital cost and the equipment delivery leadtime.

It is likely that assembly and cutting will instead be labour-constrained. The provision of additional direct labour will increase capacity, provided there are spare assembly jigs and hand tools.

The total capacity per resource or work centre is a combination of three elements:

1. The quantity of that resource, the number of machines or the number of operators.
2. The hours worked per day in that work centre. This is normally defined by a production calendar which distinguishes working days from non-working days, such as weekends, shutdowns, public holidays, etc.
3. The efficiency of the resource. This is normally expressed as a percentage, which represents that percentage of the total working hours available for production, after making allowance for all deviations from standard, including cover for unplanned maintenance, rectification work and the like.

17.4 The CRP process

The details of capacity requirements planning are best illustrated by an example. Some readers may prefer instead to refer to Exercise B4 (Appendix B) at this point. In Table 17.2 is Birdhomes' master production schedule from day 14 to day 20. In this table the MPS reflects actual customer orders up to and including day number 18. From day 19 onwards the schedule reflects forecast demand, which in this instance is level throughout the remainder of the planning horizon.

Table 17.2   Birdhomes' master production schedule

| Part | | | | Day | | | |
no.	14	15	16	17	18	19	20
A123	22	0	46	0	18	17	17
A124	0	37	5	0	0	8	8
A125	28	20	0	44	0	18	18
A126	0	0	60	0	0	12	12
A127	0	36	0	0	12	10	10
A128	54	0	26	48	26	30	30

Using the bills of materials in Table 7.2, normal MRP process logic will translate this into the schedule of planned order receipts shown in Table 17.3. Birdhomes' lot-sizing policy is lot for lot, so the planned receipts are therefore identical to the net requirements.

Using the operations data given in Table 17.1, the net requirements shown in Table 17.3 can then be expressed as workload on each of Birdhomes' four work centres, and this is shown in Table 17.4. In this table the workload in each work centre is built up part number by part number, showing the workload in standard hours. The department total is then calculated.

The Birdhomes example illustrates the methodology of MRPII's detailed capacity requirements planning, which is time-phased resource loading. In department A, the workload represented by part numbers A123 to A128 appears in the same time bucket as the planned receipt because the move time

Table 17.3   Birdhomes' planned receipts

| Part | | | | | | | Day | | | | | | |
no.	8	9	10	11	12	13	14	15	16	17	18	19	20
A123	0	0	0	0	0	0	30	60	90	0	48	47	47
A124	0	0	0	0	0	54	36	63	53	38	40	48	48
A125	0	0	0	0	0	0	28	20	0	44	0	18	18
A126	0	0	0	0	0	0	0	0	60	0	0	12	12
A127	0	0	0	0	0	0	0	36	0	0	12	10	10
A128	0	0	0	0	0	0	54	0	26	48	26	30	30
B234	0	0	0	0	0	20	123	143	38	88	95	95	95
B235	0	0	0	0	0	30	60	90	0	48	47	47	47
B236	0	0	0	0	54	36	63	53	38	40	48	48	48
B237	0	0	0	0	0	28	56	0	44	12	28	28	28
B238	0	0	0	0	0	54	0	86	48	26	42	42	42
C349	0	28	56	0	44	12	28	28	28	28	28	28	28
C350	0	54	0	86	48	26	42	42	42	42	42	42	42

Table 17.4   Birdhomes' workload by department

Part no.	8	9	10	11	12	13	*Day* 14	15	16	17	18	19	20
Department A													
A123	0.0	0.0	0.0	0.0	0.0	0.0	2.3	4.3	6.3	0.0	3.5	3.4	3.4
A124	0.0	0.0	0.0	0.0	0.0	3.9	2.7	4.5	3.8	2.8	2.9	3.5	3.5
A125	0.0	0.0	0.0	0.0	0.0	0.0	0.9	0.7	0.0	1.5	0.0	0.6	0.6
A126	0.0	0.0	0.0	0.0	0.0	0.0	0.0	0.0	2.0	0.0	0.0	0.4	0.4
A127	0.0	0.0	0.0	0.0	0.0	0.0	0.0	1.2	0.0	0.0	0.4	0.3	0.3
A128	0.0	0.0	0.0	0.0	0.0	0.0	1.8	0.0	0.9	1.6	0.9	1.0	1.0
B234	0.0	4.8	25.4	29.4	8.4	18.4	19.8	19.8	19.8	0.0	0.0	0.0	0.0
Total	0.0	4.8	25.4	29.4	8.4	22.3	27.5	30.5	32.8	5.9	7.7	9.2	9.2
Department C													
C349	0.0	2.0	0.2	0.0	0.6	1.1	1.1	1.1	1.1	1.1	1.1	1.1	0.2
C350	0.0	0.2	0.0	1.8	1.0	1.6	1.6	1.6	1.6	1.6	1.6	1.6	0.2
Total	0.0	2.2	0.2	1.8	1.6	2.7	2.7	2.7	2.7	2.7	2.7	2.7	0.4
Department P													
B235	0.0	0.0	0.0	4.0	7.0	10.0	0.0	5.8	5.7	5.7	5.7	0.0	0.0
B236	0.0	0.0	6.4	4.6	7.3	6.3	4.8	5.0	5.8	5.8	5.8	0.0	0.0
Total	0.0	0.0	6.4	8.6	14.3	16.3	4.8	10.8	11.5	11.5	11.5	0.0	0.0
Department W													
B237	0.0	0.0	0.0	0.0	2.3	4.2	0.0	3.4	1.2	2.3	2.3	2.3	0.0
B238	0.0	0.0	0.0	0.0	4.0	0.0	6.2	3.6	2.2	3.2	3.2	3.2	0.0
Total	0.0	0.0	0.0	0.0	6.3	4.2	6.2	7.0	3.4	5.5	5.5	5.5	0.0

is zero. The calculation can be demonstrated by using as an example the planned receipt of 60 units of part number A123 on day 15:

$$\text{Workload} = \text{setup time} + (n \times \text{run time})$$

$$= 15 + (60 \times 4) \text{ minutes}$$

$$= 255 \text{ minutes}$$

$$= 4.3 \text{ hours}$$

In the case of part number B234 the move time is four days. This means that production of the receipts planned for day 13 must be completed on day 9, for day 14 on day 10, and so on. All of the workload represented by part number B234 is therefore offset four days forward from the corresponding planned order receipts.

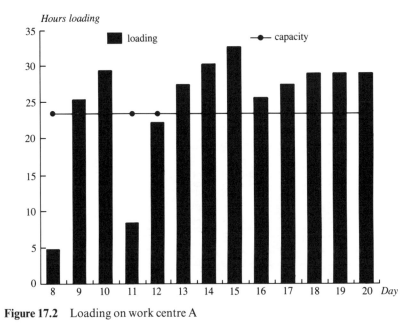

Figure 17.2   Loading on work centre A

The work-centre loading information may also be presented in barchart form, either vertically or horizontally. Figure 17.2 shows the workload on work centre A depicted in barchart form. The horizontal line indicates the limit of capacity.

Capacity utilization

For the planner it is more meaningful to have not just a statement of work-load, but rather a statement of workload in relation to the capacity available. This is provided by capacity utilization reporting. The capacity utilization is workload expressed as a percentage of capacity available, and it is normal to show also not only the overload or underload in discrete time periods, but also the cumulative overload or underload across the planning horizon.

An exercise in capacity utilization calculation can be found in Appendix B5. The results of that exercise are as depicted in Table 17.5. The detailed calculation of available hours in this example is shown in Table B5.1.

Capacity utilization may also be depicted in barchart form. The utilization of work centre P is given in this form in Figure 17.3. In Figure 17.4 the overload or underload in work centre W is shown, while Figure 17.5 shows the cumulative overload or underload for centre P.

Table 17.5 Birdhomes' capacity utilisation

							Day						
	8	9	10	11	12	13	14	15	16	17	18	19	20
Work centre A													
Available hrs	23.4	23.4	23.4	23.4	23.4	23.4	23.4	23.4	23.4	23.4	23.4	23.4	23.4
Load hours	4.8	25.4	29.4	8.4	22.2	27.4	30.3	32.7	25.6	27.4	28.9	28.9	28.9
Utilization	21%	109%	126%	36%	95%	117%	129%	140%	109%	117%	124%	124%	124%
Difference hrs	18.6	-2.0	-6.0	15.0	1.2	-4.0	-6.9	-9.3	-2.2	-4.0	-5.5	-5.5	-5.5
Cumulative	18.6	16.6	10.6	25.6	26.8	22.8	15.9	6.6	4.4	0.4	-5.1	-10.6	-16.1
Work centre C													
Available hrs	2.6	2.6	2.6	2.6	2.6	2.6	2.6	2.6	2.6	2.6	2.6	2.6	2.6
Load hrs	3.1	2.0	3.0	3.4	1.6	2.7	2.7	2.7	2.7	2.7	2.7	2.7	2.7
Utilization	117%	76%	114%	129%	61%	102%	102%	102%	102%	102%	102%	102%	102%
Difference hrs	-0.5	0.6	-0.4	-0.8	1.0	-0.1	-0.1	-0.1	-0.1	-0.1	-0.1	-0.1	-0.1
Cumulative	-0.5	0.2	-0.2	-0.9	0.1	0.0	0.0	-0.1	-0.1	-0.2	-0.3	-0.3	-0.4
Work centre P													
Available hrs	8.5	8.5	8.5	8.5	8.5	8.5	8.5	8.5	8.5	8.5	8.5	8.5	8.5
Load hrs	0.0	6.4	8.6	14.3	16.3	4.8	10.4	11.5	11.5	11.5	11.5	11.5	11.5
Utilization	0%	75%	101%	168%	192%	56%	122%	135%	135%	135%	135%	135%	135%
Difference hrs	8.5	2.1	-0.1	-5.8	-7.8	3.7	-1.9	-3.0	-3.0	-3.0	-3.0	-3.0	-3.0
Cumulative	8.5	10.6	10.5	4.7	-3.1	0.6	-1.3	-4.3	-7.3	-10.3	-13.3	-16.3	-19.3
Work centre W													
Available hrs	5.4	5.4	5.4	5.4	5.4	5.4	5.4	5.4	5.4	5.4	5.4	5.4	5.4
Load hrs	0.0	0.0	0.0	6.3	4.2	6.2	7.0	3.4	5.5	5.5	5.5	5.5	5.5
Utilization	0%	0%	0%	118%	78%	116%	131%	63%	103%	103%	103%	103%	103%
Difference hrs	5.4	5.4	5.4	-0.9	1.2	-0.8	-1.6	2.0	-0.1	-0.1	-0.1	-0.1	-0.1
Cumulative	5.4	10.7	16.1	15.1	16.3	15.5	13.8	15.8	15.6	15.5	15.4	15.2	15.1

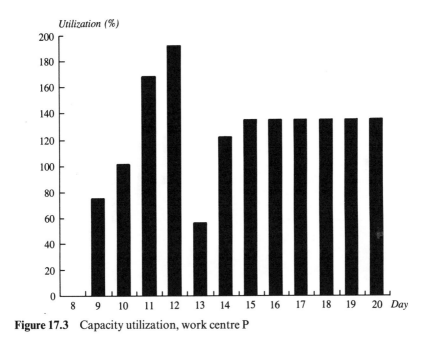

Figure 17.3 Capacity utilization, work centre P

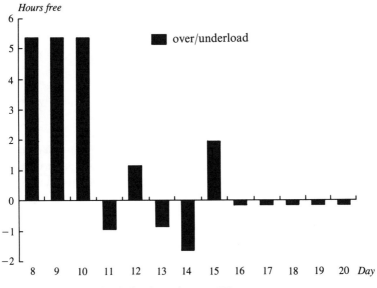

Figure 17.4 Hours over/underload, work centre W

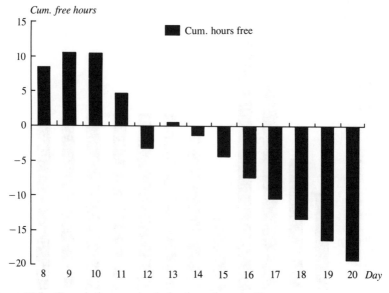

Figure 17.5 Cumulative over/underload, work centre P

CRP is normally run after each MRP run, and is intended to verify that sufficient resources are available to satisfy the workload of the works orders planned by MRP.

CRP invites only short-term response from the planner. It will help identify production bottlenecks, resource constraints, and potential order arrears problems. The planner's response to these will vary, but the most common responses are likely to be:

– an adjustment to the overtime hours worked;
– the transfer of operators between work centres;
– the transfer of production to an alternative, but under-loaded work centre;
– the transfer of production to an external subcontractor.

At this stage in the planning operation, responding by making changes on the demand side, by rescheduling order completion dates to a later date, would more often than not have repercussions reaching right back to the MPS itself. Burcher (1991) noted that just over half the users of CRP had any feedback loop from CRP to MPS.

The concept of pegging exists in CRP as it does in MRP. Most systems provide reports that peg specific orders to a specific resource load. This helps the planner identify which orders are the cause or source of resource overloads. Table 17.4 is an example of a pegged report; the load generated by individual requirements is reported in addition to the total load.

The planning horizon of CRP will normally be the same as the horizon of MRP.

17.5 Optional features of CRP

There are several options designed to make the loading information more helpful to the planner, but this information varies greatly between different software packages.

One option is that reports and barcharts may distinguish between:

- active orders—those already in process
- released orders
- planned orders

Another option allows reports and barcharts to distinguish between:

- setup load
- production load

An example of this is shown in Figure 17.6, which is Birdhomes' loading on work centre P, but broken down between setup loading and production loading.

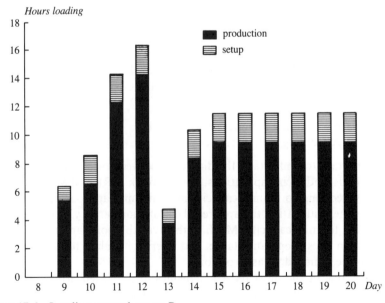

Figure 17.6 Loading on work centre P

Some systems may provide a comparison between:

- what is desirable, based on MRP's planned orders, with backward scheduling to infinite capacity;
- what is feasible, given the existing resources, with forward scheduling to finite capacity.

This comparison will indicate the repercussions on delivery promise if no action is taken. Its provision, and its use, other than in a jobbing type of business, however, is not in keeping with the correct assertion in Wight (1984) that there has to be a valid schedule in the first place. If there is, then the negative aspect of viewing the consequences of taking no action should not be necessary, and would have validity only in *force majeure* circumstances, such as a major equipment failure or other equally serious disruptions to production.

Capacity planning is very much a balancing act between what is desirable and what is feasible, and the potential conflict is neatly summed up in Figure 17.7.

17.6 Scheduling within MRP and CRP

Both MRP and CRP are based on backward scheduling to infinite capacity.

- MRP schedules backward from due date, using the planning leadtime on the parts master record, assuming there is no resource capacity limitation.
- CRP schedules backward from due date using operational leadtimes from production routings, assuming there is no resource capacity limitation.

Both of these, it will be noted, are founded on backward scheduling to infinite capacity. There are alternative scheduling methods, and these include two methods of scheduling to finite capacity:

- backward scheduling to finite capacity
- forward scheduling to finite capacity

It is important to understand the difference between these different scheduling methods, and their implications. The textbook MRP and MRPII systems regard scheduling to infinite capacity as something approaching a dogma, citing as the justification the apparent lack of transparency of the results of scheduling to finite capacity. Much of the available software in the 1990s is founded on a less dogmatic stance, and offers scheduling to finite capacity, either as the standard, or as an option.

This is one of the most recurrent themes in published articles of recent years, and will be developed in more detail in Chapter 22 when we consider non-standard approaches to MRPII.

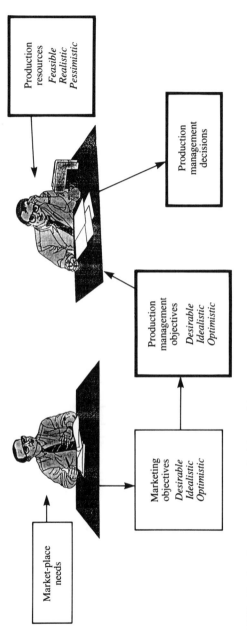

Figure 17.7 Production management decision making

Scheduling to finite capacity

In scheduling to finite capacity, work is loaded only up to the limit of resource availability. Overload situations will therefore result in a spreading backwards or forwards of workload into alternative periods. Where the immediate periods are overloaded, the effect will generally be to spread the workload forwards, and therefore to *plan* to produce later than the required date.

Scheduling to finite capacity implies observance of capacity limitations, regardless of the effect on completion date. An adverse imbalance between workload and capacity results in order arrears or lateness. The various scheduling techniques used in scheduling to finite capacity will be described in Chapter 22.

Backward scheduling

Backward scheduling is scheduling backwards from due date to arrive at planned start date. The steps in the logic of backward scheduling are illustrated in Figure 17.8.

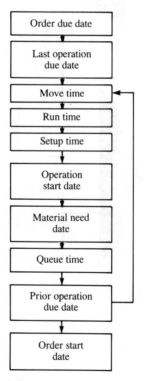

Figure 17.8 Backward scheduling

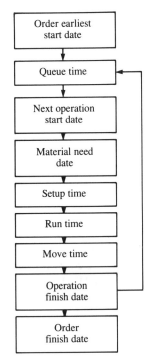

Figure 17.9   Forward scheduling

Forward scheduling

Forward scheduling is scheduling forwards from earliest start date to arrive at planned completion date, and Figure 17.9 shows the logic in this process.

Hill *et al.* (1992) point out that forward scheduling to finite capacity cannot take account of product structure relationships during scheduling, and that therefore backward scheduling to finite capacity is the more valid alternative.

Scheduling to infinite capacity

Scheduling to infinite capacity implies the observance of due dates, without regard to capacity limitations. An adverse imbalance between workload and capacity results in a resource overload.

17.7 The CRP database

The CRP module of MRPII requires two databases: production routes and resources. Production routes are the data describing:

- how a product or component part is manufactured, and in what sequence of production operations;
- which resources are used to carry out each operation in its manufacture;
- how much time of each resource is required.

The resources database defines:

- the manufacturing resources;
- the quantity of each resource;
- its production efficiency;
- the hours per day for which it will be available over the future calendar.

Production routings

We have already seen in Chapter 7 how the bill of materials defines the component part content of a part number, and is used to explode requirements for higher-level part numbers into the corresponding requirements for lower-level component parts for use in MRP. The production routing defines the manufacturing content of a part number and is used to explode requirements for a part into its detailed manufacturing operations, for use in CRP and production activity control.

Some very fundamental points to be noted at this stage are these:

- The finished product structure is defined by the bill of materials and *not* by the production routing. The bill of materials contains a set of links or parent/child relationships, providing a trail from highest-level part numbers to lowest-level part numbers, and vice versa.
- The production routing exists at discrete levels by part number only.

Some software combines bills of materials and production routings into a single database. The two databases were traditionally separate because their data sources were different:

- Bills of materials were created and provided by design engineering.
- Production routings were the result of production engineering.

In a DFM or DFMA environment these two functions of design engineering and production engineering are most likely to be combined into one, and there is therefore a prima facie case for the amalgamation of the two databases into one.

Production routing data

For each part number designated on the parts master file as a make item, the following data will be specified:

- part number
- description
- drawing number

For each manufacturing operation within each part number, some or all of the following data may be specified:

- sequence number: which denotes the consecutive flow of production operations, from the first operation to the last;
- description;
- drawing number;
- work centre;
- queue time;
- setup time;
- tool number: the tool or assembly jig used in the setup of the operation;
- production time;
- move time;
- alternative work centre;
- part number(s) of materials used on this operation.

This data will be used not only for CRP but also when producing shop-floor documentation in the production activity control module (see Chapter 19).

SETUP TIME, PRODUCTION TIME AND MOVE TIME

The significance of these data items has already been shown in the Birdhomes capacity loading exercise.

ALTERNATIVE WORK CENTRE

If the primary work centre is overloaded, this operation may instead be performed at the alternative work centre. This could be relevant if scheduling to finite capacity, or as a response available to the planner in resolving the conflict in a resource overload situation.

QUEUE TIME

This is the time it is planned that the order will wait, or queue, ahead of the work centre before production or setup is started. Queue time was accepted as normal in the era in which MRPII was conceived. It was typically quite lengthy. Surveys of MRPII users in the 1980s suggest that the typical queue times were often as great as 20 times the batch production time, and this helped to foster the inherent MRP concept that planning leadtimes can be regarded as fixed, regardless of batch quantity.

There are three opposing points of view on the whole concept of queuing:

1. Queues are necessary and desirable. They provide a buffer which ensures that there is always a choice of several orders ready to be started when the previous job is completed. In this way resource utilization is maximized. This is most likely to be the viewpoint where production supervisors are given the objective of maximizing throughput.
2. Queues are undesirable but unavoidable. This is likely to be the viewpoint of a planner faced with regular problems with the flow of work. A queue helps to buffer a work centre against any unplanned delays in the arrival of work. A safety stock of one WIP order queuing ahead of each work centre should normally be sufficient to cope with this, but many planners accustomed to bad experiences have traditionally preferred a belt-and-braces approach, and have planned for quite substantial queues in order to ensure that there is always work to be commenced when the previous batch is completed.
3. Queues are avoidable and unnecessary. They can be eliminated if supervision is encouraged to manage the flow of work rather than the throughput of the work centre. This is a major goal of JIT, and should be regarded as the standard for manufacturing in the 1990s.

Acceptance of the concept of queue times has the following effect:

- It increases the manufacturing leadtime.
- It increases the WIP inventory.
- It is associated with the management of throughput.

The effect of queue size in a pre-JIT environment is shown in generalized form in Figure 17.10.

The elimination of queue times has the following effect:

- It reduces the manufacturing leadtime.
- It reduces the WIP inventory.
- It is associated with the management of work flow and lean manufacturing.

QUEUE TIME COMPRESSION

This has nothing directly to do with queue times, but is instead a term used to describe a facility available to the planner in some systems to cope with late running orders. By reducing, or compressing, the queue times, the order is made to pass through the operations in a shorter than planned leadtime. Where queue times are accepted as the norm, this is one of the planner's more frequent responses to the expedite warning on an MRP exception report.

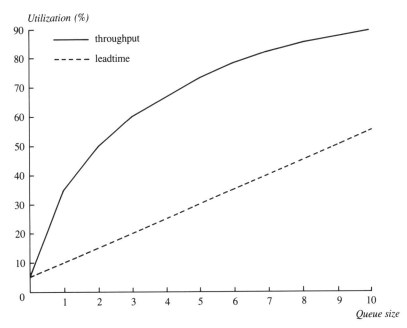

Figure 17.10 Effect of queue size

Production routing structure

There are three very different types of production routing structure which may apply to a particular product or component, and they will be decided by the way the production engineer decides the manufacturing operations should be carried out:

– sequential operations
– overlapping sequential operations
– network operations

SEQUENTIAL OPERATIONS

In the Birdhomes example (Table 17.1) each part number had only one manufacturing operation, and this is not typical. It is more common for there to be more than one operation. Part number B234 (glue sides and front to house base) could, for example, alternatively have been specified as follows:

Sequence no.	Operation
010	Apply glue to sides and front
020	Assemble sides and front to base

This is an example of sequential operations. Operation 010 is carried out before operation 020. All MRPII software makes provision for a string of sequential operations per part number. The sequence in which actual operations is carried out would be as indicated in Figure 17.11.

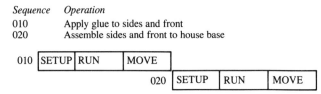

Sequence   Operation
010   Apply glue to sides and front
020   Assemble sides and front to house base

Figure 17.11   Sequential operations. Example: Birdhomes' part number B234

OVERLAPPING OPERATIONS

If one assembly operator was carrying out the gluing and another doing the assembly on an adjacent work centre, then it might not be necessary for *all* the gluing to be completed before starting the assembly. The sequence of work could instead be as shown in Figure 17.12.

Figure 17.12   Overlapping operations

This is an example of overlapping operations. Very few MRPII software packages have satisfactory provision for overlapping operations. A common technique for attempting to cater for overlapping operations is the concept of *negative move time*. This would allow operation 020 to be started a fixed time before the completion of operation 010. This may not adequately cater for all overlap situations.

NETWORK OPERATIONS

Suppose that Birdhomes made only one standard product, part number A125, and that there were no lengthy curing times involved. The advantage of numerous subassemblies would then lessen, and the product could be planned to be made in the way shown in Figure 17.13.

This is an example of a network of operations. The operations of cutting and welding the stalk can be carried out in parallel with the operations of gluing, fixing and assembly of the house shell. A network is defined in terms

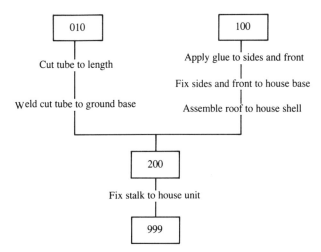

Figure 17.13   Network operations. Example: Birdhomes' part number A125

of its nodes and operations, just as it is in almost every project management system. Table 17.6 illustrates this network of operations in respect of Birdhomes' part number A125.

Most MRPII software will *not* accept networks. In that Birdhomes example it would be necessary to treat both the stalk and house unit as phantom subassemblies, and this may well be perceived as contrary to the reality of the situation. Where network operations do exist, the user should persevere in a search for a software package which supports manufacturing networks.

Resource data

For each resource or work centre, the following data will be specified:

– work centre number
– description of the operation
– the type of resource: whether it is machine or labour constrained

Table 17.6   Network production routing

Node	Sequence no.	Operation
010–200	010	Cut tube to length
	020	Weld cut tube to ground base
100–200	100	Apply glue to sides and front
	110	Fix sides and front to house base
	120	Assemble roof to house shell
200–999	200	Fix stalk to house unit

- whether or not it is a critical resource (the significance of this will be explained in the context of rough-cut capacity planning in Chapter 18)
- the quantity of the resource
- its production efficiency
- the production calendar

Many systems will have inbuilt provision for the interchangeability of labour between work centres, or for specifying fixed or variable crew sizes, but there is no standard method of specifying this data.

The production calendar may exist in several formats:

- An actual calendar, day by day, at least as far ahead as the limit of the planning horizon. The planned working hours for each working day will then be input, and subsequent changes will be made by the planner when necessary. The system should have provision for the automatic generation of new extensions to the calendar as and when required.
- A basic seven-day calendar, on which the planned working hours for each day of the week will be recorded. Exceptions or changes to the basic seven-day calendar will be specified in terms of:
    amended hours
    day number
    effective from
    effective until

Most software provides for a calendar specific to each work centre, but there are a few packages where the calendar applies to all work centres, and this may cause problems if not all work centres work the same number of hours on every day of the year.

18
Rough-cut capacity planning

Whereas detailed capacity requirements planning tests the feasibility of plans generated by MRP, rough-cut capacity planning (RCCP) tests the feasibility of plans at MPS level. In this chapter we address the functionality of RCCP in terms of both critical resources and the planner's role at this level of planning, and conclude with a brief review of the form of capacity planning that may be applied at a higher level in the planning hierarchy.

The objective of RCCP is to produce a load profile of key or critical resources. There are both similarities with CRP, and also a number of differences.

RCCP differs from detailed CRP in the following respects:

- It calculates workload only for MPS items.
- It loads only on selected critical resources, rather than on every work centre.
- It uses a bill of resource instead of the production routings.
- It may have interactive facilities to help the planner in the task of juggling production plans and capacity to achieve a balance.

RCCP is similar to CRP in the following aspects:

- It uses backward scheduling to infinite capacity.
- It provides a comparison of load versus capacity.

18.1 Critical resources

The critical resources loaded by RCCP are determined by the user, and could include any of the following:

- key or bottleneck machine centres;
- key labour skill categories;
- a variety of other key business resources, such as space, finance, costs, energy, tooling, or whatever is vital to the attainment of the top-level

production plans, provided the user can quantify for each of these the resource requirement per unit of production.

These latter may seem esoteric to many. User experiences tend to polarize between the view on the one hand that they are of inestimable value, while in very many installations they are never used. There is no middle ground. The provision for testing production plans against key business resources other than purely capacity was one of the ways in which the advocates of the standard MRPII system sought to bring all functions within the business to plan using the same set of numbers. Advances in business planning techniques have to a large extent removed the necessity for this to be accomplished within the RCCP module.

The bill of resource

A bill of resource exists for every MPS item, and defines the load profile per unit of product for each critical resource.

Bills of resource may originate in the following ways:

- *System generated*: an option in some systems allows machine or labour load profiles to be generated from the bills of materials and production routings, making allowance for leadtime offsets. This is typically triggered by a data field in the resource database record designating that resource as a critical resource.
- *Manually generated*: this is the more common method, and the only one if resources external to the MRPII database are to be included.

For example, the Birdhomes' capacity utilization data presented in Table 17.5 shows that they have two critical resources—the paint shop and the total direct labour force. The bills of resource for part numbers A123 and A125 are shown in Table 18.1. The bill of resource for part number A124 will be the same as A123, and for part numbers A126, A127 and A128 it will be the same as for A125.

The true leadtime offset in the case of labour is staggered depending on the detailed manufacturing operations. For top-level planning purposes we will

Table 18.1 Birdhomes' bills of resource

Part no.	Resource	Setup (minutes)	Production (minutes)	Offset (days)
A123	Paint shop	45	12	7
	Labour	120	22	7
A125	Paint shop	45	12	8
	Labour	155	30	8

Table 18.2 Birdhomes' master production schedule

	Day no.						
	14	15	16	17	18	19	20
A123	22	0	46	0	18	17	17
A124	0	37	5	0	0	8	8
A125	28	20	0	44	0	18	18
A126	0	0	60	0	0	12	12
A127	0	36	0	0	12	10	10
A128	54	0	26	48	26	31	31

assume that all labour is required on the longest offset. Different assumptions may be equally valid for forward planning purposes.

Birdhomes have a present manning level of 5 staff, with a working day of 10 hours per day. Making allowance for an average effectiveness of 80 per cent we can calculate that the hours available for production are 40 per day:

$$5 \times 10 \times 80\% = 40$$

Birdhomes' MPS, shown in Table 18.2, is similar to the one used in an earlier example, and the resulting RCCP report for the labour resource is given in Table 18.3.

Table 18.3 Birdhomes' RCCP report: labour resource

Day no.	Hours required	Hours available	Difference	Cumulative difference
6	46.2	40.0	−6.2	−6.2
7	43.2	40.0	−3.2	−9.4
8	63.7	40.0	−23.7	−33.1
9	73.9	40.0	−33.9	−67.0
10	24.2	40.0	15.8	−51.2
11	43.9	40.0	−3.9	−55.1
12	48.5	40.0	−8.5	−63.6
13	48.5	40.0	−8.5	−72.1
14	48.5	40.0	−8.5	−80.6
15	48.5	40.0	−8.5	−89.1
16	48.5	40.0	−8.5	−97.6
17	48.5	40.0	−8.5	−106.1
18	48.5	40.0	−8.5	−114.6
19	48.5	40.0	−8.5	−123.1
20	48.5	40.0	−8.5	−131.6

This RCCP report indicates a prevailing labour overload over the forward planning horizon. Birdhomes therefore need additional labour to satisfy the MPS requirements from day 6 onwards, plus a substantial amount of overtime or temporary labour on days 8 and 9.

As with CRP, this information may also be provided in barchart form.

The RCCP run will be done immediately after cyclical updating of the MPS and before proceeding to the next MRP run.

18.2 The planner's responsibility

The planner is responsible for resolving misfits between load and capacity. If the master production schedule is not feasible, there is no point in proceeding to an MRP run. In that event, the planner has a number of courses of action he can take, but this action is constrained by the three variables indicated in Figure 18.1.

A schedule that overloads the resources available may only be resolved by modification of one of the three variables in Figure 18.1:

1. Capacity may be varied to accommodate demand.
2. Demand may be smoothed to fit the available capacity, normally by means of a buffer stock of the finished product.
3. Delivery leadtime may be extended so as to move demand to an alternative time period where capacity is available.

It is implicit that the planner has the authority to do this. He may *not* change released or firm planned orders on the MPS.

The generalized decision-making framework within which capacity management by the planner takes place is treated comprehensively in Wild (1990: Chapter 11). A simpler framework more applicable to the routine decision making in smaller businesses is indicated below in Table 18.4.

The problems of balancing supply and demand are greatest where there is least visibility of the future, and particularly so in a jobbing business where an unpredictable product mix may have the effect of varying the short-range capacity. Very often the only feasible solution is a short-range modification

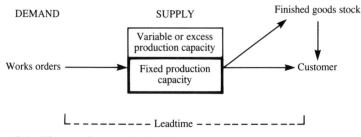

Figure 18.1 Elements in capacity decision making

Table 18.4 Capacity planning decision elements

Key criteria	Action	Applicability
End product inventory is held	Separate the management of supply and demand	Normal in make-to-stock
Capacity is flexible	Allow capacity to be varied to match demand	Needs multi-skilled workforce Normal with work cells
Capacity is finite	Build in excess capacity	Typical in JIT
	Subcontract or use overtime to extend capacity	Normal response to CRP
	Extend leadtime to fit capacity	Typical in jobbing businesses

to the marginal capacity by increasing or decreasing the amount of overtime worked or the volume of work subcontracted out. Where these mechanisms fail to attain a balance between supply and demand the extreme solution is to vary the quoted delivery leadtime, which has the downside risk of leading to loss of business.

The problems of balancing supply and demand in general tend to diminish where manufacturing strategy has been focused on the attainment of greater flexibility, particularly on the introduction of work cells manned by a multi-skilled and flexible workforce. Provided there is not a total plant overload, capacity may normally be varied product group by product group by moving staff from one work cell to another. The C&K Switches case study (Chapter 28) illustrates the effect this has had on reducing delivery arrears in a make-to-order environment. The option of maintaining excess capacity, often associated with a JIT philosophy aimed at satisfying market expectations rather than maximizing process productivity, is economically feasible only where longer-term demand is relatively stable.

To take appropriate action following the results of an RCCP run, the planner needs the following information, which most systems provide on screen:

- the loading on each critical resource;
- for overloaded resources, the loading generated by each part number on the MPS;
- the effect on the resource load of a unit change in the MPS quantity.

The corrective process may be an iterative one. Having resolved an overload on one resource the planner will move on to the next resource. Any subsequent changes he makes at MPS level may then affect the resource previously balanced. To cope with this there are various levels of support available to the planner, and these will depend on specific software packages:

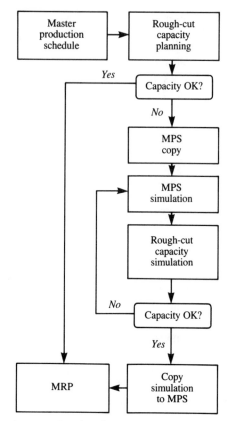

Figure 18.2   Interactive capacity planning

- *Reporting only*: the system only reports the result of the RCCP run. The planner is in effect left to perform a juggling act, perhaps having to rerun RCCP several times before he has balanced load and capacity.
- *A what if? facility*: the system shows what the effect will be of each change the planner makes. This is normally carried out using copies of the system's data files.
- *Interactive simulation*: an extension of the what if? facility, which allows the copy files to replace the original files once the planner has arrived at a feasible plan. This is by far the most user friendly option, and its logic is illustrated in Figure 18.2.

18.3 Resource planning

Where a resource planning module is available, the function of this will be virtually identical to RCCP, except that

– RCCP works at MPS item level, to test the feasibility of the MPS.
– Resource planning works at product family level, to test the feasibility of production plans by product family, and is linked to the production planning module described in Chapter 15.

19

Production activity control

Whereas master production scheduling, MRP and CRP are planning tools, production activity control (PAC) is a system module at execution level. It is driven by planned order receipts generated by MRP, and its primary task is to help the production manager execute the plans deriving from MRP.

This chapter outlines the scope of production activity control, and then presents a generalized overview of a typical PAC system module. The remainder of the chapter explains the major functionality of this module: works order release, work centre scheduling, stores issue documentation, works order documentation and control of tooling.

19.1 Scope of production activity control

The scope of PAC is generally accepted as including:

- the approval and release of works orders
- production operations scheduling and loading
- material kitting and issue
- tooling control
- order priority control in WIP
- capacity control in WIP
- the evaluation of labour and material costs
- the evaluation of production and quality performance
- closure of works orders

The MRPII standard system addressed primarily the planning functions and not the execution functions. The result is a considerable divergence between what is provided in PAC from one software package to the next, even where the core model is the MRPII standard system.

The major deficiencies resulting from MRPII's failure to properly address the system at execution level include the following:

- The absence of a standard interface with SFDC. This has evolved instead through the initiative of software suppliers.
- A lack of support to quality management. As a result very few packages offer adequate support, despite the growing importance of TQM and ISO 9000.
- Support for only simple sequential production routings. Software that supports more complex networks may not be accepted as conforming to the MRPII standard system.
- No provision for identifying individual units within a batch or order. The continuing inference is that this is important only in environments where one is the typical customer order quantity.
- No support for control of tooling. Many packages now support this, but *real* control implies accepting this as a finite resource, and MRPII is founded on scheduling to infinite capacity.

The PAC module in MRPII systems therefore varies greatly from one package to another, but within a framework dictated by the common needs of production management.

19.2 Overview of PAC module

A generalized framework of a PAC system includes the following functions:

- The release of works orders
- Work centre schedules, sometimes referred to as the dispatch list
- Stores issue documentation
- Works order documentation

A state-of-the-art system will also provide a machine-readable interface with an SFDC module.

19.3 Works order release

Works orders have been planned within MRP. They may then be mass-released by MRP, or they may be manually released by the planner on an individual order basis. With mass release, the system will automatically release all orders for which the due date or planned order release date falls within a defined forward horizon.

Release review

Before releasing works order it may be sensible to check that:

- all materials are available, and there are no shortages.
- sufficient capacity is available, and there is no overload.

Some systems therefore have a release review option allowing these checks to be carried out by specific works order before the planned order is released to production.

Trial kitting

The more common facility for checking material availability is trial kitting. This takes all the planned orders due for release, explodes them via the bills of materials, and checks the availability of inventory. The trial-kitting list identifies shortages, and is used by the planner to decide which orders should not be released because shortages exist which would prevent their manufacture.

The inference in all of this is that manufacturing capacity *is* available, because the planner will already have run CRP following the latest MRP run, and will have taken action to address short-term capacity overloads.

Releasing a works order

The release of a works order results in the physical inventory of all the material requirements being allocated. That inventory will remain allocated until such time as the material is issued. Release of the works order also triggers the production of the works order documentation and its associated stores issue documentation.

19.4 Work centre scheduling

This is the process of loading, scheduling and sequencing of works orders by work centre, and the system process differs widely depending on specific software packages. The three most common scheduling methods are these:

1. No scheduling
2. Work to list
3. Detailed production operations scheduling

User surveys by Burcher (1991) and Little and Jarvis (1993) suggest that the shop-floor scheduling function is handled by a computer package in less than half of MRPII installations. Between a quarter and one third of companies entrust this task to their shop-floor supervisors to do manually, while a further quarter make use either of a kanban system or some other physical manual aid to scheduling.

No scheduling

The system simply provides a list of the works orders in the queue ahead of each work centre, together with a list of those expected to arrive over the immediate horizon, and then leaves it to the production manager or work centre supervisor to decide what to make next.

The inference in many earlier reference works on MRPII was that the key to management at production operations level lay simply in input–output control, that is to say, in ensuring that the input to the work queue did not exceed the output from the work queue, and that in addition the output from the work queue was in line with the planned output.

The work to list

With a work to list the system provides a list of live and released works orders in a user-determined priority sequence. This is the solution adopted by the majority of MRPII software packages.

Priority sequencing

Priority sequencing may be taken into account in a simple work to list. When scheduling to finite capacity, priority sequencing is very often used as the basis for determining the sequence in which works orders are in effect allocated potentially limited production capacity.

The most common methods of prioritization are these:

– A user-selected parameter, very often order completion due date. To be valid in a jobbing business the work to list must be sequenced by planned operation due date, and not by planned order due date, and it must be noted that this is a less commonly offered software option than planned order completion date. Sequencing by planned order due date will be valid only where all works orders in a work centre are similar in terms of work content.
– The critical ratio. This is calculated as follows:

$$\text{Critical ratio} = \text{the time needed for completion}$$

$$\div \text{ the time available for completion}$$

The higher this ratio is, the more urgent the order is and the greater the priority it is accorded.
– Manual prioritization. This is normally intended as a user override where the order urgency changes after the order has been released.

A simple example can serve to demonstrate that order due date sequence is not necessarily the correct priority sequence at production operation level in order to respect that order due date. Consider two orders with production operations and times as follows:

order 123 due date: day 35
op 010:   work centre W   time needed: 6 hours
op 020:   work centre X   time needed: 3 hours

order 124 due date: day 37
op 010:   work centre W   time needed: 12 hours
op 020:   work centre P   time needed: 16 hours

Order 123 has priority over order 124 by order due date. In work centre W, operation 010 of order 123 must be started on day 34 to meet order due date, but operation 010 of order 124 must be started on day 33. That means that order 124 must be started *before* order 123, the order that would have had priority had due date been used as the sequencing criterion.

If both orders are ahead of work centre W on day 32, their critical ratios would be as follows:

$$\text{order 123:} \quad 9 \div 3 = 3.0$$

$$\text{order 124:} \quad 28 \div 5 = 5.6$$

Priority would therefore be given to order 124 because it has the higher critical ratio.

Detailed production operations scheduling

Many systems will provide for backward scheduling from operation due date, and the work to list will then be based on the planned operation start date, rather than the planned order completion date. This is very necessary in a jobbing business; even if the priority list is sequenced by planned operation due date, this may not reflect the true priority if different orders have widely differing work content. In such a case the planned operation start date will be a more valid prioritizing criterion than the planned operation due date.

Some MRPII packages may offer a choice of scheduling method, and the more common of these choices are these:

– scheduling to finite capacity, or scheduling to infinite capacity;
– backward scheduling, or forward scheduling;

In all cases where detailed scheduling is carried out, it will have the effect of making the following dates more specific:

- There will be a scheduled start date by production operation, in addition to the planned order completion date.
- The scheduled start date will also become the material need date. This may differ from the required date previously calculated by MRP.

Scheduling to finite capacity

Where detailed scheduling to finite capacity is carried out, exactly how that is done will depend on the specific software. There are three major areas of difference between systems in this respect:

1. Whether all live orders, and all orders now due for release, are completely rescheduled, or whether only the orders now due for release are scheduled around the existing live order loads. The latter is termed *residual scheduling*. It is logically similar in context to net change MRP, and just like net change MRP any errors may become self-perpetuating. If residual scheduling is used there is a need for periodic regeneration of the schedule to purge the system.
2. Whether or not the scheduling is performed before or after order release. Where it is done before order release, it is normal for the schedule to have to be confirmed by the planner before the system then releases the order.
3. The scheduling algorithms in use differ widely. There is unlikely to be ready visibility of the algorithm or its effectiveness.

Scheduling to finite capacity is regarded as a decision-making tool, and was rejected by the MRPII standard system on the grounds that it was lacking in transparency, but it may be essential in certain manufacturing environments, such as a jobbing shop, for example.

In the final analysis, simple but sound finite scheduling closely resembles what a planner would do manually on a planning board, and will normally be capable of being perceived as such, or not, as the case may be, by the planner himself.

Hill *et al.* (1992) contend that there is no algorithm which can guarantee an optimal schedule, and that there is therefore a need for a simulation model to precede finite scheduling and provide a decision-support tool which will evaluate the cost benefits of the scheduling options available. The scheduling options on the bottleneck resource would include first in first out (FIFO), shortest operation time first, critical ratio, and several others. The options for alleviating a total overload would comprise overtime working and subcontracting.

The application of scheduling to finite capacity, and the techniques used, will be discussed more fully in Chapter 22.

Table 19.1 Typical kitting list

Data item	Data source
Part Number	Bill of materials
Description	Parts master file
Quantity to be issued	Works order
Unit of measure	Parts master file
Stores location	Parts master file
Operation number used on	Production routing
Work centre needed at	Production routing
Material need date	Works order

19.5 Stores issue documentation

Stores issue documentation will normally be triggered by order release. The typical form of stores issue documentation is the *kitting list*, which is the authority to stores to issue material to production. The kitting list is produced by extending an explosion of the bill of materials by the order quantity, in the same way as gross requirements were calculated in MRP. A typical kitting list as shown in Table 19.1 will specify information for each part number required. An alternative to a kitting list may be individual material requisitions.

The material requirements of all works orders released may be batched or grouped into a picking list, typically in stores location sequence, in order to facilitate the physical picking of materials.

Inventory is allocated as a result of order release, and will remain allocated until it is issued.

Kitting lists or picking lists should have provision for the storekeeper to record what has been issued, and they should be designed as turnround documents in modern systems.

19.6 Works order documentation

Works order documentation is both an instruction, and the authority, to the works to produce a specific quantity of a product or component by a given date, and it will normally be triggered by the process of order release. The documentation is typically a travelling route card or works order routing, and it specifies three types of information:

1. Information about the order—part number, description, drawing number, quantity, due date, etc.
2. The production operations to be carried out—their sequence, description, work centre, times allowed, scheduled start and finish dates (if applicable), etc.

3. The components parts or materials to be used—part number, description, quantity per unit of production, operation where used, work centre where used, etc.

Some systems may also produce separate production operation cards for each operation on the works order. These will contain more detailed information, such as the drawing number, the detailed work instructions, and the like.

Route cards

Route cards should have provision for operator recording of the following information:

- which production operations have been completed, and when;
- the quantities produced and rejected at each operation;
- when the works order is completed—this is also when the last operation has been completed;
- the final quantity produced, and the final quantity rejected.

Production operation cards

Operation cards should have provision for operators to record the following:

- the actual time taken to complete the operation;
- the quantities produced, and the quantities rejected, at that operation;
- the dates the order arrived, was started and was completed at that operation.

Both route cards and production operation cards should be designed as turn-round documents. The actual manner in which the feedback information described above is recorded varies greatly, and is treated in greater detail in Chapter 20.

19.7 Tooling control

If dedicated tooling or jigging is required for a production operation, this is normally a finite resource. If more than one works order requires the same tooling at the same time, then it is equivalent to a resource overload. Unlike machine or labour overloads, contention for tooling cannot so easily be resolved by adjustment of overtime hours or manning levels. Only one order can be satisfied at one time, and precedence will normally be given according to the relative order priority, however that is determined.

The MRPII standard system almost completely ignores the subject of tooling control. Wight (1984) asserts that MRPII will allow planning of tooling in the same way as the planning of any other resource. In reality the MRPII planning method depends on including tooling as a resource in CRP and having the planner react manually to any contention. This will invariably necessitate a revision to the MPS in order to relieve the contention. The contention cannot adequately be addressed by RCCP because subsequent action by MRP may alter both the date the tooling is needed and also the length of time it is required for.

Many software packages do, however, make adequate provision for tooling control, but normally only in conjunction with scheduling to finite capacity. The typical features in such software are as follows:

- The tool number will be specified, by production operation, on the production routing.
- The tool will be regarded as a finite resource by the scheduling activity of the PAC module.

20
Shop-floor data collection

Shop-floor data collection (SFDC) is the feedback loop of information from both the shop floor and stores to maintain the up-to-date status of the MRPII works order and inventory databases. Little and Jarvis (1992) noted that the SFDC module is in use in only 40 per cent of MRPII installations.

In this chapter, we examine first what feedback is required from the shop floor, then more specifically what items of data are needed. Then we will note the different methods that are available to achieve this information feedback. After that we will recap on why we need this information, and will address in detail two aspects of MRPII systems which are very heavily dependent on this data feedback—performance indicators and lot traceability.

Before exploring this subject in more detail it is necessary to make a very fundamental point. The problems of data collection are minimized when system design focuses on collecting as little data as possible and leaving the bulk of the detail within a work cell. Two strategies assist in this task:

- backflushing (see page 192)
- minimizing production leadtimes: this has the effect of minimizing the volume of WIP, and hence the volume of data extant within a work cell.

20.1 Information feedback

In SFDC the information feedback consists of:

1. The confirmation to the system of all planned events. The major planned events are the receipt of parts ordered from external suppliers and the completion of internal works orders, in the correct quantities, and by no later than the planned order receipt date.
2. The notification to the system of all unplanned events. These would include, for example, discrepancies between the quantity ordered and the quantity received, or quantities rejected by inbound inspection.

With every planned event there is an associated prior output, record or document generated by one of the two execution-level system modules:

– purchase ordering
– production activity control

These generated system outputs often serve as turnround documents, for the purpose of aiding the information feedback to the system.

20.2 Data items

The major items of data which have to be collected by an SFDC module are summarized in Table 20.1.

SFDC is the key to systems data integrity. The prerequisites to that data integrity are very simple:

– Capture all relevant information.
– Capture it correctly.
– Capture it quickly.

But achieving that is often difficult. It is the prime task of the SFDC module, in conjunction with the two modules at execution level, to make it as easy as possible for the human operator to achieve those prerequisites listed above.

Table 20.1   Key data feedback

Data source	Data item	Turnround document	Information updated
Stores	Goods receipt	Purchase order	Physical inventory Purchase order Material costs
	Material issue	Kitting list	Physical inventory Allocated inventory Product costs
	Cycle count	Count list	Physical inventory
Shop floor	Labour hours	Time cards Operations card	Employee attendance Product costs
	Machine hours	Operations card	Product costs
	Operation completion	Operations card	Works order Work centre load
		And/or route card	Works order Work centre load
	Works order completion	Route card	Works order Finished inventory

20.3 Data collection methods

Data collection methods have evolved to overcome this difficulty of ensuring accuracy of feedback. The evolution towards the state of the art has been through a number of discrete steps:

1. The manual recording on preprinted forms of *all* data, followed by off-line data preparation in a computer centre and the subsequent file update in batch processing mode. This was the norm in the earlier days of MRP systems.
2. Machine-readable cards generated by higher-level systems, with static data on a punched card, and with variable data entered via the keyboard on SFDC terminals. This method was introduced in the 1960s and became increasingly common during the 1970s.
3. Turnround documents generated by higher-level systems, with the static data preprinted, and with all data entered via the keyboard on workstations in the production control office or the stores office. This also was typical of the 1960s and 1970s.
4. Data entry/enquiry terminals on the shop floor, where the source of the transaction is selected from a pop-up screen or menu, thus allowing the planned event to be confirmed, or the exception to it to be entered via the keyboard. The basic hardware will be a personal computer (PC) or a workstation on the shop floor. This method became increasingly common in the 1980s, especially as the PC became integrated into local area networks (LANs).
5. Bar-coded documents generated by higher-level systems, in which the bar coding identifies basic event details, again allowing a planned event to be confirmed, or an exception to be entered via a keypad. The hardware technology comprises a data capture terminal, which may be portable and may include a radio frequency (RF) link to the computer. This technology developed as a result of the mass automation of retail point of sale systems in the later 1980s, and is the current state of the art in terms of data capture technology.
6. Bar coding of product and materials, for automatic data capture by automated materials handling and movement systems. This is the technology now in use by industry leaders, and is likely to become the future state of the art.

The present state-of-the-art technology adopted by the majority of software packages is therefore:

– data entry/enquiry terminals; or
– data capture terminals with bar-coded documents.

Data entry/enquiry terminals

Data entry/enquiry terminals allow interaction between the system and the operator. The major benefit of this is that anomalies can be dealt with immediately. The terminals will normally be connected to the computer via a LAN. This typically involves cabling, and these terminals are therefore normally both static and limited in number.

Data capture terminals/bar code readers

This technology is one in which bar-coded information is captured by a wand, a contact scanner, or a non-contact laser scanner, and the variable data is entered via a keypad, which is typically hand-held.

Many data capture systems are programmable and have extensive data storage facilities. Some have the capability to act as a data entry/enquiry terminal, but with data display constrained by a limited (e.g. 4 × 16) LCD display. They may also be battery-powered and portable, and connected to the computer via a radio frequency link. The combination of programmable terminals with integral data storage therefore permits the capture of data on walkabout around the factory, with the subsequent batch transmission of the captured data taking place later on return to an RF transmission base or a terminal point in a conventional LAN.

A data capture system like this will normally be the most cost-effective method of data collection, especially where there are many data capture points spread over a large area.

Other data capture methods

The remaining data capture methods include:

- badge readers—for employee identification
- optical or laser scanners
- magnetic stripe readers
- automatic weighing or weigh counting, e.g. linked to electronic scales
- automatic counting, e.g. on exit from a CNC machine.

Simplification of data collection

SFDC can be simplified by avoiding unnecessary feedback. Some software has provision for avoiding feedback of the intermediate operations completion data. Feedback from milestone production operations, very often the last manufacturing operation only, can be used to automatically signal completion of all preceding operations. This is known as *backflushing*.

Hundred per cent data accuracy is most likely to accrue from a totally automated warehousing and materials handling system, where the product or components are physically bar-coded for identification purposes.

Very many systems founder due to the inaccuracy of data feedback. Simplification of data collection is key to the accuracy of data feedback. The emphasis must be on collection of as little data as possible, and the most relevant technique is that of backflushing. Minimizing the volume of extant data helps greatly, and is most easily achieved when production leadtimes, and hence the level of WIP, are minimized.

20.4 Principal feedback functions

The principal function of shop-floor data feedback is as follows:

- to update the current status of the MRPII database, including:
    parts master inventory
    open purchase orders
    open works orders
- to provide lot traceability
- to provide performance measurement information
- to generate current cost information
- to provide input for wage payment systems

20.5 Performance measurement indicators

Software packages differ in terms of their standard performance measurement reporting. Customized reporting can normally be achieved easily via the system's report generator facilities. The most common performance measurement indicators on offer include these:

- *Supplier delivery performance*: the percentage of orders on time and/or the supplier lateness profile.
- *Supplier quality performance*: the percentage of defective parts, recorded either at goods inwards inspection or by recording line rejects.
- *Inventory accuracy*: an analysis of the adjustments which have to be made following a periodic cycle count of inventory.
- *Material availability performance*: the percentage of open works orders with materials shortages at order release date.
- *Works delivery performance*: the percentage of orders produced on time and/or the works delivery lateness profile.
- *Works order arrears analysis*.
- *Works quality performance*: the percentage of rejected parts, and the reasons for rejection.

- *Production efficiency*: the times taken by work centre as a percentage of standard.
- *Analysis of queues* ahead of each work centre, compared to the specified queue times on production routings.
- *Analysis of actual times* compared to standard.
- *Work centre time activity analysis*: an analysis by idle time, setup time, run time, breakdown time, planned maintenance, etc.

20.6 Lot traceability

Lot traceability is normally an option offered with inventory management systems. It is however primarily driven by SFDC, which is good reason for considering the subject at this point. Lot traceability works as follows:

- Inventory records comprise a sub-record for each lot, or receipt batch, of the part number. Each sub-record will comprise some or all of the following data and the sub-record will be created on receipt of the lot or batch:
    part number
    lot number, e.g. goods receipt number
    additional identification, e.g. supplier batch number, test certificate number, or works order number
    the quantity received
    the date received
    the purchase or cost price
- In addition, each sub-record will contain a string of issues data, with each string comprising the following data items:
    the works order number, or despatch note number, to which the material was issued
    the quantity issued
    the date issued
- Most importantly, the lot identification is physically recorded on the materials at the time of receipt, either on the part itself or alternatively on the container or packaging it is supplied in. When materials are subsequently issued from stores the lot identification is recorded, and is captured by the data collection system. Where material is issued from more than one lot, there must be provision for recording this.

The inventory system updates the appropriate lot sub-record with every receipt and issue transaction. At any point, the balance between quantity received and the sum of quantities issued should by inference still be locatable in the stores.

There will be provision in the lot traceability system for the retention of lot sub-records for a specified period of time after the depletion to zero of the balance of the lot or batch quantity.

Purpose of lot traceability

The purpose of lot traceability may be any of the following:

1. It may be a quality assurance requirement, for example to satisfy ISO 9000 or one of the many aerospace or defence quality assurance standards. In this case the lot records may be used for the following purposes:

   (a) In the event of an end-product failure or rejection, a lot history search from the highest-level product downwards will reveal from which lots all component parts were issued.

   (b) When a component part has been identified as the cause of a product failure or rejection, the lot record will reveal which other works orders this batch was issued to, and lot record searches will then provide an upwards trail to all the customer orders which may potentially also have been affected.

2. For the controlled rotation of inventory on a FIFO basis. In this case, there may also be provision for the stores picking lists to specify the oldest extant lot, in order to direct picking to that lot.

3. For true FIFO costing.

21
The fit with just-in-time

The MRPII standard system addresses just-in-time (JIT) by the provision of a repetitive manufacturing module. Repetitive manufacturing is increasingly associated with JIT. It is positioned on the manufacturing spectrum between automated assembly lines and batch production. Under the influence of JIT there has been a migration towards repetitive manufacturing from both directions.

In this chapter we will first put MRPII and JIT in context. Then we will look at two distinct aspects of JIT:

– a manufacturing philosophy
– a specific production control method—the kanban system

This leads on to examination of how an MRPII system can support JIT. We will note that the methodology available supports both a kanban system and also the implementation of JIT without a kanban system. The vital interface with suppliers is illustrated using two case studies which illustrate a wide divergence in implementation approach. This chapter concludes by examining a model for inventory management in a JIT environment.

21.1 MRPII and JIT

MRPII was conceived before the widespread recognition of JIT in the western world. The original forms of MRPII were incompatible with JIT from the level of MRP downwards. The adoption of the repetitive manufacturing module of MRPII created an interface between MRPII and JIT, in which the repetitive manufacturing module replaces the PAC module, and supports JIT methods on the shop floor. The conventional repetitive manufacturing module available with software packages will support the JIT concept even if the kanban system is not being adopted on the shop floor.

In a repetitive manufacturing environment MRPII planning systems can provide coordination between production units and can support JIT at the medium-term planning level. More usually, however, the move towards JIT as a method of shop-floor control is associated with the following tactics, especially when rate-based scheduling has been introduced:

– Abandon MRPII in its standard form, but continue to use MRP for planning forward supplier delivery schedules. In this case MRP can be driven by forecasts or by a smoothed production plan, the uniform production rate that is the basis for rate-based scheduling.
– Plan only the final assembly operation, selecting orders from the sales order file to fulfil a predetermined rate of assembly. The more complex order-scheduling criteria associated with configure-to-order products has already been noted in Chapter 16.
– Pull subassemblies forwards from upstream processes using the kanban system.
– Pull materials from stores, or directly from suppliers, using the kanban system, and eliminate all intermediate buffer stocks.

Within this simplified overview there are two significant and contrasting approaches to the implementation of JIT, in which the main determinant is what triggers production in work cells upstream of final assembly:

– the MRPII repetitive manufacturing system
– the kanban system

The MRPII repetitive manufacturing system

In Chapter 16 we noted the alternative approaches to rate-based master production scheduling. Whichever method is adopted the net result will be the same: a rate-based production schedule will be used to drive MRP, and MRP in its turn will therefore, using the lot-for-lot principle, result in the generation of subassembly or component manufacturing schedules.

On a short-range horizon these schedules will constitute the authority to manufacture, and will result in the production of a buffer stock that will be in balance with the requirements of downstream operations, which will pull forward components or subassemblies as required.

This is a summary of the manufacturing environment described by some as JIT, but as opposed to the kanban system. It is an amalgam of the push and pull principles. Work is still effectively being pushed into the manufacturing units or work cells, but the flow of materials between the work cells is being pulled from downstream. This technique remains founded on the use of MRP principles as the basis for controlling inventory and material flow.

The kanban system

This method of shop-floor control is described in detail in section 21.3. For the moment, what concerns us is the radically different approach this implies in comparison to the repetitive manufacturing approach of MRPII.

In this type of system MRP may still be used to produce a forward manufacturing plan by work centre, but it no longer constitutes the authority to make. This authority instead passes to the recirculation of a kanban card. The crucial difference is that this marks a return to the application of an order-point replenishment technique to control the short-term supply chain. Just how the level of buffer stock is determined will be examined later in this chapter. Luscombe (1993) makes the point that the kanban parts are normally treated as phantoms, so that MRP bypasses these parts in its planning process.

The role of MRP therefore diminishes as the direct link between the planning system and execution level becomes restricted to only the final assembly schedule, with both inter-process transfer *and* manufacturing in upstream work cells being triggered by a pull mechanism. What does not diminish is the role that MRP has to play in providing external suppliers with a stable and reliable forward delivery schedule. Where material is being pulled from suppliers on a daily basis the importance of this, if anything, increases.

In addition MRP has a role to play in helping manage engineering change. Stene (1992) noted that MRP's role included:

- the introduction of kanbans for new items;
- the removal of kanbans in the case of obsolete items;
- varying the number of kanbans as the rate of demand alters.

21.2 What is JIT

Just-in-time originated in Japan in the 1960s. Toyota is generally acknowledged as the pioneer of JIT. The example of Toyota and other Japanese companies revealed a radically new approach to manufacturing strategy, especially in a number of key areas indicated in Table 21.1.

The most obvious feature, and indeed the most revolutionary feature, to western eyes *at the time* was the requirement on external suppliers to deliver

Table 21.1 Changes in manufacturing strategy

Area	Example
Product design	Design for manufacture
	Design for assembly
Quality management	Statistical process control
	Total quality management
Supplier relationships	Single source partnerships
Process layout	Group technology
Workforce involvement	Quality circles
Control of material flow	The kanban system

exact quantities on a specific date, hence the generic terminology accorded to these methods—*just-in-time*.

In reality, there are two quite distinct aspects to JIT:

1. There is an overarching manufacturing philosophy, which is fairly universally applicable across a very broad spectrum of manufacturing environments.
2. There is a production control system—the kanban system—which is appropriate *only* in very specific manufacturing environments.

JIT philosophy

The JIT philosophy is almost universally applicable, and may be regarded as an overarching manufacturing strategy, a point which has already been made in Chapter 5. This JIT philosophy has the primary objectives of producing only what is required, producing it at the required time, in the required quantities, and with 100 per cent good production, and it achieves these objectives by aiming at the following strategic goals:

- zero defects
- zero setup time
- zero inventories
- zero handling
- zero breakdowns
- zero leadtime
- a lot size of one

The relevance of these goals to both manufacturing leadtimes and to inventory levels is demonstrated in Appendix C.

JIT has often been defined as the elimination of waste in all its disguises. The point is repeatedly made that in many pre-JIT environments the true value-adding process accounts for only 5 per cent of total manufacturing leadtime, and that during the remaining 95 per cent the product is attracting unnecessary costs. JIT focuses on examining where value is added, and eliminating as much as possible of the non-value-adding activity.

For example, the relationship between waste and batch size is simply demonstrated. Large production batches lead to

- large inventories
- large storage space
- lengthy leadtimes
- high material handling costs

and reducing batch sizes will therefore contribute to reductions in inventory, in storage space, in leadtimes, and in material handling costs.

This simple logic, applied to all elements of activity that are not value-adding activities, is the foundation of the goals of JIT, as listed above.

JIT kanban system

The kanban system is applicable only in a specific manufacturing environment, that of high-volume, or repetitive, production, including assembly to order, where there are stable production plans and relatively short procurement leadtimes.

The kanban system focuses on the reduction of manufacturing leadtime and the reduction of inter-process buffer stocks, and yields the following much wider company benefits:

- a cost reduction, deriving very largely from reductions in inventory levels, which leads to a competitive advantage;
- a shorter planning horizon, deriving from the reduction in leadtimes, which places less dependency on forecasts which are inherently prone to error;
- the elimination of costly and error prone material tracking systems. When leadtimes are reduced from weeks to only hours there is very little work to keep track of.

The analogy has often been used—by Wight and others—of water level and hidden rocks to illustrate the effect of buffer stocks. If you lower the water level you expose the rocks, and by analogy if you reduce the buffer stocks you expose the many inefficiencies in the manufacturing and procurement environment. The buffer stock essentially gives protection against these inefficiencies. Removing these inefficiencies is at the very heart of JIT.

A better analogy is to regard the kanban system as the ultimate form of the transparency so strongly advocated by Wight (1984) on the planner's behalf. From the planner's perspective the task of identifying the flow of work through the factory may, in a kanban system, be compared to looking at pebbles on the bed of a clear fast-flowing stream, in contrast to the more traditional MRPII systems, where the vantage point is too often obscured by having to peer through deep, muddy and stagnant waters, or across a shop floor cluttered with queues of WIP.

A kanban system will not work satisfactorily in certain environments, especially where any of the following characteristics apply:

- Procurement leadtimes are long.
- The variability of demand is high.
- Delivery or quality performance is low.
- Material flow between production operations is not rapid.

The kanban system has two key advantages to offer from the point of view of the systems management:

- The information loops are short.
- The control is decentralized.

A kanban system is essentially a system equivalent to MRPII's execution-level modules, and must therefore be supported by overall planning at a higher level, usually by MRP. There is no logical reason why master production scheduling should not sit above MRP in the planning hierarchy, but the reader should note that the manufacturing environment to which the kanban system is most applicable is one in which rate-based scheduling will usually be more appropriate than the order-based scheduling of MRPII. These aspects have already been addressed, both in Chapter 16 and at the outset of this chapter.

21.3 Key features of the kanban system

The kanban system is typically in operation where a plant layout is product-oriented, using group technology or continuous flow methods, with line balancing, and where the material flow is based on the use of standard containers for inter-process buffer stock. It normally operates in conjunction with the direct line feed of arriving materials, the delivery of inbound materials directly to the process where they are required, rather than to a stores area.

In a kanban system the movement of materials is controlled by a circulating kanban card or container. The kanban system is a pull system in which an order triggers the final production operation, which in turn pulls materials forwards from a previous operation, which then in its turn makes to replenish the quantity pulled forward, and so on, cascading backwards all the way to external suppliers.

The flow of materials in a kanban system is synchronized with the rate of usage on the final production operation, and all material flow within the plant, and into the plant, is triggered by the circulation of a kanban.

The kanban system is a paperless system, in which a number of time-consuming and error-prone features very important in a traditional MRPII system are simply not necessary:

- There is no shop-floor documentation.
- There is no stores issue documentation.
- There are no purchase orders.
- There is no recording of receipts or issues.
- There is no recording of job flow through WIP.

Instructions and feedback in the kanban system are limited to three very basic items:

1. Supplier delivery schedules.
2. Short-term production or final assembly schedules.
3. The reporting of production completed.

All intervening material movements are controlled by the circulation of kanbans, and backflushing is used in lieu of inter-process data feedback and material movements recording.

The kanban

Kanban is the Japanese word for card. A kanban card identifies the part or material, which is *always* stored in a standard container. It is a recycling material requisition and advice note.

A typical kanban card would contain the following data:

- part number
- description
- the supplying process, or external supplier
- the destination process
- the container type
- the container capacity.

The container capacity is the quantity of parts which will *always* be placed in the container by the supply source. Only good parts will be placed in the container, and the supplying source is responsible for ensuring this. The number of containers in circulation at any moment determines the total buffer stock of the part. At an average point in time, the container being filled will be half full, and the container being emptied will be half empty. The total buffer stock is therefore:

$$\text{container capacity} \times (n - 1)$$

where n is the number of containers.

Buffer stocks in the true kanban system are determined empirically, for example by starting with five or more kanbans, and progressively withdrawing one kanban at a time until the flow of materials is no longer satisfactory. At that point the latest kanban withdrawn will be reinstated. After a period of stability the process of withdrawing a kanban at a time may be tried again, because the process of continuous improvement, a vital element of a JIT philosophy, may have led to improvements in the flow of materials.

In the western world formulae are increasingly being used to determine the optimum number of kanbans. This is best regarded as a culture buffer—adapting a superior, but alien, methodology to conform to what is believed to be sound inventory management theory. The use of a formula may give comfort that the number of kanbans is correct, but it may also divert attention away from the possibility of improving the material flow and thus further reducing the buffer stock. A typical formula for calculating the number of kanbans is given by Vollman *et al.* (1992):

$$K = (D \times L \times (1 + S))/C$$

where
K = the number of kanbans
D = demand per time period
L = leadtime in time periods
S = a safety stock factor
C = container capacity

21.4 Material flow in an MRP/kanban system

Figure 21.1 illustrates the generalized interface between MRP and a kanban system. In essence this signals a move away from a centralized MRPII system

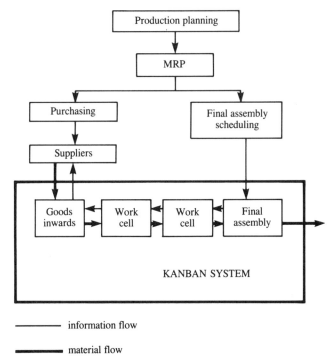

information flow

material flow

Figure 21.1 MRP/kanban interface

towards a distributed system oriented towards replenish and pull. In this alternative framework the key planning element is the forecast, the key system planning modules are production planning, RCCP and MRP, and the essential control mechanisms at execution level are final assembly scheduling and the shop-floor kanban system.

Final assembly and each production department or work cell has a short-range production schedule, covering as little as a day or a shift. How this schedule is derived, and what its data source is, will depend on the type of scheduling carried out at MPS level, or its equivalent. There are generically three options:

1. Rate-based scheduling. For longer-term planning purposes the production planning module (see Chapter 15), a rate-based form of master production scheduling (see Chapter 16), or their equivalent, will indicate the planned production rate, and this will be a rate that balances forecast demand and production capacity. Where rate-based scheduling is used, this production planning module will be run much more frequently than it would in a typical MRPII system, and will be used to plan shorter-range changes to the production rate, taking account of any divergences between the emerging firm demand pattern and the original forecast demand.

    In very simplistic terms, final assembly scheduling will then consist of selecting and extracting customer orders from the sales order file, in some form of priority sequence, to fulfil the planned production rate. This will normally be the simplest approach if the product is not configured to order.

2. Order-based scheduling, using an MPS to achieve a uniform production rate. The source of orders comprising the final assembly schedule will be selected from the MPS. This will be the case if the planned order release version of master production scheduling, described in Chapter 16, is in use. It will typically be associated with configure-to-order products.

3. Order-based scheduling, using MRP. If the production plan version of master production scheduling, also described in Chapter 16, is in use, master production scheduling will simply have been a top-level pass of the MRP system, and the final assembly schedule will derive directly from MRP. This alternative may be used where demand is insufficiently continuous to justify rate-based scheduling. The production plan version of MPS is, however, not compatible with configure-to-order products.

Inter-process buffer stock is held in the standard containers. The kanban card is attached to a full container in the arrival buffer stock of a process. The other full containers of the same component are held in the departure buffer stock of the previous process. They will move on to their destination process only when the kanban returns from the downstream process.

The final assembly process centre produces to the production schedule. It may start with a part-full container of a component part. When that is empty a full container will then be taken from the arrival buffer stock. The kanban is removed from that full container, and is returned with the empty container to the supplying process.

The supplying process will then place the kanban on a full container in its departure buffer stock, and send it on to the destination process.

The empty container now becomes the authority for the supplying process to make to replenish and fill the container. Manufacture to the schedule will halt if there are no empty containers to be filled. In this way the rate of manufacture in all of the upstream processes is permanently kept in balance with rate of usage in all of the downstream processes.

A similar process may control the material flow from external suppliers for direct feeding to the process where the component parts are required. In this case the horizon of the delivery schedule and the number of containers in circulation will take account of both transit times and the frequency of delivery. The only recording will be of physical containers leaving and entering the site, and this will be for financial accounting and payment purposes.

There are several variants of the kanban system, and one quite widely used includes two kanban cards as opposed to just one. In this case one kanban card controls the circulation of material between the supplying process and its destination, and the other controls the replenishment of the empty container at the supplying process.

In lieu of a kanban card the concept of the *electronic kanban* serves to pull replenishment from a supplier; this may be as simple as a telefax, or EDI, previously described in Chapter 10.

Within a kanban system suppliers receive regular revisions to forward delivery schedules, and these originate from MRP runs of no less than weekly frequency, and often as frequently as daily in fast-moving environments. The fact that the entire system operates within the relative stability of production rates therefore gives suppliers the necessary protection against the risk of producing to schedule but only actually delivering on receipt of the electronic kanban.

21.5 The repetitive manufacturing module of MRPII

The features of this module vary from one software package to another, but they would typically comprise the following:

– A smoothed production or assembly plan over a short-term horizon. One option will allow this to be derived from the master schedule and/or MRP net requirements, and this option will be selected when order-based scheduling is in use (see section 21.4). To support repetitive manufacturing, it is virtually essential that the MRP system be a bucketless net change system, with on-line schedule regeneration. The other option is instead to derive the production plan directly from sales order data, and this will be appropriate if rate-based scheduling is in use. The variations in approach, including those applicable to configure-to-order products, have already been discussed in Chapter 16.

- Cyclical production schedules for each manufacturing process, normally covering one day or one shift ahead. These will be related to a rate of production defined for each production process. In an assemble-to-order situation, there may be sophisticated scheduling of the product mix, and the customized optional features, to make the schedule as flexible as possible.
- The provision only for end-of-line data recording. The calculation of the material usage and the updating of inventory records will be done by the technique of backflushing. This is the automatic downdating of inventory records of all component parts and materials consumed in the manufacture of the quantity of product or component manufactured, as defined by the relevant bill of materials. Backflushing is most easily understood by imagining that the kitting list, described in Chapter 19, is calculated not at order release but instead on completion of production, and that it is then immediately used to subtract automatically the quantities on it from the inventory records.
- The provision for an electronic kanban. For each component part number the user defines container quantity and number of containers in circulation. Based on the usage as calculated by backflushing, the system then initiates the replenishment of the component from a supplier. This is an electronic kanban. For it to be effective, the information status needs to be constantly current.

The supplier interface will be discussed in section 21.6. Ralston and Reddy (1993) and others have suggested that the principle of the electronic kanban should apply only to distant suppliers. Much of the emphasis in JIT environments is directed to maximizing the use of local suppliers, and where there are local suppliers with daily delivery capability, and provided they have the security of stable and reliable forward delivery schedules, then a simple pull mechanism from the work cell will suffice. In that case a pull instruction communicated via EDI is logically equivalent to a recirculating kanban card.

21.6 The supplier interface

Two contrasting examples of how the fit between MRP and JIT extends back through the interface with suppliers are given by McKenzie (1991), in his description of the strategy at IBM Greenock, and Wilson (1993), who describes the system in operation at Mitel Telecom Ltd.

Example   IBM Greenock

The PS/1 range of personal computers is manufactured in a continuous flow manufacturing environment with build to requirement and a kanban size of one. Material requirements are pulled from suppliers by direct line feed exactly in the quantities needed for the plant's daily build programme. To avoid transport delivery congestion IBM have developed a transport pickup network based on a concept of balanced loads. One vehicle collects from several suppliers, and each container is filled with the correct quantity of components needed for assembly on a manufacturing line as soon as the vehicle arrives at the plant.

Material requirements planning is integrated with a European-wide logistics system, and a forward requirement programme at component level is generated on a monthly cycle. The material forecasts are communicated to suppliers via EDI links. On a shorter-term horizon, daily requirements diverge from these forecasts, due to changes in customer demand and also to supply constraints. A front-end scheduling module converts the immediate daily real demand into the direct line feed requirement, which is then transmitted via the EDI links to all suppliers on a daily basis.

Example   Mitel Telecom Ltd

Wilson (1993) challenges the effectiveness of MRP as a means of communicating requirements to suppliers. He reminds us that the culture of JIT is based on the use of the kanban system, and that this is no more than a modern equivalent of a two-bin system for the replenishment of shop-floor stocks. Kitting lists, and the associated data feedback, have been replaced by backflushing.

Shorter leadtimes eliminate the need to make to stock and in turn reduce the need for master production scheduling in its conventional role. The combination of flexible work methods and a multi-skilled workforce provides almost unlimited short-term variations to production capacity, and has removed the need for CRP. The reader should note the similarity between this last point of Wilson's and the Boss Trucks case study in Chapter 16; in the case of Boss Trucks, a manufacturing environment very different to Mitel, a similar flexibility in short-term capacity has also obviated the need for capacity planning systems.

According to Wilson, Mitel Telecom moved to a re-order point programme with preferred suppliers. The inference is that the majority of these do not themselves manufacture to JIT, and this is far from uncommon among component suppliers. The preferred suppliers hold specified levels of inventory on large spend items. Replenishment is triggered by a visible trigger card in the container, and replenishment instructions are communicated to the supplier via EDI. Wilson noted that most suppliers were willing to reduce their quoted delivery leadtimes when given a stable and reliable forward delivery schedule which enabled them to build in advance of replenishment orders.

In the case of Mitel Telecom the result of this approach was to reduce inventories of key material categories to between 35 and 45 per cent of their former levels.

21.7 Inventory management in a JIT environment

With a kanban system we have seen (page 202) that WIP inventory is a function of the number of containers in circulation. There will normally be no inventory of the finished product—that would be a contradiction of the concept of JIT. The remaining component of inventory is the production materials inventory. Many people assume that *all* component supplies must be delivered on a JIT basis by suppliers. In many instances this is neither practical nor desirable, and common sense will normally determine how material supplies are to be scheduled for receipt in order to satisfy a kanban system.

Example   Nissan Motor Manufacturing UK Ltd

This has been described by Hurst (1991). Using a conventional Pareto (ABC) analysis, the production inventory was classified into ABC categories:

- Class A items represent 80 per cent of usage value, or a unit cost price of more than £20. These items are controlled either by a pull control method, in effect a kanban method, or by scheduled daily call-off derived from a rate-based schedule. Class A items are collected from the supplier at least once per day, and at fixed times per day. The result is low stockholding achieved by frequent delivery.
- Examples of components in this category included wheels, tyres, headlamp units, and radiators. To this category was added all items falling within the top 80 per cent of cube storage volume, even if they did not satisfy the usage value or unit cost price criteria. The rationale for this was to make savings in both site storage and material handling costs.
- Class B items comprise the remaining items, not included in class A, but comprising a total of 95 per cent of usage value. These items are controlled by MRP in the manner described in Chapters 8 and 9. Items in class B included sun visors, locks and hinges, and wiper arms.
- Class C items—the residue—comprise such items as hoses, owners' manuals, tubes, cables, and badges. These items are controlled on a minimum/maximum basis. A relatively high stockholding goes hand in hand with infrequent deliveries.

In the Nissan model the split between the three classes of inventory was as follows:

- Class A: 625 items, or 33 per cent of all items
- Class B: 419 items, or 22 per cent of all items
- Class C: 827 items, or 44 per cent of all items

The resulting total inventory value is the equivalent of 0.87 days' usage value.

22
Non-standard solutions

In this chapter we begin by noting the assumptions made by the MRPII standard system which may not be applicable in many manufacturing environments, and this leads on to an examination of the alternative solutions. The major point of issue is the production scheduling method to be used, and the alternatives are discussed. Two of these are then examined in greater detail— backward scheduling to finite capacity and optimized production technology. The general case for adopting methods like these is stated, and the discussion then focuses on the techniques themselves. This chapter concludes with a series of case studies.

22.1 Non-universal assumptions of MRPII

The MRPII standard system is founded on a number of implicit assumptions. The following important assumptions may not hold true in many manufacturing environments:

- Future demand can be forecast to allow planning to extend beyond the limits of firm sales order cover. In many business environments there may be a high variability of demand and/or only short-term sales contracts for make-to-order or design-to-order products. In these situations conventional forecasting will be invalid or at best extremely inaccurate beyond a very short-range horizon.
- The major manufacturing processes are producing products of similar manufacturing content. MRPII evolved in an assemble-to-order environment, where the major work centres produced customized products belonging within a clearly definable and semi-standard product group. In many manufacturing operations individual work centres may have to produce products of widely differing manufacturing content. This is especially true in a jobbing shop.
- The similarity of manufacturing content in major work centres means that smoothing of requirements at master schedule level by the planner will result in smoothed production plans at all lower levels. In environments where there is wide variation in manufacturing work content, smoothing at the top level may not necessarily result in smooth plans at the level of

discrete work centres. A smooth production plan may instead depend on the smoothing of production workload at work centre level, operation by operation.

- Hill *et al.* (1992) point out that in a jobbing business the bottlenecks shift according to the product mix and that the result of this is effectively to vary the capacity available. In a jobbing business it is therefore necessary to cope with an 'irregular and unpredictable demand for an unstable mix of products in low volume'. MRPII was not designed to cope with this.
- Where order prioritization is provided for, it is often based on order due date sequence. Where product variety involves a widely differing mix of production operations and work centres, the correct priority at operation level may *not* be the same as the priority at order level.
- MRPII does *not* assume infinite capacity, but the inference that smooth production plans will follow from the smoothing of the master schedule by the production planner leads to the inherent principle of the subsequent scheduling to infinite capacity in the interests of transparency. When this assumption is not true, there is a need for more detailed scheduling. In many cases that will imply scheduling to finite capacity, at least in the bottleneck work centres.
- MRPII assumes that production times are short in relation to setup and queue times, and that a fixed planning leadtime is therefore valid, regardless of batch quantity. This will not be true where effort has been made to reduce setup times and/or better manage the flow of work as opposed to work centre throughput.
- In MRPII all required dates are calculated by offsetting the fixed planning leadtime from due date, assuming scheduling to infinite capacity. Where scheduling must take account of finite capacity, then MRP's order planning may be invalid unless it takes account of scheduled start dates.
- MRPII expects the planner to ensure that what is planned does happen. The possible impact of material shortages on production plans is virtually ignored. Where supplier delivery reliability is uncertain, better control may result if production plans take account of when receipts are now expected as opposed to when they were originally planned to be received.

The general case for acceptance into the MRPII systems framework of scheduling techniques that recognize the need to address finite capacity is made by a number of authors.

Little and Jarvis (1993) noted that almost half of the users surveyed used computer packages for shop-floor scheduling, and that these packages were more modern than the MRPII system itself.

In asserting that finite capacity scheduling is a desirable, but not essential feature of production control, Norton *et al.* (1993) had this to say:

MRP's main assumption is that manufacturing takes place in the fairytale world where due dates are met. At best the interface with the shop floor from MRP can be an unrealistic and unachievable work to list. If finite capacity scheduling is used, the work to list can be achievable and realistic at the point of production. Finite capacity scheduling takes account of constraints, . . . including the fact that due dates may be unachievable.

Little and Jarvis (1992), noting that shop-floor scheduling was the third tier in a planning hierarchy below MRP and master production scheduling, recognized that 'adjustments have to be made to cope with the real world problems not predicted by the plans'.

Referring specifically to jobbing shops, Hill *et al.* (1992) noted that there is an inherent flexibility in a jobbing shop which, properly used, is a strategic advantage. It should be possible to rearrange the current plans to accommodate a new customer order with the minimum of inconvenience. This requires finite capacity scheduling. To attempt this using infinite capacity scheduling results in wide variations in load that lead to a nervous system.

Mitchell (1992) made the point that the demand for shorter leadtimes created a need for the optimum time sequencing of works orders, and that scheduling to finite capacity helped eliminate queues by sequencing production so as to minimize the queue time.

Stene (1992) described misfits between MRPII and real-life manufacturing environments. He made the point that in MRPII the emphasis is on planning and managing inventory, and this may not correspond to the major objectives of manufacturing management. In discrete batch production, Stene noted that the key management criteria were usually productivity and throughput, and concluded that 'the solution for many has involved replacing the infinite capacity based CRP with a finite capacity scheduling suite'.

Harrison (1992) noted that 'MRPII effectively launches work into the plant and then loses control'. He asserted that there was by now a general acceptance that within MRPII there was a major gap in terms of shop-floor control, and that this gap is 'now being filled by finite capacity scheduling systems'.

22.2 MRPII non-standard solutions

Many software packages address the needs of these manufacturing environments which do not conform to the assumptions implicit in the MRPII standard system. They vary widely in terms of their structure and detail, but their two most common features are:

– a works order file driver of MRP
– a finite capacity production scheduling module, interfaced between the works order file and MRP.

The generalized schematic of this was illustrated in Figure 12.1.

Works order file driver

A works order file replaces the MPS as the driver of the system. In a properly integrated system there will be provision for the planner to release orders in a systematic manner from the sales order system to the works order system. Batching of orders or lot sizing will be achieved in a fairly unsophisticated manner, for instance by the planner grouping together a set of discrete sales orders for the same part number. The logic of this approach has validity where the two main features of master scheduling are not relevant:

- The balancing of demand and supply, the smoothing of a production plan—this will be carried out instead by a production scheduling module which works at operation level by work centre.
- The consumption of the forecast by actual sales orders, a technique of importance only in an assemble-to-order environment. The works order file will then have the same driving effect as a mixture of planned and firm planned orders on the MPS.

Production scheduling module

A production scheduling module is interfaced *between* the works order file and MRP. Its two main functions will be:

- The scheduling or smoothing of the workload by production operation in each work centre. This will use the same production routing and resource database as the CRP and production activity control modules of MRPII.
- The calculation of planned start dates by production operation and by order. These dates will then be taken by MRP as the material requirement dates, instead of the due dates obtained by the normal systems technique of time phasing using a planning leadtime. Where material shortages exist or are expected, there is normally provision for the planner to enter delayed start dates. In this way production scheduling is able to take account of material unavailability.

Relating specifically to a jobbing shop, Hill *et al.* (1992) point out that this scheduling model must be dynamic because of the dynamic nature of jobbing production. Only by a dynamic model can the need for continuous re-scheduling be supported by an information system which at all times reflects the current status of the plant.

A what if? version of this module may provide the planner with workload information similar to the CRP module of MRPII. This enables the planner to make capacity adjustments before proceeding to the detailed production scheduling run. Hill *et al.* (1992) describe the what if? capability as a discrete simulation model, comprising three steps:

1. Identify shortages or surpluses of capacity within the planning horizon.
2. Simulate the various possible adjustments to capacity.
3. Report on the systems performance, to enable the planner to test the various options on a what if? basis.

22.3 Production scheduling techniques

Production scheduling techniques are founded on a mixture of logic and mathematics, and represent the specialist skill of the operations analyst. The availability of computer power from the early 1960s enabled more complex and sophisticated techniques to be applied, but the central strategy of operations analysis as applied to production scheduling was logically very simple and two-fold:

1. Identify production bottlenecks.
2. Then devise the most effective scheduling algorithm to maximize bottleneck resource utilization.

The application of this methodology in the 1960s and 1970s did not always work, and it often failed on two counts:

1. In maximizing throughput insufficient attention was given to observing customer delivery requirements.
2. There was both a language and a learning barrier between operations analysts and production planners. The planners did not understand the methodology and the operations analysts were often incapable of explaining it in the layman's terms the planners might have understood. This led to a central theme of the MRPII standard system—the systems logic must be transparent to the planner, and in turn to the promotion of a standard system founded exclusively on the principle of backward scheduling to infinite capacity.

Despite that, the *need* for the operations analysis approach did not disappear, especially where there were real production bottlenecks that were difficult to resolve by the planner at the levels of RCCP or CRP. The advent of *optimized production technology* or OPT (OPT is a registered trademark of Scheduling Technology Group Ltd.) in the early 1980s helped restore the element of legitimacy to the analytical approach, after a decade when MRPII had been in the ascendancy.

The production bottlenecks that have to be addressed vary in nature. Some are relatively fixed bottlenecks, and may be caused by an imbalance between the capacities of different processes. Financial constraints often lead to a serial approach to the introduction of new process technology rather than the upgrading of every process, and somewhere in the chain is the limitation on the throughput of the whole plant. Even where production lines have flexible capacity there are often finite constraints within the whole system. One example is engine assembly, where line speed and therefore capacity can be varied, but where assembly is followed by testing on a fixed and finite number of test beds. Another is a metal rolling mill, where the finite limitation on what can be produced is more often the number of pre-heat furnaces than the capacity of the hot mill.

The complexity of the problem facing the analyst largely depends on *where* the bottleneck exists, and whether it is fixed or variable. Where a fixed bottleneck exists and is the very last operation in sequence, the task is simply to schedule that last operation, and given planned transfer dates into that operation, MRP is then perfectly capable of scheduling the remainder of the production operations.

If the bottleneck is the first operation, then scheduling that first operation establishes planned transfer-out dates, which can be used to schedule forward the remaining operations, although this poses the additional problem that with forward scheduling it is difficult to recognize dependencies in the product structure.

Where the task grows in complexity is when the bottleneck is midstream, or where there is more than one bottleneck, or, worst of all, where the bottleneck is not fixed but variable. The classic example of this is the jobbing shop, where a variable product mix in effect alters the real available capacity from one period to another, and quite often shifts the bottleneck around from one work centre to another.

Identifying bottlenecks is easy; the RCCP or CRP modules of MRPII will do that without difficulty. The analyst's task is that of finding the most appropriate scheduling technique which will strike a balance between the need to maximize throughput at the bottleneck and still accord priority according to order due date. Where that task is most complex of all is where the bottleneck can shift according to the mix of work, and where one single scheduling technique may not be appropriate for all the different patterns of work flow associated with the various production processes.

Wild (1990) identified 12 different production scheduling techniques and attributed their appropriateness to different manufacturing environments as summarized in Table 22.1.

With the exception of the MRPII standard system, *all* of these techniques schedule to finite capacity in specified work centres. These different production scheduling techniques reviewed by Wild in effect constitute the inventory of techniques available to systems designers when formulating the scheduling algorithm at the heart of finite capacity scheduling packages. Which specific technique has been adopted in a software package is not always visible to the potential user, and may not in many instances be revealed by the authors.

Table 22.1 Production scheduling techniques

Scheduling technique	Project	Manufacturing environment		
		Jobbing	Batch	Flow
MRPII	?	?	yes	no
OPT	?	?	yes	yes
Backward scheduling	yes	yes	yes	no
Forward scheduling	yes	yes	yes	no
Sequencing	no	yes	?	no
Dispatching	no	yes	?	no
Assignment	?	yes	?	no
Timetabling	no	no	no	yes
Network analysis	yes	?	?	no
Batch sequencing	no	no	yes	?
Line of balance	no	no	yes	no
Flow scheduling	no	no	?	yes

Source: Wild (1990)

These different scheduling techniques can be summarized briefly:

- *OPT*: a scheduling technique which concentrates on flows through bottleneck production operations. This is explained in more detail in section 22.5.
- *Backward scheduling*: scheduling all production operations backwards from due date (see Figure 17.7).
- *Forward scheduling*: scheduling all production operations forwards from a given date, or earliest start date (see Figure 17.8).
- *Sequencing*: determining the best sequence in which to process a group of jobs through a process. Its objective is to minimize total leadtime, queue time and idle time.
- *Dispatching*: determining which job in a queue is best processed next. Its objective is to minimize the leadtime and lateness.
- *Assignment*: allocating the available jobs against the available resources. Its objective is to minimize leadtime and to maximize the resource utilization.
- *Timetabling*: a schedule that indicates when resources will be available for the work requiring them.
- *Network analysis (or critical path analysis)*: a technique for scheduling interdependent activities in a complex project, so that slack, or free time, and the critical path are identified. This is the method extensively and successfully used in most proprietary project management software.

- *Batch scheduling*: determining optimum batch sizes and a schedule for their production. This is very similar to the part-period balancing lot-sizing technique described in Chapter 9.
- *Line of balance*: a technique calculating quantities to be completed by an intermediate date in order to satisfy a final delivery schedule.
- *Flow scheduling*: a technique for meeting output requirements in terms of cycle time, and for balancing the use of resources within the system.

22.4 Backward scheduling to finite capacity

The scheduling technique in MRPII non-standard systems varies according to the software package. The most common of these techniques is backward scheduling to finite capacity. The basic scheduling steps are shown on Figure 22.1.

How *well* the system schedules depends on the scheduling algorithm used to smooth overloads, and there is little or no immediate visibility or transparency of this. The smoothing of load can be an iterative process, involving rescheduling of downstream production operations and/or the rescheduling of higher priority orders until a feasible smoothed load results. Unlike the basics of MRPII, which are founded on simple logic, scheduling to finite capacity is a methodology associated with a level of competence in operations analysis at MSc level or higher.

BASIC SCHEDULING STEPS

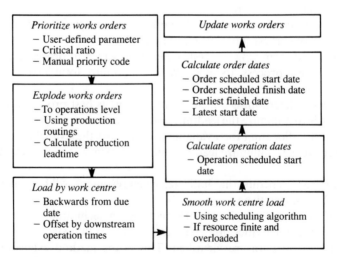

Figure 22.1   Backward scheduling to finite capacity

Backward scheduling to finite capacity results in the calculation and reporting of a number of significant dates for each order:

1. Scheduled start and finish dates. These are the dates on which the system has scheduled the works order to be started and finished, by scheduling backwards and taking account of both finite capacity and the loading generated by higher priority orders. A comparison of order scheduled finish date with order due date will indicate planned lateness.
2. Earliest finish date. This is the earliest date this order could be completed, if started now, and even if it received priority over all other orders.
3. Latest start date. This is the latest date on which the order could be started and still meet customer due date, even if it received priority over all other orders.

Residual scheduling

Provision may be made for residual scheduling, which is the scheduling of new works orders around an existing workload which has already been scheduled to finite capacity.

On a what if? basis this can be used to answer *ad hoc* delivery enquiry promises, and it is logically synergistic with net change MRP.

Pros and cons of scheduling to finite capacity

The respective case for both methods of scheduling can be summed up as follows. Scheduling to finite capacity implies that:

- it does not allow resources to be overloaded;
- the smoothing of the production load takes precedence over respect for customer delivery dates;
- when capacity is full the next available start date extends farther and farther into the future, and delivery leadtimes become longer and longer;
- it works best when manufacturing to stock;
- it offers no solutions when there is an existing order arrears situation;
- it is realistic, pessimistic, and is founded on feasibility;
- it is a production-oriented tool.

Scheduling to infinite capacity, on the other hand, has the following implications:

- it accords precedence to order due date, except when the order is already overdue;
- it gives no indication of what is actually possible, as opposed to what is desirable;

- it requires the planner's intervention to resolve contention—by delaying start dates to relieve bottlenecks or to create gaps in the loading;
- it is idealistic, optimistic, and is founded on desirability;
- it is a market-oriented tool.

On balance, the market orientation of scheduling to infinite capacity, by virtue of the precedence it accords to due dates, makes it the preferable of the two scheduling methods. Scheduling to finite capacity should therefore be the *in extremis* solution, applied primarily in a make-to-order environment where contention between workload and capacity is so high as to render infeasible the manual juggling act required of the planner following a CRP run.

22.5 Optimized production technology

OPT is a technique for optimizing production schedules in order to increase throughput, decrease inventories, and reduce operating expense. OPT distinguishes between bottleneck and non-bottleneck resources. It combines realism and optimism, and offers the best balance between desirability and feasibility.

Developed in Israel in the late 1970s, OPT attained public visibility at APICS conferences in the early 1980s, and the definitive work is Goldratt and Cox (1986). The emergence of OPT as a distinctive approach should be viewed in the context of a series of progressions which all, in the broadest sense, coincided chronologically:

- a wider visibility and adoption of kanban systems in the western world;
- the marketing drive by its advocates to promote MRPII as a standard prescriptive solution;
- an increasing degree of disappointment with the MRPII standard system, especially as visibility of failed systems emerged;
- the emergence of OPT itself.

This led to much philosophical debate as to which was the best way forward: MRPII, kanban or OPT? The reader is cautioned against accepting that there has to be a *best* choice from these three, and more recent debate has come to focus on how they complement each other. The best strategy will always be the one that best fits the user's specific manufacturing environment, and the good news is that there is now a much greater element of choice.

In many respects the rise of OPT signalled the re-emergence of operational analysis as a respectable skill, and destroyed the MRPII claim that backward scheduling to infinite capacity was the *only* valid scheduling technique. This point of view is reinforced by Luscombe (1993), who argues that an OPT/MRPII hybrid is still MRPII because the hybrid process is still under top management control through a structured closed loop methodology.

Like JIT, OPT has by now come to mean two different things:

1. A proprietary system, comprising an innovative approach to production scheduling.
2. A set of rules, founded on a deep insight of the central production scheduling problem and embodying a great deal of common sense. Quite separately from the OPT production scheduling system, these rules have by now attained the status of received wisdom.

The OPT scheduling algorithm is reputedly a closely guarded secret, and is available only with a relatively expensive proprietary software package. This limits its usage, but the principles on which OPT is founded are well publicized and provide by far the most logical framework for production scheduling in most types of manufacturing environment.

The major steps in OPT scheduling are, in order:

1. Schedule backwards to infinite capacity to identify bottleneck resource(s). This first step is virtually identical to the MRP process.
2. Schedule bottleneck production operations to the OPT finite scheduling algorithm, of which there is no visibility in the public domain.
3. Schedule production operations downstream of the bottleneck forward to finite capacity, also using the OPT finite scheduling algorithm.
4. Schedule upstream operations backward to finite capacity.
5. Finally, test capacity loadings to ensure that new bottlenecks have not emerged as a result of scheduling downstream. If they have, then further passes of the logic will take place until all the bottlenecks are eliminated.

The rules of OPT

The rules of OPT are worth stating, if only because they encapsulate by far the best principles of common sense yet articulated in the context of production planning and scheduling.

1. Utilization of non-bottleneck resources is constrained by something other than their own capacity. It follows that there is no benefit in trying to schedule non-bottlenecks to 100 per cent loading.
2. Efficiency and effectiveness of a resource should not be confused. What is effective is to use bottleneck resources efficiently. The efficient use of a non-bottleneck does not increase the effectiveness of the overall system.
3. Time lost at a bottleneck is time lost throughout the entire manufacturing system. It follows that 100 per cent utilization of bottleneck resources is effective. One way to achieve this is to maximize batch sizes on bottlenecks and thus reduce the number of setups.

4. Time saved at a non-bottleneck does nothing to improve the throughput of the system as a whole. The number of setups on a non-bottleneck resource therefore does not matter, so neither does the batch size at these processes.

5. Bottlenecks determine the total system throughput. They also determine the total level of inventory in the system, because the level of WIP will depend on how much of a work pipeline, or queue, is needed to keep the bottlenecks at 100 per cent utilization.

6. The transfer batch quantity does *not* have to be equal to the process batch quantity. The overlapping of process operations and the splitting of batches from one process to another can therefore be effective.

7. Batch quantities should be variable, not fixed. The batch quantity may vary operation by operation, and from one order to the next.

8. Capacity and priority are interrelated. Leadtimes are not fixed, but variable. Where capacity is limited, leadtimes and priorities must take account of the limitations to capacity.

9. Production scheduling should aim to balance the material flow, and not to balance capacity. This helps to identify bottlenecks, where management attention and action can then be directed.

10. Performance measurements should be related to the total system, the output that flows from final assembly, and not from its individual components, or specific work centres.

These rules are now increasingly being incorporated in customized software. MRPII/OPT hybrids are an emerging technology, and may possibly represent the state of the art for the 1990s. A significant degree of expertise is required when engineering such hybrids founded on OPT principles.

In addition to these rules of OPT there are other models for good scheduling. For example, Harrison (1992) stated eight rules of good scheduling which, like OPT, focused on the identification of bottlenecks. His eight rules can be summarized:

1. Identify bottlenecks.

2. Balance the flow of work to and from the bottlenecks. On no account schedule work into a bottleneck if there is not the capacity to process it.

3. Sequence the non-bottlenecks to an MPS that takes account of both demand and production bottlenecks. The final assembly schedule will reflect the planned sequence through the bottleneck.

4. Use time as a buffer ahead of the bottleneck, rather than a volume of work, and ensure that there are no queues ahead of non-bottlenecks.

5. Plan small batches to ensure the smoothest flow of work.

6. Take account of setup dependencies between jobs at the bottleneck, and modify the sequence to reduce setup times.

7. Allow for the constraints on production to vary, for example, between machine capacity, labour capacity, or tooling or assembly jigging.
8. While an accurate bill of materials is essential, do not worry about the accuracy of operation times. A tolerance of plus/minus 15 per cent will not invalidate the results of scheduling.

22.6 Examples of non-standard solutions

Case study   Short Brothers: an OPT/MRPII hybrid system (AT&T Istel 1992)

A hybrid system combining OPT and a conventional MRPII type system is in use at Short Brothers, Belfast. Used from late 1991 to schedule high-pressure ovens for the curing of carbon-reinforced components such as aircraft wing and rudder sections and aero-engine nacelles, the OPT system is part of a complete operational management and control system, encompassing the manufacture of sheet metal components, machined parts, metal bonding, composites, and tool manufacture, developed and installed by AT&T Istel. These five manufacturing areas presented 'very different manufacturing environments and so demand different systems functionality'. The resulting software design offers 'hundreds of optional functions all integrated seamlessly with a core database'. The systems development was part of a £200 million investment programme undertaken after Bombardier Inc. acquired Shorts, and was in support of the company's long-term objective of achieving world-class manufacturing standards.

In the manufacture of composites, the traditional bottlenecks were three autoclaves: high-pressure ovens for the curing of composites, where the curing time could be as long as nine hours. OPT-type dynamic scheduling is used to schedule these bottlenecks to ensure that they operate at full capacity, and this is followed by scheduling backwards and forwards to meet MRPII due dates.

The result is that MRPII requirements are satisfied and that short-term capacity problems are overcome. In the case of Short Brothers this solution led to adherence to schedule improving from around 60 per cent to a constant 98 per cent, with throughput of composite components increasing by 50 per cent, from 400 units per week to 600 units per week.

Case study   Aluminium Corporation Limited: finite capacity scheduling (AT&T Istel 1993)

Part of the British Alcan Group, Aluminium Corporation (ACL) has 300 employees, is located at Dolgarrog in North Wales and produces rolled aluminium products for niche markets such as aerospace and kitchen holloware.

The manufacturing environment is one that comprises small production batches on short leadtimes critical to maintaining a competitive level of customer service. The typical works order book comprises a large number of small batches, with complex decision making needed to control work in process. The major decisions involved in scheduling production include:

- Is there sufficient stock ahead of the hot mill?
- Is the order due within a three-week planning horizon?
- Is the raw material available?
- Is a pre-heat furnace available?
- Is WIP within pre-defined limits at specified buffers?
- What alternative routes are available if queues are too long?

In addition the scheduling system had to be capable of handling emerging demand on short leadtimes, and to have the ability to sequence production batches so that setup times could be minimized. ACL selected finite capacity scheduling as the most appropriate means of addressing these complex scheduling decisions. The software in use is AT&T Istel's Provisa system, which handles finite capacity constraints on multiple resources, including machines, labour and buffer stock space. In ACL's case all work centres are modelled for capacity planning purposes using the Provisa system, but the production plan defines only the sequence in which jobs are started, and not the sequence through each work centre. Sequencing at individual work centres is the responsibility of shop supervisors, whose freedom is constrained by the limitations on buffer stock inbuilt into the scheduling rules.

The benefits of implementing this system were as follows:

- WIP reduced from 1000 tonnes to only 700 tonnes.
- Production leadtime reduced from eight days to four days.
- Productivity improved by 15 per cent.

Case study   Thurne Engineering: an integrated non-standard solution

A Norwich company founded in 1968 and manufacturing food processing machinery, Thurne Engineering decided in 1983 to install an integrated manufacturing planning system to replace earlier systems running on a minicomputer. Eighty per cent of the typical product comprises a common bill of materials and the remaining 20 per cent is made up of customized features and options. The manufacturing environment is a mixture of make-to-stock and make-to-order, although items made-to-stock normally require customized additions or accessories prior to despatch.

In replacing their previous system, Thurne Engineering had these objectives:

- inventory reductions
- WIP reductions
- shorter manufacturing leadtimes
- productivity improvements

In addition to these, scheduling to finite capacity was perceived to be most in keeping with the manufacturing environment, and the use of bar-coded documents was regarded as an essential element of shop-floor data collection.

The system installed by Thurne Engineering in 1985 was Kewill's Micross system. A generalized overview of the modules installed is shown in Figure 22.2. This serves as an example of a robust integrated system achieving the objectives of MRPII, but in a way that differs in detail from the MRPII standard system. At a planning level MRP is

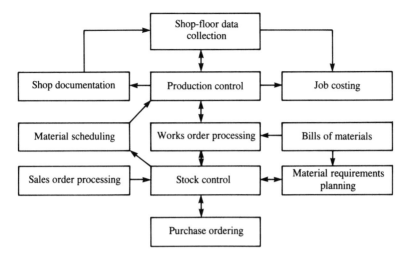

Figure 22.2   Non-standard form of MRPII system

incorporated, and the full MRP logic described in Chapter 8 is achieved by the interaction of the MRP and stock control modules. The driver of the materials planning process is the sales order database, a driver mechanism described in Chapter 12. There is no direct equivalent of master production scheduling, and the real balancing between demand and supply for capacity is addressed in a production control module which schedules to finite capacity, and is driven by a works order file derived from the MRP and stock control logic.

This system is based on a PC and DOS platform. The system has 30 users, connected since 1989 by a Novell/Ethernet LAN. There are two file servers, one serving the manufacturing database and the other the accounts database.

Interfaces to and from the Micross system include the following:

– Customer delivery performance data is maintained using Lotus 1–2–3.
– Company business planning is also a Lotus application.
– Sales history, for demand forecasting purposes, is maintained using dBase IV.
– A more recent link in 1992 was between AutoCAD and the Micross bill of materials module.

The interfaces between Micross and both Lotus and dBase were originally achieved by data interchange in ASCII format, pending the incorporation into Micross of an SQL interface.

The results of the system used by Thurne Engineering are indicated by these performance figures:

	1985	1991
Sales revenue	£3.5 million	£7.0 million
Inventory	£750 000	£500 000
Stockturn	5	12

23
Distribution resource planning

Distribution resource planning (DRP) was not originally an integral part of the MRPII standard system, but evolved in the mid 1980s as the logical extension of the application of MRPII techniques to an integrated downstream distribution system. While DRP can feasibly support an operation solely involved in distribution, its relevance in this book is in the context of a systems module totally integrated with the rest of MRPII, sharing common databases with the other MRPII system modules. Some MRPII software packages support this integrated DRP module, and this will be the approach most relevant to companies with integrated manufacturing *and* distribution operations. This is therefore the environment assumed in this chapter.

This chapter begins by examining the nature of distribution, and moves on to a functional overview of DRP and the integration of MRPII and DRP. The remainder of the chapter describes in detail the DRP functions illustrated in the overview.

DRP is an alternative systems methodology to an order-point system for the planning and control of distribution inventories. The arguments for using MRP instead of order-point systems, articulated in Chapter 2, apply equally to DRP. In the case of DRP the fundamental distinction between dependent and independent demand is as follows:

- The demand at the point of sale, or end customer shipment, is independent demand.
- The demand at resupply depots and at the manufacturing plant is dependent on the demand at the point of sale, and is therefore dependent demand.

DRP is now commonly available as a standalone package, very often as a module of a wider distribution management system (DMS). Standalone DRP packages are more commonly used by companies where distribution and manufacturing are *not* closely integrated at a planning level. As already stated, this chapter is concerned only with the application of DRP in an *integrated* manufacturing and distribution operation.

23.1 Primary distribution and secondary distribution

The business of distribution comprises two distinct aspects:

- *Primary distribution*: the distribution of a product from locations within the manufacturing system to locations within the distribution system, and/ or between locations within the distribution system.
- *Secondary distribution*: the distribution of a product from locations within the distribution system to the end customers of the business.

The DRP module of MRPII supports only the primary distribution network. It will however support any of the following scenarios:

- multiple distribution warehouses,
- which may exist at multiple levels in the distribution pipeline,
- and may be supplied from multiple supply sources,
- by multiple distribution routes.

23.2 The DRP module of MRPII

The principal functions of the DRP module are the following:

- the planning and release of resupply orders
- the tracking of resupply orders
- the allocation of supply
- shipping capacity planning

If DRP is used along with MRPII's demand forecasting module, it will also handle the following functions:

- the generation of future demand forecasts
- the calculation of safety stock levels

DRP incorporates inventory management methods similar to those available with MRP, including lot sizing, and it also assists in planning the distribution of inventories within the total distribution system.

Where the DRP module is a component of an integrated DMS, as opposed to MRPII, the following additional functions may typically also be supported:

- the management of the secondary distribution network, e.g. vehicle scheduling and delivery routing
- warehouse management, e.g. stores location planning
- warehouse location planning, or siting

The DRP module as described in this chapter implies a number of very important concepts:

1. The complete integration of MRPII and DRP.
2. The sharing of a common database.
3. A system that is integrated by a common master scheduling module.

23.3 Integration of MRPII and DRP

That integration of MRPII and DRP is based on five common elements:

- a common parts master file
- a common master scheduling system
- a common sales order entry system
- a common inventory management system
- a common demand forecasting system

The unique functions of DRP are supported by a unique resupply ordering module, and this requires the following specific systems elements:

- a distribution routings database;
- a unique shipping capacity planning module
- which in turn requires a shipping calendar;
- a unique resupply order tracking module;
- a unique supply allocation module;
- an addition to the inventory management module to support network-wide inventory distribution planning.

It is implicit that all locations in the distribution network are linked to the MRPII and DRP systems by a wide area data communications network.

By way of example, suppose that the demand for Birdhomes' six finished products, first described in Chapter 7, had grown substantially in volume and was now manufactured in two different factories—factory A and factory B—and that to be competitive and meet its customer service demands distributed inventories were now held in a distribution network like the one shown in Figure 23.1. This is fairly typical of the integrated manufacturing and distribution network which an integrated MRPII/DRP system can support.

Inventory records

In this network, in Figure 23.1, Birdhomes have stock of finished products in ten locations—location A B C D E F G H J and K. For each finished product, Birdhomes will now have separate parts master records for each combination of part number and location, each of them containing details of inventory of a specific part in a specific location. Separate records will also be maintained of inventory in transit between specific supply and destination locations.

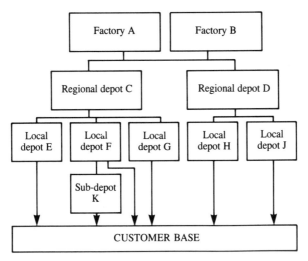

Figure 23.1 Distribution network

Master schedules

In an integrated MRPII/DRP system there will be separate master schedules for each combination of part number and location. Master scheduling controls the planning and release of resupply orders. In MRPII, master scheduling is the link between manufacturing resource planning and distribution resource planning, and it is also the driver of material requirements planning (MRP). A simplified overview of integrated MRPII/DRP is given in Figure 23.2.

The combination of MRPII and DRP makes possible the coordination of

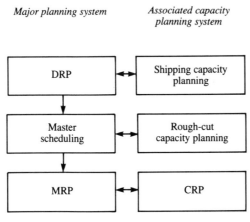

Figure 23.2 Integrated MRPII/DRP

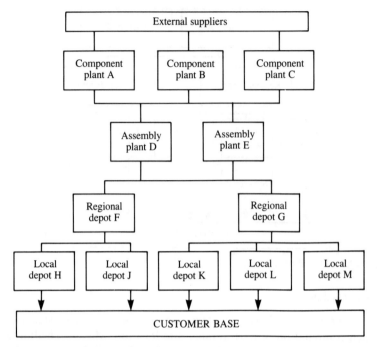

Figure 23.3   Integrated manufacturing and distribution network

materials planning within a complex manufacturing and distribution net-work, such as the one shown in Figure 23.3. This example has the following characteristics:

– End-product inventories are stocked in locations F to M.
– End-product assembly takes place in locations D and E.
– Component-part manufacture takes place in locations A, B and C.

Systems integration is made possible very simply by prefixing location number to part number on the key to all the product-related databases, for example:

– parts master records
– bills of material
– master schedules
– MRP requirements
– open orders

and by appending the location number to the resource identification on all of the resource related databases.

23.4 Sales order entry and demand forecasting

Sales order entry

The factories and regional depots may supply both customers and resupply depots. Which customers are supplied from which location is determined at sales order entry, according to the company's procedures. The sales order, once entered into the sales order processing (SOP) system, is specific as to location as well as part number, quantity and date required.

The interface between SOP and MRPII/DRP results in the creation of an actual customer order demand on a master schedule item at location level.

Demand forecasting

Sales analysis is performed by location, using the location attribute on the sales order data. This allows demand forecasting to be performed location by location, and leads in turn to the creation of forecast demand data on a master schedule item at location level for all locations involved in secondary distribution.

23.5 Master scheduling

The principles of master scheduling are exactly as described in Chapter 16 in the context of MRPII. These principles include:

- the balancing of demand and supply;
- the consumption of the forecasts by sales orders;
- the choice between a regenerative mode or a net change mode;
- the choice between a bucketless system or a time bucketed system;
- the planning horizon and the time fences;
- the netting of requirements against projected inventory;
- the exclusion of safety stock from projected inventory;
- an available-to-promise calculation;
- the pegging of demand to planned supply;
- the lot sizing rules.

At the lowest level in the Birdhomes distribution example—locations E, G, H, J and K in Figure 23.1—the demand side of the master schedule will comprise only the actual customer orders and the forecast. At all higher levels it will be the sum of two factors:

- the actual customer orders or forecast, and
- the resupply requirements of all locations at a lower level in the network.

23.6 Distribution routings

The resupply routes within the system are defined by the distribution routings, which typically comprise the following data:

- part number
- the receiving location
- the supplying location
- the percentage of resupply to be supplied by this supplying location
- the planning leadtime
- the in-transit leadtime
- a shrinkage factor

This structure has the flexibility to handle complex distribution routes, which may vary from one product to another. For example, it allows the following situations to be catered for:

- It allows resupply to be divided, if applicable, between different sources according to the specified percentage split.
- It allows for a distribution route which bypasses discrete levels in the network, or crosses over from one limb of the network to another.
- It allows for a manufacturing specialization by factory.

23.7 Resupply ordering

The basic steps in the resupply ordering logic are shown in Figure 23.4. Master scheduling begins at the lowest levels in the network. The resulting planned resupply orders are generated by supply location, part number, planned receipt date and quantity, and will depend on total demand, the percentage split by supply source, and the lot-sizing method in use.

Where a planning leadtime is indicated on the distribution routing, planned receipt date will be offset from the required date by the planning leadtime. This is normally used to provide for a buffer stock of a number of day's requirements, as an alternative to, or in addition to, any safety stock which may be specified on the parts master record. It may very often simply reflect the delay between replanning runs, the system leadtime.

Due shipping date at supply location is calculated by offsetting the in-transit leadtime from the destination location's planned receipt date. The due date is then checked for feasibility against a shipping calendar (see below).

Where a shrinkage factor is specified on the distribution routing, the resupply quantity will be grossed up to take account of planned shrinkage. This may be used to protect against loss or damage in transit.

These planned resupply orders are then inserted as resupply demand on the source location master schedule.

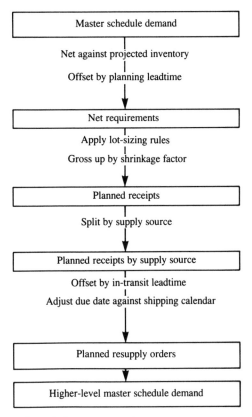

Figure 23.4 Resupply ordering

This process continues until all of the resupply requirements have been cascaded back up to the highest levels in the network. At these highest levels master scheduling will drive MRPII as previously described in Chapter 16.

Resupply order release may be manually controlled or it may be controlled by the mass release of all planned orders within a specified due date horizon. Order release results in the released orders being transmitted simultaneously to both supplying and receiving locations.

Shipping calendar

The shipping calendar may be specified in one of two ways:

1. It may specify on which dates one location is planned to ship to another. The due date is then adjusted to the nearest shipment date on or before due date. In this case the shipping calendar is specified in terms of the combinations of supply location and destination location.

2. It may simply distinguish between shipping days and non-shipping days. If the due date falls on a non-shipping date, the due date is then adjusted to the preceding shipping day in that supply location. In this case the shipping calendar is specified only in terms of the supply location.

23.8 Shipping capacity planning

Shipping capacity planning is very similar in purpose and method to CRP, which was described in Chapter 17.

For each supplying location the system calculates the shipping load by both shipment date and receiving location, based on both released and planned resupply orders. The calculation of shipping load is a function of quantity and unit load. The unit load is recorded on the parts master record, and it may be expressed in any of three ways:

- the quantity per pallet, allowing number of pallets to be calculated;
- the unit weight;
- the unit volume, or cube.

The resulting shipping load information may then be used by the transport manager to plan or adjust planned shipping capacity. As in other planning modules of MRPII, the facility of pegging is available to allow the pegging of shipping load to the specific order, or orders, generating the shipping load.

Where provision is made for the maintenance of shipping resource data, the number of vehicles and their carrying capacity, then comparisons of the shipping load versus its capacity will be provided, just as CRP will provide a comparison of the production workload versus the production capacity. These comparisons of shipping load versus capacity may also be presented in graphical form. Shipping resource data is typically specified by discrete dates on the shipping calendar.

23.9 Resupply order tracking

The function of resupply order tracking is to maintain visibility of orders in transit between supplying and destination locations. Stores issue at the supplying location triggers the following system events:

- the subtraction from physical inventory at the supply location of the quantity issued;
- its addition to in-transit inventory;
- the recording of the issue against an open resupply order.

The subsequent shipment from supplying location triggers recording of the shipment details on the open resupply order. Finally, the receipt of the shipment at the receiving location triggers the remaining events:

- the addition to physical inventory at the receiving location of the quantity now received;
- its subtraction from in-transit inventory;
- the closing entry of recording of receipt details on the open resupply order.

23.10 Supply allocation

The purpose of supply allocation is to handle the allocation of supply between depots if there is an overall shortage of an item within the distribution network. The system in effect recommends a fair share among destination locations of the supply available at the supplying location. The calculation of fair shares is normally biased in favour of actual customer orders, as opposed to forecast demand, in line with principles of opportunity costing.

Where insufficient supply exists at the supplying location to cover all actual customer orders downstream, the system may recommend inter-depot transfers.

Supply allocation is an inexact science and it frequently requires manual intervention by the planner if it is to be effective.

23.11 Inventory management

The inventory management methods available within DRP are the same as those available with MRP, and described in Chapter 11. The actual level of inventory at each distribution location will be influenced primarily by the following parameters:

- the lot-sizing rules being used
- the level of safety stock
- the planning leadtime

Safety stock may be calculated by a demand forecasting module, and this will take account only of independent demand, or end-customer demand, by location, and not resupply demand, otherwise the generation of resupply orders within DRP would lead to doubling up of demand, and therefore of safety stock, at each step in the network.

This implies that safety stocks would be distributed around the network, depending on where actual customer demand is serviced. This may not be the most effective distribution. Total safety stocks of an item in that case may be greater than if all safety stock were instead held at a central location, because the variability of demand, and therefore the safety stock, should decrease as a result of aggregating demand from all customer service points. But central safety stocks may not satisfy the desired customer delivery response.

Research reported in Vollmann *et al.* (1992) indicates that customer service levels will be highest if all safety stock is distributed, and only slightly lower if it is split between a central point and the distribution points. That research shows that holding all safety stock in a central location is not a sensible choice.

Distributed inventory planning

Whereas MRP was primarily concerned with these two questions:

1. *How much* material do we need?
2. *When* do we need it?

DRP is also concerned with the question of: *Where* should we hold the inventory?

This is what the DRP inventory planning function addresses. It will help to optimize the distribution of safety stocks within the total distribution system, in order to:

- achieve the minimum total safety stock needed to satisfy the desired customer service level;
- maximize the level of customer service across the total distribution system.

24

Distributed MRP/MRPII

Distributed MRP/MRPII (DMRP) is essentially an implementation method based on a cellular manufacturing organization, in which each manufacturing cell is an autonomous mini-factory dedicated to a product family or to a functional process. Each work cell may be organized according to the manufacturing method most suitable for the product or process—for example, kanban in one cell, and MRPII in another; a flexible manufacturing system (FMS) in one cell, or a process-oriented jobbing shop in another. Each work cell has its own local database, and its own decentralized MRPII system. Each cell has responsibility for bottom–up planning, and is linked to a central MRPII system to which data is regularly uploaded.

DMRP is increasingly becoming a favoured implementation method arising from the application of other state-of-the-art business methods such as benchmarking and business process re-engineering. It has a strong fit with flatter organization structures, and as an implementation method is likely to contribute to substantially reduced implementation leadtimes.

After a brief introduction, we will then examine in turn the key features of DMRP and the benefits of adopting this approach to implementation.

24.1 Problems addressed by DMRP

DMRP addresses a number of fundamental problems:

- Manufacturing organizations in earlier decades had become increasingly complex. MRPII computerized that complexity, rather than simplifying it. Despite that, MRPII is nonetheless a valid systems tool, and it works well in the hands of managers capable of understanding and using it.
- There is a high failure rate among MRPII installations. The most successful organizations had simplified their manufacturing operations *before* the implementation of an MRPII system. Adoption of a cellular manufacturing organization is the key to simplification.

- The repetitive manufacturing module of MRPII is adapted to high-volume production where stable production plans exist. It is not appropriate to discrete batch production in a make-to-order environment.
- MRPII is insensitive to leadtimes and to capacity. In MRPII, planning leadtimes are typically fixed, and the planner's response to recurring problems of transient capacity overload is usually to add a safety margin to the planning leadtime. This degrades delivery performance and causes an increase in WIP inventory.
- Centralized MRPII systems are user-unfriendly. They are often associated with lengthy, and therefore infrequent, MRP regeneration runs. There is often not sufficient time left over for the what if? capacity planning runs. The system users therefore often do not have correct up-to-date information for planning and management purposes.

24.2 Key features of DMRP

The principal features of DMRP are as follows:

- Production planning and control are decentralized to a local MRPII system and database, focused on individual work cells.
- Specialization by cell allows simplified production routings and bills of materials to be used. The bill of material structures in DMRP are typically only a single level in depth. Figure 24.1 illustrates the principle of decentralizing bills of materials, and shows the consequent reduction in the depth of the product structure.
- Production managers are responsible for their own local MRPII database. This element of real ownership helps to foster a high degree of data accuracy.
- Decentralized MRPII run times are greatly reduced. This makes possible much more frequent MRP and CRP processing runs, and allows sufficient time for the what if? capacity planning runs.
- DMRP works on the principle of feed-forward and feedback of information. Sales orders are accepted on the basis of a tentative delivery promise, to be confirmed by the manager of the final assembly or final process work cell, taking account of the existing capacity load attributable to firm customer orders in that cell.
- The technological leadtime is used to estimate start and finish dates. The technological leadtime is setup time plus process time. It does not include any element of queue time.
- Dynamic scheduling is used to schedule a new order around the existing workload, and thus offer a firm delivery promise. If necessary, this can be done manually, based on the latest capacity utilization information reported by the DMRP system.

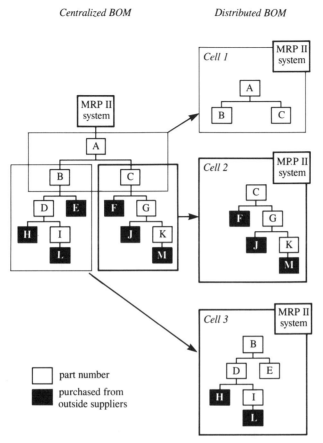

Figure 24.1   An example of distributed bill of materials (BOM)

– Subassemblies or component parts required from an upstream work cell
will be handled by the immediate downstream work cell passing a tentative
order to the immediate upstream work cell, and by rescheduling their own
customer order if the firm delivery promise from the upstream work cell is
later than the order required date.

Figure 24.2 depicts this mechanism at work, and Figure 24.3 shows the communications network in which a DMRP system operates.

24.3 Advantages of DMRP

The advantages of DMRP compared to conventional MRPII, given by
Barekat (1990), are as follows:

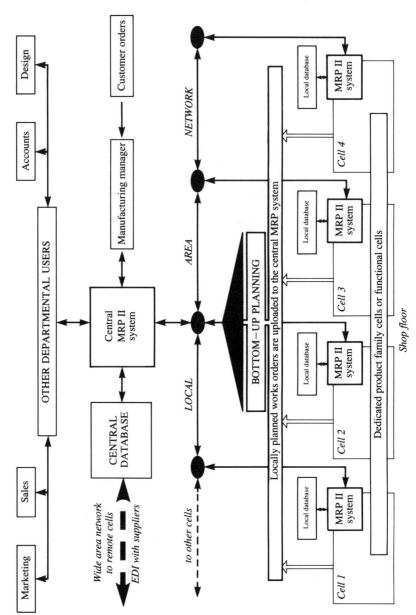

Figure 24.2   DMRP mechanism at work

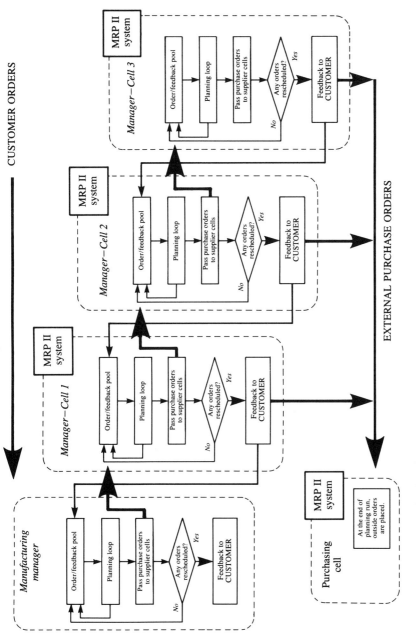

Figure 24.3 Data communications in DMRP system

- DMRP resolves leadtime and capacity problems.
- The local ownership of data overcomes problems associated with inaccuracy of production routings, bills of materials and inventory data.
- Computer processing time limitations are removed. More rapid and frequent what if? analyses can then be performed.
- DMRP overcomes the problems of transient bottlenecks in capacity.
- Daily planning and control is in the hands of shop-floor managers. The total system therefore reflects the true state of the factory.
- The practical difficulties of implementing and managing MRPII are greatly reduced, by virtue of the much more limited data structures and the reduced number of system users at each work cell.
- DMRP is highly flexible. The local systems can be tailored to the exact needs of each cell. Depending on the organization of each work cell, it is feasible to use the standard system in one cell, the fit with JIT in another, and the make-to-order model in yet another cell.
- DMRP can be implemented using existing MRPII software, or by acquiring inexpensive commercially available packages.
- The implementation of TQM is also simplified.
- DMRP moves the political centre of gravity away from the data processing department and towards the shop floor.

The movement towards JIT is highlighting the need for distributed computer systems and communications on the shop floor. A JIT approach is more difficult to operate within a completely centralized computer environment, and DMRP is therefore much more supportive than traditional forms of MRPII implementation.

DMRP case study   Chadderton Aerostructures

Chadderton Aerostructures, a part of British Aerospace Regional Aircraft Ltd, is steeped in aviation history—the former site of A V Roe, it was famous for production of Lancaster bombers during the Second World War. Today there are five business units within Chadderton Aerostructures, and this case study focuses on one of these—the Aerostructures Components organization (AerCo). The AerCo business unit manufactures and supplies airframe, wing and control surface components and subassemblies, mainly for civil aircraft, both to other British Aerospace business units and to independent aerospace companies.

AerCo's production is organized around advanced manufacturing cells, whose customers include downstream AerCo manufacturing cells, other business units within Chadderton Aerostructures, and other British Aerospace companies making the 146 regional jet airliners and the ATP turboprop airliner. The components manufactured range from small brackets up to assemblies which can be carried by two people, and include wing parts for Airbus Industrie, the Anglo-French consortium. The supply of components and subassemblies on a subcontract basis to independent customers is a growing facet of AerCo's business.

To stay ahead in the highly competitive and rapidly changing global market-place of the 1990s, Chadderton Aerostructures has adopted business re-engineering as a corporate tool. Within AerCo this was known as Project Interlink, and was represented by six teams of twenty people, designing new ways of working and developing more appropriate organizational structures to meet business needs.

In a trial scheme to test a viable alternative to centralized mainframe IT services, AerCo has downsized to a comprehensive PC-based MRPII system, based on software from Fourth Shift UK Ltd. Aimed at cost reduction, better business control and local data ownership, the pilot system was operational within ten weeks of delivery of the software, and is an important contribution to Project Interlink's employee objective of fostering teamwork as the alternative to traditional lines of functional demarcation within the organization.

The move toward downsizing stemmed directly from the corporate business re-engineering objective. Over many years British Aerospace had constructed a centralized corporate computer system, known as overall business architecture (OBA). This is a massive array of individual software applications serving each functional requirement of the business, encompassing almost every application from personnel management to manufacturing and financial accounting. A complex network of interfaces links the software modules, enabling data to be exchanged within Chadderton and other British Aerospace sites.

Under the new business organization, comprising cellular profit centres and matrix management, each business unit was obliged to pay for its share of the centralized computer services. For the business units this was both costly and inflexible. Central response to software or data problems was slow because of the queue of problems that built up, to be addressed by a central systems department on a priority basis. What local users needed and wanted was more control, and especially the local ownership of both the tools and the data, to enable them better to resolve problems quickly and keep the business running efficiently.

To address and resolve this problem, British Aerospace established Project Prometheus, a project to offer downsizing away from the mainframe to PC systems operating on LANs (local area networks). The focus of the trial project was to enhance planning capabilities, and it followed that this was based on the MRPII system. AerCo's Airbus customer support operation was chosen as the starting point; it was a manufacturing centre serving one customer, but had multiple suppliers, both in-house and external.

Selection of the new MRPII software was begun by the Project Prometheus team, who compiled an extensive software requirements specification, from which a software vendor questionnaire was produced. On the basis of replies to the questionnaire, 75 per cent of the potential vendors were eliminated. The next stage brought AerCo personnel into the selection team in order to make a shortlist, as a result of which four vendors were invited to make presentations. A team made up of systems engineers, AerCo production controllers, stores and engineering staff evaluated the detailed proposals and narrowed the shortlist down to two suppliers, whose products were subjected to exhaustive demonstrations and workshops. From this process Fourth Shift's MRPII software emerged in December 1992 as the software whose capabilities most closely matched AerCo's requirements. Simplicity and ease of use were key criteria used by AerCo in their evaluation process.

The implementation phase began in January 1993 with AerCo establishing a project team, and the pilot project, embracing eleven modules of Fourth Shift's manufacturing software series, was implemented in ten weeks. Training of staff relied extensively on the use of video training packages. As implementation proceeded, there was parallel running of the old system and the new, and at the beginning of the eleventh week AerCo's Airbus operations moved over entirely to the new MRPII system.

A major benefit of the new system is that its users can now see the whole picture, and this is aided by having a limited number of comprehensive display screens. With the former OBA system tasks were compartmentalized; individuals had set and discrete tasks to do, and the wider implications of their activity was always someone else's responsibility.

Under the old system, leadtimes were subject to global rules, which in effect padded the manufacturing leadtime. With the new system, users can specify leadtimes based on a knowledge of the real and current situation. The result has been a dramatic reduction in the manufacturing leadtime, and this in turn has led to a reduction of £200 000 in inventory level. The combined effect of shorter leadtimes and less work in progress means that changes to the schedule can be made more easily; this is helped by the fact that users have greater visibility of the overall picture when doing so. The ability to react quickly to change is a major benefit. With OBA any change meant awaiting a weekend run of the MRPII system before the implications were known. With the new system there is immediate visibility of the impact of change, and local staff can detect problems immediately rather than having to await periodic reports from the central system.

The higher level of responsiveness matches more closely the demands of JIT manufacturing, and AerCo are now planning to develop their existing MRPII system to include the Kawasaki Production System, which will combine the power of MRPII's longer-term forecasting and planning—the 'push' system—with the 'pull' methods of a JIT execution environment.

The case study cited here illustrates very clearly the developing nature of the DMRP concept. From the initial studies of Love and Barekat (1989), which focused on a systems-implementation method supportive of cellular manufacturing, DMRP has moved into the mainstream of corporate business process re-engineering, in which downsizing from mainframe to open systems PC network IT platforms is a key feature. This is a process that is being driven by advances in technology, in which 'manufacturers of open systems are halving the cost per transaction on an annual basis [and have] added a factor of 100 to the price/performance ratio of a computer system' (Bennett 1993).

25

Interfaces with costing and accounting systems

The two key financial interfaces supported by MRPII are:

– product costing
– inventory evaluation

In this chapter we shall first examine the alternative costing methods, then look at features common to these methods, such as the concepts of cost elements and cost buckets. We move on to see how products attract costs, and how these are directed into the relevant cost buckets. The key data for product costing is then summarized, after which the major costing methods—standard costing and current costing—are explored in greater detail. The extension from product costing to cost of sales analysis is described. After that we briefly address the question of inventory evaluations, and this chapter concludes by examining the implications of the newer concept of activity-based costing.

25.1 Product costing methods

There are three methods of product costing in use today:

1. *Standard costing*: what the cost *should* be.
2. *Current costing*: what the cost actually is, or was. This is sometimes referred to as actual costing, or historic costing.
3. *Activity-based costing*: this will typically be used in conjunction with either standard costing or current costing, and is addressed in detail in section 25.9.

The difference between standard costing and current costing may be summed up in this very simplistic way:

Standard cost $\pm$ variances from standard = current cost

When applying current costing to manufactured items, inaccuracies in SFDC will lead to inaccuracies in product costing, and very often to an extreme

243

variability in the perceived product cost from one works order to the next. Where real variances in cost from one order to another do exist, these are much more likely to be process-related than product-related, and it may not be wise to penalize only the order or orders that have suffered as a result of process inefficiency.

With standard costing there is at least consistency of management accounting over time, but there will inevitably be variances between the actual and the standard over time. The variance reporting associated with a standard costing system directs management attention to the things that have gone wrong, in a way that is virtually impossible if current costing is applied.

Most of the available software packages will maintain *both* standard and current costs. Optional standard costing methods supported by some software include the following:

- *Simulated standard costs*: for use in analysing the effect of changes to the cost structure, for example, when direct labour rates are to be changed.
- *Engineering standard costs*: used by design engineering to estimate the impact of changes in the product design or by production engineering to estimate the impact of changes to the production process.
- *Future standard costs*: what the impact would be of replacing the existing standard costs by the current costs at all lower levels in the bill of materials.
- *Previous standard costs*: a reference set of standards retained after an earlier revision to the standard costs.

25.2 Cost elements and cost buckets

The cost content of most products falls into three major categories:

- material costs
- direct labour costs, or machine centre costs
- overhead costs

What is provided by way of cost content by software packages varies between these three elements only, and a variable number of user-specified cost buckets. Some packages will support up to 30 cost buckets. These can be used to isolate cost elements of importance in specific manufacturing environments, for instance:

- subcontract costs
- different categories of labour
- packaging
- freight
- shrinkage
- scrap

- works overhead
- administration overhead

25.3 Direction of cost; attraction of cost

The direction of cost to the appropriate cost bucket is normally achieved in the case of externally purchased components or materials by the specification of a cost-centre or cost-bucket code on the parts master record, and in the case of manufacturing operations on the work centre database.

The attraction of cost into the appropriate cost bucket is triggered by production or by the receipt of an externally purchased item. In the case of manufactured items, the point in time at which cost is attracted depends on the major cost category:

- Material costs are attracted when materials are issued to a works order.
- Direct labour costs are attracted when labour or machine time is incurred on a works order manufacturing operation, and for convenience this is normally when discrete operations are completed.
- Overhead costs are assumed to be attracted pro rata to one or other of the two direct costs.

Three options are typically allowed for the apportionment of overhead costs:

1. As a percentage of labour or machine hourly rates. This is the option most commonly used.
2. As a percentage of the total manufacturing cost.
3. A fixed value allocated to works orders pro rata to the units of production or the hours of production capacity used.

The apportionment of overhead costs pro rata to direct labour originated in an era when processes were heavily labour-intensive. Increasing automation has reduced direct labour content to a small percentage of total cost. In many industries it is now too small to be a valid basis for the apportionment of the very much larger overhead costs. The emerging technique to replace this is activity-based costing, and this is treated in more detail in section 29.5.

25.4 Key cost data

Both standard costing and current costing are dependent on two sets of data:

1. *Labour or machine-related cost rates*: the cost per hour to be attracted to work completed. This is specified by work centre for each cost bucket, and may include one or more overhead cost buckets.
2. *Material cost prices*: the unit cost of component parts or materials. Most software packages will provide for a choice of pricing method.

The most common pricing methods are these:

- *Standard price*: this is normally used only in conjunction with standard costing.
- *Current price*: the latest purchase price of buy items, or the latest current cost of make items.
- *Average price*: this is normally recalculated after every receipt and the calculation is as follows:

$$\text{B/F inventory quantity} \times \text{B/F average price}$$

$$+ \text{ receipt quantity} \times \text{actual price or current cost}$$

$$\div \text{ C/F inventory quantity}$$

$$= \text{ C/F inventory average price}$$

- *First in first out* (*FIFO*) price: this is normally calculated by preserving visibility of actual price, or current cost, by receipt date sequence of lot or batch received, and then by pricing material issues on the principle of exhausting the oldest batches first. The system mechanism for handling a FIFO pricing method is very often combined in practice with that of lot traceability, which was described in Chapter 20.

25.5 Current costing

Current costing is driven by the data feedback from an SFDC module. The key data feedback consists of:

- *Stores issues*: for each issue, the cost attraction is quantity issued times unit price.
- *Shop floor feedback*: for each production operation completed, the cost attraction is time taken times hourly cost rate(s).

These costs accumulate from the point of order release right through to order completion. At order completion, the accumulated costs will be divided by the good production quantity to give the current costs per unit of production.

Because of the inherent unreliability of current cost data a common convention following order completion is as follows:

1. To allow the cost accountant to analyse the accumulated costs, and to make amendments if appropriate.
2. Next, to update the current cost on the parts master record.
3. Then, and only then, to close or cleardown the open works order.

25.6 Standard costing

Whereas the accumulated build-up of current costs accrues from a data feedback loop, the generation of standard costs is an integral function of MRPII.

For any item on the parts master file, an explosion against the bill of materials gives the lower-level parts content. For each component part in the bill of materials structure:

- extending the quantity of the child per unit of the parent by the standard price of child gives the standard material cost
- explosion against the production routing gives the standard times by each production operation, and for each operation extending the standard time by the cost rates of the appropriate work centre(s) gives the standard machine or labour costs.

The sum of these individual standard cost elements is the standard cost of the parts master item. It will comprise all the cost buckets attributable to materials, labour and overheads. This is how standard cost generation works within MRPII. In both explosions a parts master item quantity of one is used, in order to calculate unit standard cost.

At production operation level both queue times and move times are ignored. The only complication concerns setup time, which is normally fixed in MRPII regardless of batch quantity. It therefore follows that the unit standard cost of setup is a variable cost element, depending on production batch quantity. It is normal, therefore, for the generation of standard costs to be based on a user-specified standard lot size by part number. The standard unit cost of setup will therefore be the setup standard cost divided by the standard lot size.

Generation of standard costs

The generation of standard costs within MRPII is normally done one level at a time, beginning at the lowest level in the product structure, as defined by the level number on the parts master record. At each higher level in the bill of materials structure, a roll-up of standard cost takes place. In this way the standard costs of *all* lower-level child components are added into the standard costs of their parent parts.

For each discrete part number, the accumulation of standard costs is done in operation sequence number. The first production operation attracts labour or machine standard costs. These are rolled over as the carry-forward to the next operation, and so on. This technique also makes possible the evaluation of the standard labour cost of WIP, depending on which operation of an open works order has just been completed.

Table 25.1   Cost of sales model

Calculation element	Data source
Sales revenue	Sales order processing system
− Material costs	Parts master record
− Direct labour costs	Parts master record
= Gross margin	
− Works overhead costs	Parts master record
= Works contribution	
− Admin overheads	Parts master record
= Profit before company overheads and variances	

In Exercise B6 (Appendix B), the reader is invited to calculate the standard costs of the Birdhomes' products, first described in Chapter 7.

25.7 Cost of sales

Depending on the costing method in use, either current costs or standard costs will be used as the basis for periodic or end-of-month cost of sales analysis. This will be triggered by sales invoices in both a make-to-order environment and a make-to-stock environment. The MRPII costing methods will have resulted in the current costs or the standard costs being available on the finished product parts master record.

This cost-of-sales analysis may be by individual sales order, by finished product part number, by customer, by works, or for the company in total. It will be similar to the model given in Table 25.1, although different companies may use slightly differing terminology and different accounting definitions, which will reflect in the presentation of this data.

25.8 Inventory evaluation

Periodic inventory valuations will be produced for financial accounting purposes. The two sources of this information are as follows:

− *The parts master file*: the physical inventory will be extended by whichever costing or unit pricing method has been adopted, and this will encompass:
   finished product inventory
   stores inventories, including both purchased parts and manufactured parts or subassemblies.
− *The works order file*: which is the source of work in process inventory evaluation. Each works order will be evaluated in terms of
   the actual costs attracted to date, in the case of current costing, or

the standard material costs plus the rollover of standard labour costs, in the case of standard costing.

25.9 Activity-based costing

The traditional methods of incorporating company overhead costs into product costs depended on a supposed relationship between these overhead costs and the costs of the production departments. The normal method, inbuilt into most MRPII-type systems, has been explained earlier in this chapter—against the hourly machine rate or labour rate in each work centre there was provision also for an element of overhead cost attribution.

Cost accountants typically determined this overhead cost rate by apportioning the total of annual budget overhead costs to each individual work centre according to a formula perceived to be equitable—most commonly pro rata to the total direct and indirect costs of the various work centres—and then dividing the resulting lump of overhead cost by the planned hours available, in order to arrive at an overhead cost per hour.

In the days when work was labour-intensive and products relatively unsophisticated, the direct hourly rates were typically high relative to the overhead element, and the side effects of the crudeness of the technique had a relatively insignificant impact on the total product cost, and on product pricing policies which in turn used the data.

The two trends over recent decades which have invalidated this traditional method of overhead recovery are:

1. Advances in process technology have greatly compressed the technological leadtime—the hours of machine time needed to manufacture the product—while the associated automation of processes has reduced the size of crew, and therefore the labour hours associated with the manufacturing process. The net result is that the direct costs of manufacture have reduced dramatically.
2. Products have become dependent on more advanced product technology and a much higher degree of quality engineering, and this has led to a growth in many of the support functions within the business. The indirect costs of product development and ensuring product integrity have grown quite considerably as a result.

There has been, therefore, a shift from a more traditional environment, in which overhead cost rates were relatively minor in comparison to direct costs, to the situation most prevalent today—where the overhead cost rate can be several times that of the direct cost rates. The arbitrariness of the traditional method of determining overhead cost rates means that this can no longer be accepted as a valid method of arriving at total product cost.

Different products indent on overhead costs in different, and often complex, ways. The biggest contrast is very often between products at different stages in their respective product life cycles:

– The *cash cow* product nearing the end of its product life cycle, where both product technology and process technology are mature. Such a product will typically have a low dependence on overhead activity, and the traditional costing method will exaggerate the total product cost and understate the gross margin, with major implications for product pricing. Believing the cost figures, and in consequence setting too high a price, may in fact accelerate the end of the life cycle, and with it the substantial positive cash flow from a cash cow which may be helping to finance the development of the products of the future.

– The *star* product in its early stages of product development and market penetration. A very large part of the company's overhead activity is likely to be focused on these products. Product technology, process technology and quality engineering will be being continuously fine-tuned for quite some time after the product first appears in the manufacturing plan. The use of traditional costing methods tends to lead to underpricing of new products in their early years, at the very time when the market-place is normally not so price-sensitive, with potentially disastrous implications for company profitability.

In addition, much of the overhead activity supporting the newer products in manufacture will also be being used to support future product development, and this is an activity which has no bearing on the cost of today's products, but is likely to be included if the traditional costing method is applied.

Activity-based costing (ABC) is the technique that has been developed to address this fundamental problem of how to associate logically and objectively overhead activity cost with product cost. It begins with an extensive analysis of the activity undertaken in each function, and in the process leads to an understanding of what drives the activity, and hence its impact on product costs, in these functions. In most instances the relationship which emerges will be two-fold:

1. The volume of activity, and hence the cost, will vary significantly between different product groups or product families. The contrast cited above between mature products and newly developed products is a typical example of this.

2. Within a product family the activity is most likely to be determined by some aspect, or aspects, of the product technology or product features. For example, in a company assembling personal computers using industry-standard bought-in components, there will be a high volume of activity directed at ensuring the product integrity, both in product design

and quality engineering, and this will largely be determined by the product features, such as RAM memory, fixed disk, floppy disk drives, maths co-processor, integral modem, to name but a few.

The result of ABC is to determine a cost relationship between the overhead activity and:

– the presence or absence of a product feature, or
– the quantity of a feature or component.

In the example given above, the relationship will be influenced, for instance, by the number of floppy disk drives.
These relationships will then be expressed in terms of:

– the product family
– the product feature or component
– the feature or component quantity
– the overhead activity time per unit of the end product

From the extension of activity time by activity cost rate the activity-based cost per unit of end product is derived, and from the aggregation of all feature-associated costs is derived the total activity-based cost for one unit of the end product—the substitution for the traditional overhead cost element.
Proprietary software packages, mostly PC-based, are available to aid the activity and cost analysis underpinning ABC. The incorporation of the activity-based costs themselves within MRPII systems, and in a way that pre-serves system integrity, is another matter, and one where there is as yet no clear industry standard. At the time of writing only a small minority of MRPII-type packages made specific provision for ABC.
The expedient solution is simply to create within the parts master record a series of activity-based cost buckets, but while this enables ABC to be incor-porated with little or no MRPII systems development cost, there are a number of serious disadvantages arising from this approach:

– The data has to be inserted on each of the parts master records within a product family.
– Each parts master record must be updated when the cost structure alters, or when the activity cost rates alter.

There is therefore likely to be considerably more effort involved in maintain-ing activity-based costs within the MRPII system than there is with the remainder of its integral standard costing facility, where periodic updates to machine or labour rates are automatically reflected in standard product costs by the integral system features of product explosion and roll-up of standard cost elements.

The most appropriate solution to the problem will be the two-way inter-facing of the ABC software packages with the MRPII database, rather than the replication within the MRPII system of yet another structural database, associating product feature or component quantity with unit of activity. This is one of the more important challenges facing software systems engineers at the present time.

PART FOUR
PLANNING,
IMPLEMENTATION
AND MANAGEMENT

The planning, implementation and management of manufacturing planning systems is a big subject, and itself merits an entire book. In these concluding chapters, the reader's attention is simply focused on the more salient features.

There are two key questions that users must address very shortly after the implementation of an MRPII system:

1. Does the system work?
2. Is the company achieving benefits as a result?

We start in Chapter 26 by examining the variable success rate of MRPII-type systems, the reasons for failure, and what the critical factors for success are. In Chapter 27 we go on to examine the question of software selection. Chapter 28 addresses the key factors in making the system work and, in conclusion, Chapter 29 is concerned with the question of benefits arising from implementation and use of the manufacturing planning system.

26

Introduction to planning, implementation and management

26.1 Success and failure

Since the definitive works on MRPII first appeared, various user surveys, most of them conducted in the USA, have been documented and indicate a number of alarming conclusions:

- MRPII has a success rate of less than 60 per cent.
- There are a large number of failed MRPII systems.
- There is a wide divergence from one user to another in terms of the benefits achieved.
- There can be a damaging effect on the business if MRPII is applied badly.

26.2 Reasons for failure

The major reasons for failure are also well documented, and the reasons most commonly given are these:

- a lack of management commitment
- a lack of education
- inaccurate inventory records
- inaccurate forecasts and/or inaccurate master production schedules
- inaccurate leadtimes
- inaccurate bills of materials
- out-of-date data
- quality deviations
- material shortages

With most of these reasons the link between cause and effect is self-evident, but a number of observations are nevertheless pertinent at this point.

Lack of management commitment

Among MRPII software suppliers the lack of management commitment is frequently singled out as the most common reason for a failed MRPII system. It is a theme that has been laboured on a fairly regular basis since Wallace (1986) devoted an entire publication to the subject. Management commitment is addressed in more detail in Chapter 28, but the salient observations are these:

– Management teams that are successful in general at introducing new systems normally do not fail with MRPII. Those that have difficulty in implementing more basic systems, such as a financial accounting package, are likely to fail quite spectacularly when it comes to the implementation of an MRPII system.
– What is different about MRPII is the scale of its impact across a very broad spectrum of company activity. It is a company-wide system, and not merely a departmental system.
– Because MRPII addressed, and by default helped preserve, product and process complexity, the commercially available software reflected this complexity while attempting to conform to a standard system, which was itself an inappropriate model for many manufacturing environments. The author's contention is that there is a direct correlation between commitment and relevance; if the system appears esoteric and complex in relationship to what actually happens, commitment can be *expected* to be lacking.

Much of the failure stems from a misfit between the MRPII standard system and the real needs of production management, and this is compounded by the aggressive marketing of software packages which may not be the best fit with specific manufacturing environments. MRPII was conceived within the world of IBM and it fits best in that type of assemble-to-order environment. At the opposite end of the spectrum, managers of jobbing shops have good reason to suppose that the originators of the MRPII standard system did not fully understand the very different needs of their type of business.

The argument has been stated in Chapter 13 that if it was legitimate for the originators of MRPII to amend their definitive or standard system *post facto* to fit with JIT, it is equally legitimate now to redefine MRPII to encompass techniques accessible with software commercially available in the 1990s, and which fit with a jobbing type of environment. This is especially so where the contention between workload and capacity is high, and the constraints of finite production capacity have to be faced. Scheduling to finite capacity may be both necessary and desirable, and it is wrong to discount it because it is at odds with a standard system that was propounded in the 1980s, but that was based on a model developed as far back as the 1960s.

Inaccurate master production schedules

If the MPS is heavily dependent on forecasts, then it will be less reliable as the driver of the remainder of the MRPII system. The usefulness and potential accuracy of forecasts was summarized in Chapter 14. The antidote to inaccurate forecasts is not so much better forecasting, but rather to adopt a manufacturing strategy that reduces leadtimes and thereby lessens the dependency on closer-range forecasts.

A high dependency on forecasts is likely to mean that what is pulled out of the system by the emerging demand will be different to what was pushed into it on the basis of the previous forecast. This in turn is likely to lead to shortages, longer leadtimes, and higher WIP inventory. Shortages that derive in this way may be a major *cause* of system failure.

The concept of master production scheduling is perhaps the least thoroughly understood of all the building blocks of MRPII. The confusion that arose from the acceptance (Orlicky 1975) of several *de facto* master scheduling practices has been covered in Chapter 16. What is crucial to the successful installation and use of MRPII is the selection of the appropriate scheduling method, and this in turn requires appropriate supporting software which fits the manufacturing environment at MPS level or its equivalent. The conclusions of Chapter 16 are worth restating here:

1. The seemingly complex master scheduling modules of packages which conform to the MRPII standard system are relevant *only* in an assemble-to-order environment, or in a make-to-stock environment where the products are feature-dependent.
2. For most other manufacturing environments the system logic will work perfectly well by regarding master production scheduling as a top-level pass of the MRP system. In that case a software package that combines MPS and MRP will be the *best* fit, despite the fact that it is at odds with the standard system.
3. This will also produce the best fit in a low-volume assemble-to-order environment. In that case the fit is completed by treating the product structure as design to order. The additional overhead of configuring design-to-order bills of materials will be more than compensated for by the resulting simplicity of logic.
4. At the jobbing shop end of the make-to-order environment there is a prima facie case for omitting master scheduling in its entirety, and opting for a package that allows MRP to be driven directly by the sales order file. The less visibility there is of forward demand, the greater will be the merit of this approach.
5. Where rate-based scheduling is in use, smoothed production rates will be established by the production planning module, and the final assembly

schedule will be derived directly from the sales order file. Master production scheduling in its MRPII context will therefore be bypassed completely.

Inaccurate leadtimes

Actual manufacturing leadtimes are a function of batch quantity, scrap rates, capacity utilization, production efficiency, and workforce motivation. In many companies, leadtimes that are attainable will be longer than the theoretical technological leadtimes, and this may result in the inflation of the planning leadtimes by the planner to reflect what is perceived to be regularly attainable. There is a complex interrelationship between leadtime variance and material shortage or excess, and between inter-process work queues and WIP inventory, which is quite frequently not fully understood by production management. The MRP concepts of fixed planning leadtimes, and a material need date equal to planned order release date, as opposed to operation scheduled start date, do little to foster real understanding.

Quality deviations

When yield and scrap rates are predetermined as data item parameters, there is little or no incentive to manage quality performance. MRPII was supposed to be about closing loops. One of many significant loops not closed is the feedback loop between quality management systems and MRPII. If nothing else, the requirements of BS 5750 and ISO 9000 now predicate the urgent revision of both the textbooks and software packages to bring this within the scope of MRPII, and thus build a long overdue interface between the production management system and the quality management system.

26.3 Key factors for success

Failed MRPII systems evoke the following typical user responses:

- People are the problem.
- There needs to be a culture change.
- There is too little understanding.
- There was too little user involvement.
- 'They attack MRP as a computer system, rather than as a people system' (Wight, 1984).

With that in mind we should ask: what therefore needs to be right in order to ensure success?

For the MRPII system to be successful and yield benefits, five things above all need to be right:

1. The selection of appropriate MRPII software. The software must fit the manufacturing environment. The MRPII standard system will only be the best fit in very specific instances, and this is not fully appreciated, especially by some software suppliers who conform religiously to the standard system for commercial reasons. Software selection is addressed in Chapter 27.
2. A commitment to making it work. However laboured this theme may be, it is nevertheless very vital to the success of an MRPII system.
3. The education, training and motivation of all users.
4. Accurate data. The topics of commitment, education and data accuracy are reviewed in Chapter 28.
5. An understanding of the business. The problem regarding planning lead-times has already been mentioned in this chapter. The performance of MRPII systems hinges on many of the parameters given to the system, and this is developed in Chapter 29. Thinking of a number, in order to satisfy the system, is a recipe for disaster.

27

Choice of MRPII software

In this chapter the choice between in-house systems development and use of proprietary software is considered. After that we examine the key constraints on software selection, beginning with the implications of the IT platform, and then looking in more detail at the selection of software which fits the manufacturing environment. The chapter concludes by examining a model for the selection process itself.

In this chapter the subject of IT technology is addressed in a level of detail that is intended to provide the layman with a broad understanding of the technology supporting manufacturing planning systems. This technology advances fairly swiftly, and this chapter is believed to present a fair picture of the state of the art as of 1993. The reader must, however, be aware that some aspects of this will inevitably become dated as the technology advances.

27.1 In-house systems development and proprietary software

There is a basic choice between:

– in-house systems development—the do-it-yourself method, and
– the acquisition of a proprietary software package.

In house development

The do-it-yourself solution is generally reinventing the wheel at a high cost. It is the course large companies have followed in the past. It allows personalization of the system to the company's specific manufacturing environment, but it needs detailed knowledge of both MRPII and the environment. Above all it needs competence in both systems engineering and computer programming skills.

The typical costs of a do-it-yourself solution may vary depending on the type of programming language used:

- Using a traditional high level programming language, such as COBOL, the total costs of development may be in the range £250–500 000.
- Using a 4GL, the costs would more typically be in the region of £25–100 000. Apart from the costs, the major drawbacks of a do-it-yourself solution are the lengthy elapsed time associated with the systems development project, the risk of the system not being bug-free on implementation, and the fairly substantial burden of ongoing maintenance throughout the future.

Proprietary MRPII software

A wide choice of proprietary software packages is available. One user claimed to have identified about 100 packages; the author is acquainted with more than 50.

The total costs of a bought-in solution will include the following:

- the software itself;
- any modifications to the software to fit the user environment. This will be charged at a day rate;
- the computer hardware: the host computer or file server, data terminals or PCs, and a data communications network;
- any training and consultancy proposed by the supplier.

These costs may sometimes be bundled or packaged together.

The actual software costs will usually depend on a number of parameters:

- The number of system modules acquired. The cost per module may vary according to the complexity of the particular system module.
- The number of users of the system, and this may be either the maximum number of data terminals allowed access to the system, or the maximum number of users simultaneously logged into the system.

The software costs for a full MRPII system will typically be in the ranges shown in Table 27.1, which are based on 1991/92 price levels.

In addition there will be an annual maintenance charge of between 10 and 20 per cent of initial purchase price.

Table 27.1 Software costs for a MRPII system

	IT platform	No. of users	Purchase price
Low	PC based	4	< £20 000
Mid	UNIX platform	12	£40–120 000
High	Mainframe	50 +	£250 000 or more

27.2 Constraints on software selection

The major constraints on software selection include those at both a macro and a micro level. Micro-level constraints are best described as looking under every stone at data item level, whereas the macro-level constraints include the following:

- the IT platform
- the degree of openness
- the system performance
- security
- modularity
- user report generator facilities
- vendor quality assurance
- the degree of fit with the manufacturing environment

27.3 The IT platform and open systems

The IT platform is the combination of the host computer and its operating system. If the IT platform and migration path are already decided, this may be a limiting factor on the choice of MRPII software.

The MRPII software currently available subdivides into four approximately equal groups by IT platform, and this is by number of packages, and not by number of users, which is very difficult to quantify with any degree of accuracy:

- IBM mid-range (AS/400) platform;
- DEC-VAX/VMS platform;
- UNIX platform;
- the rest of the field, and this encompasses mainframe computers at one extreme, and PC-DOS platforms at the other, but with no single distinct platform approaching the significance of the first three listed above.

Only a small minority of packages cross the frontiers between these platforms, and where they do, they generally span at most two types of platform, very often one of these pairs:

- IBM mid-range and IBM mainframe
- DEC-VAX and UNIX
- UNIX and PC-DOS

This presents a finite limit to choice if the IT platform is predetermined.

The market share held by the different types of IT platform is undergoing a dramatic shift, away from mainframes and mid-range computers and

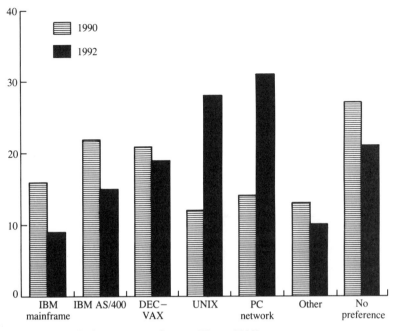

Figure 27.1   IT platform: user preference (Xerox 1992)

towards the greater flexibility of UNIX and PC platforms. Market research undertaken by one software vendor (Xerox 1992) revealed the substantial shift in user preference shown in Figure 27.1.

The proportion of users indicating a preference for UNIX or PC networks had grown from just over a quarter in 1990 to almost 60 per cent by 1992, a very substantial movement in just two years. At the same time the proportion preferring a mainframe solution had fallen from three quarters to not much more than 40 per cent. This coincided with the loss of near-monopoly power by IBM. '[IBM's] gross profits—the vast majority of which came from mainframes—fell from $24.6 billion in 1990 to $14.1 billion in 1992' (Cassidy 1993), as the company moved from net earnings of $5.97 billion to a net loss of $4.97 billion. The decline of IBM has wide-reaching repercussions in terms of MRPII software: the one company that did so much to promote the below MRPII standard system, as Figure 27.2 testifies, no longer exercises monopoly power, and is unlikely ever to regain it. The availability of MRPII software packages in the future may be expected to respond to such shifts in market preference for IT platform; non-prescriptive MRPII solutions which fit the manufacturing environment are more than likely to outstrip packages based on the MRPII standard system throughout the remainder of the 1990s.

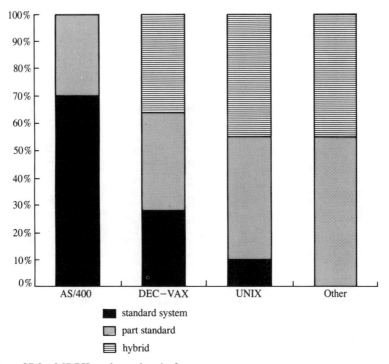

Figure 27.2   MRPII packages by platform

Of much greater significance is the generic type of MRPII system on offer with the various types of platform. The packages of which the author has visibility have been classified into three categories, following the generic classification adopted in Chapter 13:

- the full **MRPII** standard system;
- a part-standard system, in which there is little or no support at or above the level of master scheduling;
- a non-standard system, covering the scope of **MRPII**, but not conforming to the standard system.

The barcharts on Figure 27.2 indicate the distribution of these categories by type of platform. The extent to which an **IBM** mid-range platform goes hand in hand with *only* the standard system is quite remarkable, and this in turn presents a potential problem for many users already locked into an **IBM** mid-range platform. By contrast, the degree of choice increases quite markedly as one moves away from the **IBM AS/400** to a **VAX, UNIX** or **DOS** platform. The shift in user preference for IT platform illustrated in Figure 27.1 is therefore likely to lead at the same time to a much greater user choice in terms of the type of MRPII system. There will be much less danger in future of users becoming locked into the MRPII standard system by default.

Openness

Systems are open systems if they satisfy questions like these:

- Will the MRPII software bought for the current or proposed IT platform be portable to a different platform?
- Will it be portable to a different vendor's platform?
- Can this platform communicate with the wide variety of PCs and other terminals which may already be installed in the company?
- When we add new terminals to the network can we select these without having to worry about compatibility?
- Can we take advantage of new technology without having to scrap our existing investment in software and starting all over again?
- Can we simply change the technology as and when the company grows and the existing platform is no longer powerful enough for the job?

Open systems should in theory make all that possible, but it is not easy for the layman to assess just how much openness there really is. To ensure openness there really needs to be openness at three distinct levels:

1. Open software
2. Open operating systems
3. Open data communications

Openness implies industry standards, and at present there is no universal set of standards. There is instead a mixture of:

- ANSI standards
- ISO standards
- *de facto* industry standards
- emerging standards

Some computer manufacturers avoid the issue of openness. Others pay only lip service to it. A closed system ties the user to that manufacturer for the indefinite future, and this can be intended for the manufacturer's commercial advantage.

Open software

On mainframe and mid-range platforms, the degree of openness will depend on the programming language in which the software has been written, for example:

- Software written in ANS COBOL may in theory be recompiled to run on any other platform that supports ANS COBOL.
- Software written in IBM AS/400 Native Code is unlikely to be portable outside the IBM mid-range. One in four MRPII packages at present therefore effectively ties the user throughout the future to the IBM mid-range series.

On PC and minicomputer platforms, openness will depend on which database language the application software has been built around. The MRPII software will be portable if the database language is portable, and the database language will be portable if it operates under an operating system designed to industry open standards.

Open operating systems

Until now POSIX has been the industry open standard, and it now incorporates an industry standard for file access, C-ISAM, which was originally developed by Informix. For example, the following operating systems are POSIX-compliant, but this is not intended to be an exhaustive list:

- most versions of UNIX
- XENIX—the operating system for SCO platforms
- VMS and ULTRIX, both serving DEC platforms
- AIX—the version used with IBM RISC platforms
- DRS–NX—serving ICL DRS platforms

Software designed for a POSIX-compliant operating system may, however, still have to be recompiled if it is ported to another POSIX-compliant environment.

At the date of writing it had just been reported by Fujitsu (*Daily Telegraph* 1993), that 'the major European, American and Japanese computer companies' were about to announce their agreement to adopt UNIX as the industry standard operating system.

The concept of open architecture may obviate the need for such recompilation. Two examples of open architecture are these:

- the IBM AT/XT, which became the *de facto* industry standard for the PC;
- the industry standard RISC (reduced instruction set computing) processor chip, which is incorporated in platforms by IBM, DEC, Hewlett Packard, Sony and Apple, for example.

Open data communications

MRPII systems are most likely to operate within a multi-user network. In a multi-user network there will be three elements:

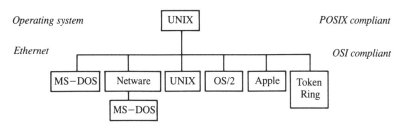

Figure 27.3 DEC pathworks

– a host file server;
– client terminals;
– a LAN, linking together the file server and the user terminals.

In a multiple-site installation there will be a LAN in each site, linked to the LAN of the file server by a wide area network (WAN).

The file server hosts the MRPII database and is the platform for the MRPII software. Industry standards also apply to the server-client interface:

– *Data interchange*: the standard is structured query language (SQL). Developed by IBM, this is now an ANSI standard.
– *Network connectivity*: the emerging standard is ISO–OSI (open systems interconnection). Ethernet is the proposed ISO–OSI standard for LANs, and the market is presently dominated by Ethernet and IBM Token Ring, both of which have a market share of about 40 per cent. There is no industry standard for WANs, but OSI-compliant examples include DECNet and Hewlett Packard OpenView. The physical network requires a network manager, and an example of an OSI-compliant network manager is OSLan (ICL).

Open systems networks have been developed by several manufacturers to allow file servers to communicate with the wide variety of existing PC operating systems and network protocols. A typical example is DEC Pathworks, which is represented in Figure 27.3.

27.4 Other software constraints

Performance

The overall system performance or response will be a function of two factors:

– *The capacity*: for instance, processor cycle time or channel carrying capacity.
– *The load*: the number of transactions and their arrival pattern.

The system performance will be constrained by the load on the bottleneck resource, just as it would be in a manufacturing plant, but the management of these types of resource does not fit with the types of resource planning described in Chapters 17 and 18. The bottleneck resource may be any of those three:

- hardware
- data communications
- software

HARDWARE

The computer hardware itself is becoming more easily reconfigurable with the advent of open systems. With PC-based networks the cost of hardware upgrades is fast becoming a cost element of only marginal significance. The cost of processing on a PC, as measured by millions of instructions per second per dollar, has decreased 25-fold over the period 1979–1993 (*Sunday Times* 1993). It is when this is taken in conjunction with the availability of larger and faster fixed-disk storage systems that the real benefit accrues to the user.

For example, a PC with a 486 processor and one gigabyte (1000 megabytes) of fixed disk has more than ten times the processing power of the typical mid-range mainframe of the early 1980s. With a retail price often as low as £2500, in contrast to a price tag of up to £25 000 for an early 1980s mid-range mainframe, the present state-of-the-art PC therefore represents at least a hundred-fold improvement in the relative cost performance ratio over the last ten years. Just as important, 'according to an industry consultancy [Gartner Group], raw computing power on an IBM mainframe now costs between five and eight times that of equal capacity on microprocessor based systems' (Cassidy 1993). For most smaller users opting for a PC-based system the cost of hardware is now likely to be less than the cost of the software.

THE DATA COMMUNICATION NETWORK

Here again the cost performance ratio is moving rapidly in the user's favour. The cost of installation or reconfiguration is becoming more heavily weighted towards the cost of the engineer's time, and less heavily weighted towards the cost of the network materials. The development of fibre optic and laser technology means that by 1994 or 1995 the typical network carrying capacity is likely to increase tenfold, from 10 megabytes per second to around 100 megabytes per second.

SOFTWARE

In contrast to hardware and data communications, the software is unlikely to be so easily reconfigurable. The most frequent software bottleneck is often the file access performance of the database language. The general characteristics of database file access performance are these:

- A drop in performance as the number of users increases, and often out of all proportion to the increased load on the physical resources of the system.
- A wide variation in the overall performance between different database languages. Published reviews indicate relative performance ratios in the range 5:1 between the best performer and the poorest.
- A wide variation in their relative performance depending on which database function is being carried out. For example, some database languages which perform well on file updates are relatively sluggish when carrying out database queries, while a few that lead the field in database query performance are lower down the performance tables in terms of file updating.

Security

The three major aspects of systems security are these:

- *Backup*
- *Password control*: normally offered as a user-controllable means of determining who is allowed access to specific programmes, specific data files, specific records within a data file, and in some instances, specific data items within a record.
- *Lockout*: normally predetermined within the application software as a means of avoiding conflicting user activity within the system. Lockout may occur at the levels of data file or data record. The user-friendly but failsafe convention is this one:

    batch programming file update, such as an MRP regeneration run—lockout at data file level;

    on-line record add, update or delete—lockout at data record level;

    on-line record read only—no lockout.

Software that unnecessarily locks out users causes great frustration.

Modularity

There are some key questions concerning the modularity of an MRPII software package:

- Can we buy and install only the system modules we actually need?
- Which other modules are necessary to support these?
- Can we use one module to begin with, get that working and producing benefits, and then move on to the next? Or do we have to make *all* modules work together in order to make the system do anything?

User report-generator facilities

Despite the mountain of reports available from most MRPII software, the need may often arise for user-defined reports. Most software packages include a report generator. This will be used by the company to produce user-defined reports.

The report generator is normally a facility of the database language, and not the MRPII software itself. The critical question is this: does it allow the user to join or relate two or more databases for reporting purposes? For example, suppose the managing director asks for a list of all customers whose orders are delayed by material shortages from supplier X. This report can be produced by relating in turn the following databases: supplier, purchase order, MRP net requirements, sales orders, customers.

In some database languages, the standard report generator is limited to one database only. Most *ad hoc* needs of the user relate to more than one.

Vendor quality assurance

Key questions concerning vendor quality assurance include:

- Will the software be bug-free on delivery?
- Will future releases also be bug-free on delivery?
- What degree of support will be available if problems emerge?
- Will there always be someone available on a hot line?
- Is all of this verified by unbiased users?

27.5 Fit with the manufacturing environment

This requires the greatest attention of all. No two software packages are identical in terms of their detailed functionality. Many suppliers claim that their software supports specific industry types. This is often because the initial version did not, and had to be modified. This is now seen as a selling point, but it begs the question of how many versions there are now of this package.

The great variety of the available software reflects the fact that there is no single production management method that is best for any individual environment, and this in turn improves the potential user's chances of finding a system that *does* fit.

The question of functional fit revolves around marrying requirements and options on two sides of a balance sheet:

- What is the functional need of the business?
- What are the functional features and options of the available software packages?

This is a process that will therefore vary greatly from one business to another, and the user must always bear in mind that it is simply a planning tool that is being selected. As we have seen in Chapter 5, it is not a substitute for a manufacturing strategy, nor is it a substitute for sound management practice. In this chapter we can do no more than to highlight the salient elements of choice, and we will do this in the form of a simple checklist, beginning with issues of a strategic nature, and concluding with issues of a more detailed type.

Strategic issues

1. Is the IT platform predetermined? If it is, and if it is an IBM mid-range platform, the user must recognize that the available software will have a bias towards a solution based on the MRPII standard system (see page 264).

2. Is there an integrated manufacturing and distribution environment? If there is, and the user wishes to apply an integrated MRPII and DRP solution (see Chapter 23), then the choice of software packages reduces dramatically, and these will by definition also be based on the MRPII standard system.

3. Is the market environment conducive to demand forecasting? This was addressed in Chapter 14. If it is, and only if it is, then the system should include a demand forecasting module. Otherwise the actual firm demand available to either master production scheduling or MRP should instead be supplemented by the manual addition of forecasts produced by the company's marketing function.

4. Is rate-based scheduling in use? If it is, then the standard system may well not be appropriate. The production planning module (see Chapter 15) should be used to derive production rates, and this should then be used as the driver of MRP. Master production scheduling will not be relevant, and there may be a need to customize the interface between production planning and MRP. Final assembly schedules will be derived directly from the sales order file, and this may be accomplished by the repetitive manufacturing module of MRPII (see Chapter 21).

5. Is the environment assembly to order, or make to stock of feature-dependent products? Provided rate-based scheduling is not being used, then this environment will be well satisfied by packages conforming to the MRPII standard system. Master production scheduling will be required; it will be the planned order release option (see Chapter 16), and must have provision for configure to order. In this case the software must make provision for the production of final assembly schedules, as these will not be produced by MRP.

6. Is the environment make to order, but not a jobbing-shop environment? The key in this case is to use the planned production option at MPS level

(see Chapter 16). The best solution may be to select a package for which the presentation format allows master scheduling to be performed as the top-level pass of MRP, rather than opting for a separate MPS module.

7. Is the environment a jobbing shop? If it is, then the entire process of master production scheduling will be irrelevant to the needs of the business. The best solution will be to select software which allows MRP to be driven directly from the sales order file (see Chapter 12). The principal element of scheduling will then take place at work centre level, operation by operation, and this will require a production scheduling module (see Chapter 22), which will in turn provide MRP with material need dates.

    If there is also a high degree of contention between workload and capacity, then there may be a requirement for this module to schedule to finite capacity (see Chapter 22). Where there are known bottlenecks, and where the interrelationship of the works processes are complex, a solution embodying the principles of OPT (see Chapter 22) may yield benefit, but this will invariably require expert external advice in order to arrive at a cost-effective fit with the available software.

8. Is the shop floor controlled on a push principle? The PAC module will be required (see Chapter 19). In this case consideration should also be given to the methods of shop-floor feedback (see Chapter 20), and the most relevant question may be whether or not the software provides for the generation of bar-coded documents.

9. Is a kanban system in operation? If it is, the first question will be how the final assembly schedule is to be derived, and this will depend on whether rate-based scheduling or order-based scheduling is used. Rate-based scheduling was addressed in question 4. If order-based scheduling is used, then it depends on which MPS option was selected (see Chapter 16). If the planned order release option is used, then the final assembly schedule must be produced by the MPS module, and if the planned production option is used, then it will be produced by the top-level pass of MRP.

    For the kanban system to work the principle of backflushing must be adopted (see Chapter 21), and this will be accomplished by the repetitive manufacturing module of MRPII or an equivalent offered by a specific software package.

10. Is there integration along the supply chain? If there is, then the software must provide for EDI (see Chapter 10). Before selecting EDI software it is necessary to first establish what EDI standards are being used by the major partners in the supply chain. If a kanban system is in use, consideration should also be given to whether an electronic kanban is required, and what provision for this exists in the software on offer.

11. Is the system to be decentralized? If so, the concept of DMRP will be applicable (see Chapter 24). If the organization of the various work cells varies considerably, more than one type of MRPII approach may be

needed, and the user may require more than one of the possible solutions indicated by the preceding questions. Consideration should also be given at the outset to the technical issue of how the uploading of the decentralized databases is to be accomplished.

Detailed level issues

The list that follows is by no means exhaustive, and there may be many more questions which are relevant in specific manufacturing situations:

1. Are fixed planning leadtimes acceptable? If they are not (see Chapter 11), then the user should note that there are very few packages conforming to the MRPII standard system which support variable planning leadtimes. By contrast, non-standard systems almost without exception allow for variable planning leadtimes.
2. Are products heavily feature-dependent? If they are, then the MRPII standard system will cope with these better than any variant will. The concepts of planning bills and consumption of the forecast will be of especial benefit (see Chapter 16).
3. Is the factory heavily product-family oriented? If it is, then there may be benefit in considering the MRPII standard system modules above the level of MPS (see Chapter 15).
4. Is the balancing of MPS and capacity requirements complex? If it is, then the user should seek a RCCP module which provides for interactive simulation (see Chapter 18).
5. Is a bucketless net change MRP system desirable? The advantages, and disadvantages, were addressed in Chapter 11. If it is desirable, then ensure that the software provides for it.
6. Are there production routing networks? These were described in Chapter 17. If there are routings in the form of networks, the user should note that only a mere handful of software packages will support networks. The alternative is to treat each limb of the network as a phantom subassembly (see Chapter 7), and this may be less than desirable.
7. Is there a need for tooling control? If there is, then this is normally a very finite resource and the planner's task will be eased by the inclusion of scheduling to finite capacity (see Chapter 22).
8. Is lot traceability required? This was described in Chapter 20. Despite the widespread application of ISO 9000, lot traceability has yet to be included in some software packages.
9. What interfaces are needed with costing and accounting systems? This subject was examined in Chapter 25. The available software varies greatly in terms of the interfaces with these systems. If standard costing is used, the user should ensure that the MRPII software does provide for the generation and updating of standard costs.

10. Is activity-based costing in use? The user should note that this has yet to be addressed by the majority of software packages.
11. In a make-to-order environment, is there a need for an interface with a project management system? Where large-scale and complex one-off production orders are normal, there is merit in using a project management system to provide the overall control, but with a link to MRP to provide for the procurement of materials. Only a very few software packages allow for this interface.
12. Does the design department use a CAD system? If so, then the user should seek a package with an automatic link between the CAD system and the bill of materials module (see Chapter 7).
13. Is a CAD–CAM system in use? If so, the interface should include not only bills of materials but also production routings (see Chapter 17). There may be merit in considering software which combines bills of materials and production routings into a single database (see Chapter 17).
14. Does the level of material scrap vary from work centre to work centre? If it does, the user should ensure that this data is specifiable by production operation, and not by product.
15. What performance measurements or indicators are needed? The main source of these is normally the production activity control module. There is no standard set of indicators. The user should check what is provided, and what report generator facilities are available to cater for those that may not be provided.
16. Is a production efficiency feedback loop desirable? This is a loop not closed by most systems. Ask software suppliers for ideas.
17. Is a quality feedback loop desirable? This too is a loop very rarely closed. In an ISO 9000 environment, there is a prima facie case for closing it. Ask the software suppliers for ideas.
18. Is there provision for the recalculation of safety stocks, taking into account supplier and works performance? This is another loop that is very rarely closed in MRPII. Again ask the software supplier for ideas.
19. Is the choice of lot-sizing methods satisfactory? Where demand is highly variable, part-period balancing (see Chapter 9) may be very cost-effective, but it is not often available.

27.6 Micro-level constraints

At a micro level will be a great many points of user detail, such as these:

− Are all relevant data fields both present and large enough?
− Are all print formats either acceptable as they are or modifiable to the user's specific needs?

By way of example of micro-level detail, here is a sample of detailed level misfits that were found during one MRPII installation:

- Production routes allowed standard times to be expressed only in *whole* minutes, but the typical production rates were in a range 500 to 5000 per hour. This would have required times to be expressed to three decimal positions.
- Queue time was specified in *whole days*. The typical queues ahead of most work centres were one batch, or roughly two hours' production. Rounding up queue time to one day would have added several days to the manufacturing leadtime.
- The parent/child relationships were assumed to be integral relationships, with one or more integral units of a child being required for one unit of the parent. There were many relationships like that of the Birdhomes' tube, described in Chapter 7, where a unit of the parent required only a fraction of the stock-keeping unit of the child.
- Production routes were based on an assumed unitary relationship within each production operation, that is to say, each operation was assumed to be carried out for each *unit* of production. In fact many production operations were performed *n* variable and later subdivided into discrete units. For example, the process included screen printing where the unit of production was a sheet of plastic containing as many as several hundred identical images, each of which would later be cut into unitary components.
- Provision for yield existed only at works order level, and was therefore a constant from the first production operation to the last. The real-life material wastage occurred at each setup and therefore varied by operation. The yield on materials issued to the first operation was therefore considerably poorer than the yield on materials issued to operations closer to final assembly.

These are examples of micro-level constraints. They require prior and detailed examination data item by data item.

27.7 Software selection methods

In Chapter 5, we noted that manufacturing strategy was frequently described in terms of the strategic planning process, and that the difficult part was more likely to be selecting which strategies to adopt. It is the same with software selection. Thus far in this chapter we have examined in detail the elements of choice, or the constraints on the selection of MRPII software. What is needed to bring this together is a systematic model for carrying out that process of software selection.

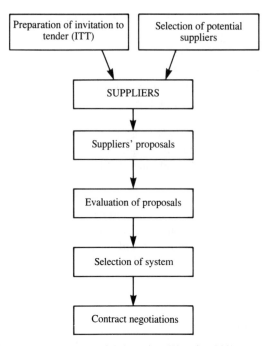

Figure 27.4   Software selection model (based on Mundy 1992)

There are many well-proven models, especially among management consultancies and government procurement organizations. The more formal of these focus at some stage on the *invitation to tender* (ITT), and a generalized summary of the steps in the selection logic are illustrated in Figure 27.4.

Invitation to tender (ITT)

Mundy (1992) recommends that this document should comprise four sections:

1. Company details.
2. The functional requirements: these will address the business needs, in much the way that earlier in this chapter the reader was advised to match the variants or options of MRPII type systems to the needs of the particular manufacturing environment. Mundy advocates classifying these functional requirements as follows:
   (a) business critical
   (b) desirable
   (c) nice to have
   (d) future requirements

3. Technical requirements: for example, the IT platform, data file volumes, data input and enquiry levels and patterns.
4. Assessment criteria: the criteria against which evaluation of suppliers' proposals will be made, for example, price, the level of support available, how well proven the system is, the number and types of users of the system, and the people resources of the supplier.

Selection of potential suppliers

This process of pre-selection begins with defining the key criteria which will merit the inclusion of a potential supplier on the ITT list. These criteria will include the fit between the software and the business need, the IT platform(s) that are supported, and other attributes such as number of installation and the apparent backup support available from the supplier.

Using these criteria, a search for potential vendors will be undertaken, and those who satisfy the criteria will be sent the ITT. At this point Mundy (1992) advocates holding a vendor conference. This ensures that each is given the same information.

Evaluation of proposals

The suppliers' proposals will be evaluated against the key criteria of the ITT—the functional requirements, the technical requirements, and the assessment criteria. This initial evaluation should result in a shortlist of suppliers.

The next step in evaluation should be for the shortlisted suppliers to demonstrate their system. This will normally result in a preferred supplier emerging, but Mundy (1992) suggests that at this stage the shortlist should comprise both the preferred supplier and a backup supplier.

Selection of the system

The model offered by Mundy (1992) breaks this down into two steps:

1. A functional fit study. For both shortlisted suppliers this will consist of 'a detailed simulation of how the system would handle specified business transactions using company data'. This will result in a statement of the following:
   (a) those functions covered by standard features;
   (b) the changes needed to the system;
   (c) any issues not resolved.
2. Selection of system with the best functional fit. This will be based on visits to other users of the system, and taking account of their experiences.

Having selected the best-fit solution in this way, the final step in the process is to proceed to the negotiation of a contract with the software supplier.

For many very small companies this software selection methodology may seem top-heavy and time-consuming, and there will be a natural temptation to short-circuit the process. The basic elements of that selection process described by Mundy are not options but necessities if the best solution is to be found. What can be done is to make some of the elements of the selection process less formal. The advice given by one small company (Thurne Engineering, Norwich—see Chapter 22) with the benefit of hindsight is as follows:

- Allow plenty of time for planning the selection of software.
- Produce a written specification of what is required.
- Look for flexible report-generator facilities.
- Examine as many software packages as possible before making a decision.

28
Making the MRPII system work

Having selected the appropriate MRPII software, the essentials in making the system work are then these:

- commitment
- education
- accurate data
- a sound implementation plan
- effective management of the system, and coordination of its users

28.1 Commitment

Commitment was the keynote message of the MRPII evangelists, possibly in response to a high failure rate among MRPII installations. Commitment is essential to making any system work, but it is of especial importance in the case of MRPII systems, and for these reasons:

- MRPII affects a larger number of people, and across a larger number of company functions or departments than most other computer systems do. In that sense it has an impact comparable to the introduction of standards such as ISO 9000 or Investors in People.
- It invokes a culture change in many areas, not least of them being in the area of expediting.
- It replaces a number of informal systems, many of which are well tried and may work tolerably well.
- It depends on top management, who must create an environment which supports the introduction of MRPII, and the changes it implies.

Making MRPII work will be easier if three pre-conditions are assured:

- Top management actually understand both MRPII and its interaction with the business they are managing.
- The introduction of MRPII is incorporated in the company's business strategy.

– Top management is prepared to spend as much time actually making the system work as it does at the outset on promoting the change.

Organizations that have successfully implemented standards like ISO 9000 or Investors In People will already have understood both the change in culture and the level of commitment needed to make MRPII work, and the company culture is most likely to be supportive of an MRPII installation. Those who have failed to gain, or to retain, these accreditations, or who have shied away from them on the basis of the effort needed, will be likely to lack the level of commitment needed to make a success of MRPII.

Ralston and Reddy (1993) present a very simple list of the key criteria for successful implementation:

– a knowledge of the company and its people;
– an understanding of some basic techniques;
– common sense;
– a willingness to get everybody involved.

28.2 Education

Successful MRPII users spend as much on education and training as they do on software. Making an MRPII system work properly requires the motivation of a large number of people. They will be more motivated if they have an adequate understanding, and this implies a substantial programme of education and training. The similarity in this respect with a quality standard such as ISO 9000 has already been noted.

The goals of MRPII education should be these:

– to support the overall business objectives, which will include the introduction of MRPII;
– to cultivate a perception of the end results that are being sought;
– to acquire a technical knowledge of the principles and methods of MRPII systems, at different levels of detail and breadth depending on individual job functions;
– to create an atmosphere of company-wide cooperation.

The aims of the education and training will be to provide a large number of people at different levels in the organization with a *sufficient* understanding of both the principles and methods of MRPII in order for them to work successfully with the system.

An outline of a textbook education and training programme structure is given by Comber (1992). He identifies three layers:

1. *Communication*: which should be concentrated at four points in time—the start of the project, the start of the preparatory work, implementation, and post-implementation.
2. *Education*: this comprises four distinct areas of education—management education, education of the implementors, specialist education (in master production scheduling and inventory control, for example), and user education.
3. *Training*: this should focus on three distinct groups—the implementation team, the information systems team, and users.

Case study   C&K Switches Ltd, Kettering

The training strategy adopted by C&K Switches focused on the principle of cascading the training from management level down through the organization, and is a model that may be relevant to small to medium-sized companies which do not have substantial in company training departments. Key to its success was that there were no financial constraints placed on the training plan.

The training comprised four waves:

1. *The project team*: this comprised 10 staff and was a part-time multi-disciplined team led by a senior company executive, and including a senior member of the financial division. The company's aim was to establish experts in the system at the highest possible level in the company. The project team received intensive training off-site, followed by extensive hands-on system testing experience.
2. *User education*: all 70 users of the system were given general systems education. This was provided in classroom sessions, and included an overview of the entire system, and the interrelationship of all its parts. It was general and not job-specific.
3. *Intensive user training*: this comprised job-specific training at a detailed level, and was oriented around detailed procedures written by the department manager, who was himself a member of the project team.
4. *On-the-job-training*: provided for the occasional user, on the job, at the time of need.

Other aspects of the implementation of MRPII at C&K Switches are dealt with in greater detail in Chapter 29.

Case study   Sara Lee: MRPII and Investors in People

Sara Lee Household and Personal Care employs around 750 people in three locations in the UK and has a turnover in excess of £60 million. Based in Slough, it has a manufacturing facility in West Yorkshire and distribution facilities in Leicestershire.

The company has a core range of toiletries, household, shoecare and cosmetic products, many of which are household names: for example, Radox, Kiwi, Amplex, Matey, Meltonian and Vapona.

In the world of FMCG, companies need to be highly adaptable if they are to be competitive, and in the late 1980s Sara Lee implemented an MRPII system. At that time the business was becoming more complex and customers were becoming more demanding. These pressures from within the company, coupled with market demands, meant rapid changes, and employees had been carried along without any real formalized training programme.

At this point Sara Lee realized it had to invest in its people, rather than simply a new piece of hardware or software, in order to survive as a business in the 1990s. 'Alongside MRPII we needed to create a company culture that drove our business towards agreed objectives, through continually improving quality whilst lowering costs.'

In response, Sara Lee developed a policy setting out the future direction of the organization, the success of which depended substantially on educating and training all employees in vision, culture and operational processes. The company began a massive training programme along with a commitment to all employees to continuously improve their training, rewards and development.

The company's training programme consisted of external and internal courses and, like that of C&K Switches, was implemented by cascading the learning process through the company. Just-in-time, TQM, continuous improvement methods, MRPII and training in new software were all important components of the programme. For the company, becoming an Investor in People has been an essential part of keeping it ahead of its international competition, and has already led to significant improvements in company performance and profit.

28.3 Accurate data

Accurate data is essential throughout the MRPII database. It needs positive effort if that is to be achieved. It is often most difficult to achieve where feedback from the shop floor is concerned. To achieve data accuracy requires discipline in four key areas:

1. To ensure that bills of materials and production routings are correct. The accuracy of this information is assisted by the linking of data from engineering systems to MRPII, for example by engineering data management (EDM) systems, or by more limited interfaces between CAD or CAD–CAM systems and MRPII.
2. To maintain accurate inventory records.
3. To report accurately and promptly both order completion and order receipt events.
4. To report *all* planned events and *all* unplanned events.

The key to data integrity in these latter areas will depend on the SFDC system (see Chapter 20).

Capturing the data promptly is as important as capturing it correctly. In the context of physical inventory checking, for example, it is exceedingly difficult to reconcile cycle count information to inventory records if the information being audited is other than right up to date.

A high degree of data accuracy will usually be easier to attain if:

- leadtimes are reduced;
- there is a frozen period in the MPS;
- individual responsibilities are clearly defined;
- responsibility is decentralized, under DMRP for instance;
- backflushing is used.

That high degree of data accuracy will be more difficult to attain if:

- MRP is not run frequently;
- net change MRP is operated, but without periodic regeneration;
- there is a time lag between events and their corresponding data entry;
- responsibilities are centralized;
- currency of information status depends on a mass of paperwork recycling from the shop floor.

Data accuracy tolerances

The question is often posed: what degree of data accuracy is required in order for MRPII to operate successfully? In the Oliver Wight classification system (see Chapter 29) the following standards of data integrity are expected of class A users of MRPII:

- inventory records: 95 per cent or better
- bill of materials: 98 per cent or better
- production routings: 95 per cent or better

It can be argued that if the bill of materials is anything other than 100 per cent accurate then the kitting list will not contain the parts actually required for manufacture or assembly. The only concession to accuracy in a bill of materials should be in the case of bulk issue parts, or consumables, such as fasteners.

Likewise if the production routing is less than 100 per cent accurate then the shop-floor documentation, in any environment other than repetitive manufacturing, where permanent work instructions are feasible, will not assure that manufacture or assembly is carried out correctly.

The more the environment is positioned towards make-to-order, the greater becomes the need for 100 per cent data integrity of bills of materials and routings.

In the case of inventory accuracy a balance must be struck between the value of the materials. Using a conventional ABC analysis, the class A items, or those top 20 per cent of items accounting for around 80 per cent of total inventory value, should have zero tolerance when measuring the accuracy of inventory records. That is where perfection of stock recording is essential. By contrast, most systems will be tolerant of errors of 5 per cent or more on low-value class C items; in many instances these may be controlled more cost-effectively by two-bin systems and not by MRP.

28.4 Implementation plan

A model for the key steps and tasks in an MRPII implementation plan is suggested in Table 28.1.

Project definition

This first step on the implementation plan begins with a clear and concise definition of the business needs. This will focus on what the overall objectives of implementing an MRPII system are, and what the desired end results will be.

The process of management education will sell these objectives and predicated end results and should aim to lead to the cross-functional commitment to the project, and to its inclusion in the company's business plans.

Table 28.1 Implementation plan

1. Define the project	1.1	Define business needs
	1.2	Educate management
	1.3	Select project team
	1.4	Define training plans
2. Select software	2.1	Assess, shortlist and select
	2.2	Define and select IT platform
	2.3	Define and select file server and client network
	2.4	Define software modifications
3. Prepare to implement	3.1	Install and review software
	3.2	Educate senior staff
	3.3	Review data collection procedures
	3.4	Build key databases
	3.5	Plan pilot project
4. Develop and prove system	4.1	Run and prove pilot project
	4.2	Formulate and develop changes
	4.3	Train all users
	4.4	Plan detailed implementation
	4.5	Audit data accuracy
	4.6	Audit data collection procedures
5. Implement system	5.1	Cutover—by module, by product, by factory
6. Operate new system	6.1	Monitor results
	6.2	Maintain system

The project team has a key role to play. The members of this team must have the qualifications to take part. They must be given responsibility, accountability and authority. They must believe in teamwork and practise it.

Training plans must be evolved at the very outset. These plans will address both the skills and knowledge needed by individuals at different levels in the organization, and the skills and knowledge they already possess. A sound model for planning the training and education of staff is to be found in the Investors in People standard.

Selection of software

This step has already been described in detail in Chapter 27.

Preparation for implementation

The project team will install the software, and will become thoroughly familiar with it. Using sample company data, a working demonstration model will be built. This will be used in the education of senior staff.

The existing data collection procedures must be reviewed, and changed if necessary to help ensure the degree of data accuracy needed for the proper working of the system. At this stage the key company databases will be built—the parts master file, bills of materials and production routings being the most critical. Having been built they must, from then on, be maintained to a high level of accuracy.

The final preparatory step is to plan a pilot project, in a limited area of the business, perhaps in just one work cell. This pilot will be used to develop and prove the system.

Development and proof

Running and proving the pilot is key to the containment of major problems associated with implementation. During the pilot the accuracy of the databases will be proved, the effectiveness of data collection will be proved, the interaction between people and the system will become understood, and, in short, the barriers to the wider implementation will be removed. The business of proving the accuracy of the database and the data collection procedures will entail an extensive auditing and, more often than not, some form of corrective action to the new procedures themselves.

Only when the pilot project is proven is the time right to commence the training of all users of the system. They must be trained on a system that works and has the confidence of the pilot users.

The experience gained in the pilot project will be invaluable in planning the full-scale implementation of the system.

Implementation of the system

The key question is to determine how the change or cutover from the old system to the new is to be accomplished. In a business of any size it cannot be done all at once, and so the plan must address whether the cutover will be done system module by system module, and whether it can be done product by product. In a decentralized operation, the most logical cutover method is work cell by work cell, especially if DMRP is the chosen solution.

Operation of the new system

After implementation there is a need for an overall system manager to coordinate all users of the system, and maintain the integrity of the system. The focus will then move to the key questions postulated at the beginning of Chapter 26.

- Is the system working? If the software has been chosen wisely, if the commitment has been there, and if a well-trained staff are now operating in the aftermath of a sound and logical implementation, there is no reason why the system should not be working satisfactorily.
- Is the system yielding the desired benefits? This is a matter we now consider in more detail in Chapter 29.

29
Achieving business objectives with MRPII

Making the system perform will depend first of all on making the system work. The question of performance or benefits then has to be put in perspective. In this concluding chapter we once again examine the limitations of a planning tool as the key to real benefits, and we then challenge the historic assumptions as to which benefits are desirable and attainable. Next we will look at contrasting approaches to the identification of tangible objectives. In passing we must note the Oliver Wight classification system, but will move on to examine what is achieved by leaders in the implementation of MRPII. Then we will examine more critically just which benefits are attainable by using MRPII, and which factors influence the performance of MRPII.

29.1 The limitations of a planning tool

MRPII is not a panacea for underperforming manufacturing operations. At best it is a system tool which, if used in conjunction with the appropriate manufacturing strategies, may help achieve limited objectives.

In Chapter 3 the functionality of MRPII was compared to the goals of JIT. In general, where JIT sets a goal or objective, MRPII more or less accepts the *status quo* and computerizes it. In Chapter 5 the importance of manufacturing strategy as the key to real benefits was stressed, and the limited influence of MRPII—the system tool—is reinforced in Appendix C, where the real driving forces behind inventory levels and manufacturing leadtimes are analysed.

The results of system-user surveys cited later in this chapter all strongly suggest that the benefits are very considerably greater where a substantial change in manufacturing strategy preceded implementation of the MRPII system.

Tompkins (1989) made the distinction between three categories of users, and offered succinct advice to each of these categories:

1. *Successful users of MRPII*: they should simplify their MRPII systems.
2. *Unsuccessful users of MRPII*: they should discard their MRPII system.
3. *Potential users of MRPII*: they should first aim at winning manufacturing before implementing a systems planning tool. An example of the successful adoption of this recommendation is illustrated by the second C&K Switches case study (see below).

Tompkins went on to identify where these different users should focus their activity.

Successful users

They should concentrate on three things:

- Make MRP time buckets much shorter.
- Schedule focused departments, and not individual machines.
- Improve material tracking and control systems.

Unsuccessful or potential users

Their activity should focus on a number of important factors as a precondition to the implementation or reimplementation of an MRPII system:

- Achieve a synergy between marketing and manufacturing.
- Simplify the product design.
- Reduce leadtimes.
- Reduce production lot sizes.
- Reduce uncertainty.
- Aim for balanced focused departments and factories.
- Reduce inventories.
- Move to continuous flow manufacturing.
- Improve material tracking and control.

For many would-be users of MRPII, Tompkins' advice to first reduce inventories will be astounding; for many, that may well be what they seek to achieve by implementing MRPII. To unsuccessful users, the advice to discard their system, reduce inventories, and then try again, may seem even more astounding, and yet his advice is founded on the same logic developed in Appendix C—inventory is essentially a function of demand over leadtime. Reduce the leadtime and you reduce the level of inventory.

On a different note, readers should note that Luscombe (1993) recommends the implementation of TQM prior to the implementation of MRPII.

Case study C&K Switches Ltd, Kettering

C&K Switches' progression from non-user to successful MRPII user followed the general approach suggested by Tompkins (1989), and described above. The three strands in the company's strategy were:

1. A manufacturing strategy aimed at reducing inventory prior to the implementation of MRPII. In the case of C&K this was achieved by the introduction of work cells to replace conventional production lines.
2. Careful selection of an MRPII package which addressed the special needs of their product structure.
3. A professional approach to implementation planning and the education and training of users at all levels in the company. This has already been described on page 281.

The company's core product is electrical switches. This product range comprises 40 basic models, each of which is configured to order by the customer using C&K's product catalogue. The combinations of switch function, actuator, termination, and other features allows potentially millions of options, and results in upwards of 8000 live bills of materials in any year. The manufacturing environment is assembly to order, using assembly jigs. There is little setup time, and product cost is thus not very dependent on batch quantity. For customer convenience, a standard delivery leadtime of three to four weeks is offered, depending on the type of switch. Order quantities vary from ones and twos to 10 000 or more, with the average being in the range 350–400. Distribution of the product is through a network of agents and distributors, with over 75 per cent of total production being exported.

C&K's previous software was custom designed, and the sales, manufacturing and financial modules were not integrated. In the late 1980s, the product range was extended. A UK acquisition brought the Unimax range of safety switches to the production plant at Kettering, and at about the same time the company entered the growing membrane switch market, and opened a new production plant adjacent to the existing plant. With membrane switches came a design-to-order environment along with an essentially jobbing type of production. These events prompted the company to look to MRPII as the system that would provide consistency of management information across the three types of product.

Before doing so, C&K tackled the manufacturing strategy on their core product, and this was done in stages. Production had originally been organized into six production process departments, and each works order had to move progressively through each department to completion. All the subassemblies were produced in the relevant process department and were then routed to a stock room. Production operators tended to be trained for specific tasks.

The first major change in strategy resulted in production being organized into four production lines, with each product being built entirely within one line, as a result of which the stock of subassemblies was greatly reduced, and these were stocked within the production lines. Visibility of the buffer stock then allowed replenishment to be balanced to usage and eliminated the planning leadtime as well as the time and costs of handling and storage. The result of this was that WIP was reduced by about 50 per cent. Production operators were still largely trained for specific skills, as before.

Finally, production was split up into nine work cells, each building a specific range of switches to completion within the cell. Some cells are service cells, making the commonly used subassemblies with stockholding controlled on the kanban principle, or for special processes like sealing. Production operators are now trained as multi-skilled workers able to perform any task within the cell. Short versatile assembly tracks are used extensively throughout the work cells. All inventory is now held within the work cell, and is backflushed as the finished product is received into stock. As a result of this, WIP has reduced by a further 50 per cent.

The planning of this latest stage in manufacturing strategy occupied several months, but the physical reorganization was accomplished over two weekends. Hand in hand with this went an extensive retraining programme to multi-skill the workforce. At the same time an incentive payment scheme was replaced by standard wage rates, and C&K now have the flexibility to adjust capacity on any product line by moving staff between work cells.

All stock is now held at the work cells, and the space and costs associated with a materials store has been eliminated. Subassemblies common to more than one product are produced in a dedicated work cell, and buffer stock is controlled by a kanban. Downstream cells simply withdraw from the kanban the quantity required for a works order, and the subassembly cell then makes to replenish the quantity withdrawn.

The total WIP is now only a quarter of its original level. The minimum manufacturing leadtime has reduced to about 30 per cent of its previous figure, and arrears have all but disappeared. Standard times and standard costs have not altered; the technological leadtime is the same as before, but all inter process queuing has been completely eliminated.

Customer orders are classified according to whether or not delivery will be accepted before due date, and if necessary the production load is smoothed by pulling forward orders that may be delivered prior to due date, in marked contrast to the past when transient overloads resulted in producing late.

To support the reorganized manufacturing facility, C&K Switches then decided to install an MRPII system which would support all product lines. The choice of software was constrained by two major criteria:

1. The decision to replace the earlier IBM System 36 with an IBM AS/400 platform, in order to have compatibility with the US parent company and sales agents across Europe.
2. The need for a powerful configure-to-order option to cater for the complex configuration of customer orders.

Selection of software was entrusted to a part-time multi-disciplined team, led by a senior company executive, and including a financial executive. From a shortlist of three packages, and after extensive hands on testing, CGI's LS3 package was selected, and comprises integrated sales administration and distribution, manufacturing and financial systems.

The implementation was completed in May 1993, 17 months after the start of the project. Cutover was by each of the three product lines, and in successive months. The initial cutover was achieved using discrete BOMs, but a second phase, to be introduced nine months after the original cutover, was planned based on the development of a configurator facility which searches for features and dependencies within the product number, and establishes the combinations leading to a configured BOM, routing and selling price.

Commonality of parts content between different configuration options is catered for by the extensive use of phantoms at first level in the bills of materials, although these are not discrete subassemblies as such. The configure-to-order logic composes the specific bill of materials by the combination of a range of phantoms.

The basic implementation focuses around MRP and the configurator, and produces daily work to lists in due date sequence plus works orders. Already, a new order can be loaded into a work cell within an hour of order receipt. Backflushing is in use on both switch and safety switch production, while stores issue recording continues to be used in the case of membrane switches.

The next stage in implementation, just being planned at the date of publication, is to extend the system to include capacity planning in the membrane switch production unit, where a jobbing-shop type of problem has to be addressed, and to establish reporting of cost variances by work cell.

29.2 The historic assumption of benefits

Where such advice, to first address manufacturing strategy, is not followed, then the impact of MRPII as a planning tool has to be considered, and in particular its impact on three key business criteria:

- inventory levels
- leadtimes
- delivery performance

As far as inventory levels are concerned, the impact of MRPII will be limited to removing any excess inventory inherent in the logic of previous inventory management systems, such as an order-point system, for instance. It was inventory reductions of this nature that led Wight (1984) to claim that 'a company getting two inventory turns without MRP should expect to get three inventory turns with MRP'.

This has been the basis used ever since for the financial justification of an MRPII system, and the logic is somewhat naively repeated in the current (1993) version of the DTI *Managing into the 90s* publication on MRPII, where a 33 per cent reduction in inventory carrying costs, based on Wight's predicted attainment of an annual stockturn of three, is assumed. A stockturn of three is 120 days' stock, or 100 times higher than the stock level in Nissan, described in Chapter 21. As will be seen later in this chapter, a three times stockturn is on par with the performance of the laggers in the implementation of MRPII; the leaders, even if they do not match Nissan's example, at least better this by a factor of four, and even the average is 50 per cent lower than that three times stockturn—hardly a recipe for managing into the 90s.

Such glib assumptions fail to address the key question—what really drives inventory?

In moving from an order-point system to MRP, the real benefits may be greater or less than that yardstick given by Wight (1984). Inventory levels in an order-point system are in the main a function of demand over leadtime, just as they are in real life. A greater precision is given to this at dependent demand level in MRP by virtue of the fact the system logic is founded on future visibility of demand, and not historical usage. This is important in preventing both shortages and stock obsolescence in an environment where the level of demand over the future differs from that of the recent past, or where there is an incidence of engineering change arising over the future.

The excess inventory in an order-point system arises from its safety stocks, calculated mathematically to give protection against the variability in the historical pattern of usage. A safety stock calculated in this way also gives protection against any deviation between actual supply and planned supply of materials. Where there are deficiencies in delivery or quality performance on the supply side, the MRP system will also need safety stocks, and safety stocks of this nature were accepted as legitimate by Orlicky (1975).

The real reduction in inventory arising from the replacement of an order-point system by MRP will therefore hinge on a number of factors:

- How great was the variability of usage in the past? If production levels were relatively stable, an order-point system would have relatively low safety stocks, and therefore less excess to be purged out of the system in the future.
- How reliable is the supply side, including the shop floor? If this is unreliable, a significant level of safety stock will be required in order for the MRP system to prevent shortages arising.
- How great is the incidence of engineering change? The higher it is, then the greater scope there is under MRP for preventing stock obsolescence.
- Whether or not planning leadtime and queue time parameters given to MRP are factual or inflated.
- The lot-sizing method. If the order-point system's EOQ is perpetuated as the lot-sizing method in MRP, there will be less benefit than if lot for lot is adopted.

29.3 Contrasting approaches

We must now examine what is likely to happen in these key areas of inventory level, leadtime, and delivery performance as a result of implementing MRPII, and why it is likely. Before doing so, it is worthwhile considering what our expectation may be. This is something that we can approach from two different directions:

– Where are we coming from?
– What should we be aiming for?

Where are we coming from?

With this approach we will see benefits in terms of the change that takes place after implementation, for instance the change in inventory level or in delivery performance. What must be realized is that the greatest scope for improvement will be where the pre-implementation performance was poorest.

Where pre-implementation performance is low, it is likely that very basic business problems exist. A new system may not eliminate these problems, but merely computerize them. It may therefore be better to ask instead: Where are we going?

What should we be aiming for?

There are four possibilities:

– achieving specific business objectives
– becoming a class A user
– reaching world-class manufacturing standards
– setting a benchmark

ACHIEVING SPECIFIC OBJECTIVES

These could be defined in the company's business plan, and could include, for example, target levels of inventory and target levels of delivery performance. If these are achieved then no one has immediate cause for dissatisfaction. The trouble is that many business plans are developed within a four walls mentality. For the future security of the business it may instead be better to set sights on some external yardstick, something that will ensure the future competitiveness of the business.

BECOMING A CLASS A USER

For the sake of completeness, the Oliver Wight classification system is described in this chapter. It does set a yardstick by which MRPII installations may be judged. The problem is that it was specifically designed to promote the concept of the MRPII standard system, and therefore focuses much more heavily on the inputs to the system rather than the outputs, or results. Where the standard system is inappropriate, and therefore is rejected as a system option, the user by definition stands little or no chance of becoming certified as a class A user.

REACHING WORLD-CLASS MANUFACTURING STANDARDS

This has become something of a buzzword. Recent years have seen a flood of published material, much of which attempts to set definitive standards for inventory levels, delivery performance, and the like. Two problems are generally overlooked. A commitment to never-ending improvement by industry leaders will have moved the goalposts onwards and upwards before the date of publication of such material. And, just as important, specific standards are process dependent; even with a JIT kanban system, WIP levels *cannot* be less than the level of demand over the technological leadtime. No one has yet suggested that technological leadtimes should be equal, regardless of the process technology, and so it follows that there can be no universally applicable standard. What is relevant, however, is what is being attained by competitors within the same industry.

SETTING A BENCHMARK THAT BETTERS THE INDUSTRY LEADERS

This is the surest way of joining the leaders, and is the approach now taken by successful companies. Benchmarking was described in Chapter 5, and should be regarded as the state of the art tool in this respect.

29.4 Oliver Wight user classification

The classification devised in 1981 by Wight is based on four aspects of the MRPII installation:

- the technical capability of the software
- the data accuracy
- the *amount* of education carried out
- the results achieved

The checklist of 25 questions listed in Table 29.1, each inviting a straight yes or no answer, is used as the basis for this classification. Of these 25 checklist questions, Browne et al. (1988), intentionally or otherwise, highlighted five which together serve as a good indication of the effective use of MRPII, and they were:

- planning buckets of not more than one week;
- replanning on a weekly or more frequent basis;
- material shortages have been eliminated;
- delivery performance is in excess of 95 per cent;
- improvements have taken place in inventory levels, productivity and customer service.

Table 29.1   MRPII Checklist

Technical
1.   The time periods for MPS and MRP planning are weeks or smaller.
2.   MPS and MRP are run weekly or more frequently.
3.   The system includes firm planned orders and a pegging capability.
4.   The MPS is visibly managed, not automatic.
5.   The system includes CRP.
6.   The system includes a daily dispatch list.
7.   The system includes input output control.

Data integrity
8.   Inventory record accuracy is 95% or better.
9.   Bill of materials accuracy is 98% or better.
10.   Production routing accuracy is 95% or better.

Education
11.   Initial education covered at least 80% of all employees.
12.   There is an ongoing education programme.

Use of the system
13.   The shortage list has been eliminated.
14.   Vendor delivery performance is 95% or better.
15.   Vendor scheduling extends beyond the quoted delivery leadtime.
16.   Shop-floor delivery performance is 95% or better.
17.   MPS performance is 95% or better.
18.   There are regular, at least monthly, production planning meetings between the general manager and his staff, including manufacturing, production and inventory control, engineering, marketing, and finance.
19.   There is a written MPS policy that is adhered to.
20.   The system is used for scheduling as well as ordering.
21.   MRP is well understood by key people in manufacturing, marketing, engineering, finance, and top management.
22.   Management really uses MRP to manage.
23.   Engineering changes are effectively implemented.
24.   Simultaneous improvement has been achieved in at least two of the following three areas: inventory, productivity, customer service.
25.   The operating system is used for financial planning.

The answers to the checklist in the Wight system led to a user classification, which can briefly be summarized in Table 29.2. This classification system forms the basis for the present APICS certification, for which a charge is made.

Table 29.2 Oliver Wight classification

Class A user
> Uses MRPII to manage the business.
> MRPII is used in virtually all areas of the business.
> Achieves outstanding results.

Class B user
> Uses MRPII to schedule and load.
> MRPII is used mainly in manufacturing and materials planning.
> Achieves very good results.

Class C user
> Uses the system to order.
> MRPII works mainly in production/inventory control department.
> Achieves fair to good results.

Class D user
> MRPII works in data processing department but nowhere else.
> Viewed as another computer failure.
> Waste of time and money.

29.5 Leaders in the effective use of MRPII

An A. T. Kearney and Institute of Materials Management (IMM) survey (1991) noted a big gap in performance between leaders and laggers. The major characteristics of the leaders were these:

- They achieve the highest levels of service with the lowest levels of stock.
- They lead in terms of quality assurance along the entire supply chain.
- They have the most highly developed supplier relationships, based on supplier quality assurance (SQA) and the elimination of goods inwards inspection.
- They have eliminated waste in the production process, including wasted time.
- They use JIT techniques, mainly group technology and kanban systems, and have reduced WIP levels to a quarter of the industry average.
- They have weekly replanning.

These findings support a view that MRPII will yield best results where:

- basic business problems are addressed before implementation;
- pre-implementation improvements in plant layout and organization have taken place;
- there has been a substantial move towards a JIT manufacturing philosophy.

This yet again demonstrates the vital importance of seeing manufacturing strategy as the key to benefits, as opposed to believing they will accrue from the implementation of MRPII, the planning tool.

29.6 What benefits are attainable?

The Kearney/IMM survey highlighted the relative performance of leaders and laggers across the key results areas influenced by MRPII systems. About 25 per cent of respondents were identified as leaders, and their attributes in performance terms were as follows:

- Ex-stock customer service levels of 97–100 per cent, compared to under 90 per cent for the laggers and an average company performance in the range 91–95 per cent.
- Manufacturing delivery performance of 98 per cent or more, compared to under 80 per cent in the case of laggers and an average in the range 80–95 per cent.
- Total inventories of just over six weeks' stock, compared to about 20 weeks' stock in the case of the laggers.
- WIP inventory of under 1.5 days, compared to about 5 days in the case of the laggers.

The survey also noted that the leaders usually measured supplier delivery performance and had suppliers operating SQA systems, but that typically the laggers more commonly did not.

Effect of introducing MRPII

From data presented in the Kearney/IMM survey it can be seen that the average results of introducing MRPII systems is as follows:

- *Finished inventory*: virtually no change.
- *WIP inventory*: around 50 per cent reduction.
- *Purchased material inventories*: a reduction of about 10 per cent.
- *Ex-stock customer service*: an apparent deterioration of about 10 per cent.
- *Manufacturing delivery performance*: a deterioration of about 5 per cent.

What is at first sight surprising is the observed deterioration in delivery performance. It therefore forces us to look in some detail at the factors that influence the performance of MRPII systems.

29.7 Factors influencing MRPII performance

In global terms the key factors influencing the performance of the MRPII system will be the following:

- a system that works;
- accurate inventory records;
- reliable forecasts and master production schedules;
- accurate and up-to-date bills of materials.

Inventory levels

In Part One we noted that MRP is concerned with managing the flow of materials rather than managing the level of inventory. In Appendix C, the fairly minimal impact that MRP *per se* has on the level of inventory is noted. Its major influence is through data parameters communicated to the system. With MRP systems the actual level of inventory will mainly be determined by:

- the lot-sizing techniques in use (see Chapter 4);
- safety stock decision rules (see Chapter 6);
- the span of time buckets in a bucketed MRP system (see Chapter 8).

Survey results indicate that in general, the implementation of MRP will result in:

- inventory reductions at the level of dependent demand;
- little or no change at independent demand level.

But yet again it has to be repeated, as Appendix C shows, that the most elementary formula for the reduction of inventory is to reduce leadtimes, not to rely on the MRP planning tool.

Leadtimes

Manufacturing leadtimes with MRPII systems will depend on planning leadtimes, which are typically fixed, regardless of batch quantity. The planning leadtime as defined by Wallace (1980) includes:

- order preparation time
- queue time
- setup time
- run time
- move time
- inspect time
- put away time

With MRPII planned manufacturing leadtimes are just as likely to increase as they are to decrease. An increase in planned leadtime can be caused by the use of fixed planning leadtimes (see Chapter 11) or the incorporation of lengthy fixed queue times (see Chapter 17). As far as queue time is concerned it is worth remembering that in a typical pre-JIT environment only 5 per cent of activities are value-adding activities, and that non-value-adding activities have the following effect:

- They add to costs.
- They increase inventories.
- They increase the quality loss.

Again, it has to be stressed that reductions in leadtime primarily accrue from an appropriate manufacturing strategy, and not as a result of implementing a planning system. Some of the appropriate manufacturing strategies were outlined in Chapter 5.

Manufacturing delivery performance

Under MRPII systems manufacturing delivery performance will be influenced by three factors:

- supplier performance, in the case of buy items (see Chapter 10);
- works performance, in the case of make items;
- the balance between workload and capacity (see Chapter 17).

With MRPII, delivery performance is just as likely to worsen as it is to improve. A worsening in performance could be because:

- Actual leadtimes may be longer than planned leadtimes, especially where planned queue times have been either eliminated or reduced to a minimum.
- Scheduling takes no account of any finite capacity limitations. This may be especially true in a jobbing business.
- Scheduling takes no account of the actual material availability. This will be important where supplier delivery or quality performance, or upstream manufacturing performance, is unreliable.

It must be stressed that MRPII is only about *planning* the availability of materials and production capacity. A planning tool cannot make things happen, it can only provide accurate information to those who do make things happen. The management culture is critical to making things happen when they should, and how they should. A management strategy incorporating TQM is much more likely to ensure a high level of delivery performance than a planning tool.

Critical parameters

The overall performance of MRPII systems will depend very largely on how a number of critical parameters are specified, particularly planning leadtimes and queue times. This requires real knowledge of the manufacturing environment. Thinking of a number to satisfy the system is a step on the route to failure.

29.8 Conclusion

The parting message is very simple indeed.

1. A manufacturing planning system is no more than a planning tool. It is not itself a manufacturing strategy. The key to achieving real competitive benefits lies in the selection of an appropriate manufacturing strategy (see Chapter 5). The implementation of the manufacturing strategy should *precede* the implementation of a manufacturing planning system.
2. There is no universally applicable standard system. The connection between MRPII and the standard system should be consigned to history. MRPII is *de facto* a systems framework encompassing a variety of manufacturing planning methods. Selecting the generic variant that has the best fit with the manufacturing environment is critical to success. The allowable variants include those that support rate-based scheduling, at one extreme of the spectrum, and jobbing businesses requiring scheduling to finite capacity, at the other.
3. Decentralization of the MRPII system—DMRP—is increasingly likely to become the state of the art during the 1990s.

Appendix A
MRPII—an objective assessment of the standard system

The dilemma—how to treat MRPII?

The greatest problem facing authors of a work like this is just exactly how to treat MRPII (manufacturing resource planning) which, after all, is not just a manufacturing planning system, but the most widely installed manufacturing planning system. The problem is that it is prescriptive in its methodology, and its acolytes have promoted it as the standard system. In turn the standard system has been used as the basis for a majority of the proprietary software packages available at the start of the 1990s.

Almost every author on this subject of the last decade has therefore invented a new name, in order to avoid confusing his own master plan with MRPII, and each time a new acronym follows. We have had manufacturing control system (MCS), production management system (PMS)—far too easily confused with project management system—production and assembly control system (PACS), and so on.

Vollmann *et al.* (1992) succeeded in tackling the subject under the title of manufacturing control system (MCS) while mentioning MRPII only once in 844 pages, and ignoring it in the index; for all its faults MRPII deserves better than that, especially as the book was dedicated to the memory of Joseph Orlicky and Oliver Wight. Browne *et al.* (1988) at least elevate MRPII to the status of one of three competing manufacturing planning systems, the others being the JIT kanban systems and OPT (optimized production technology).

The simple answer to this problem is to adopt MRPII as the manufacturing planning system. This is what this book does, and the manufacturing planning system is referred to throughout as MRPII. But in the process MRPII is redefined. It becomes, not a heavily prescriptive standard system, but instead a generalized systems framework, both relevant and applicable, and without problems, to the vast majority of manufacturing environments.

Throughout the content of this book, MRPII equals the manufacturing planning system. Where necessary, the reader is alerted to inherent features or weaknesses in the standard system which may have adverse repercussions in specific production environments.

This particular treatment of MRPII is quite likely to cause outrage in many quarters; there are many who have vested interests in MRPII. It did after all lead to something of a commercial empire along the way, and the position of IBM on the subject of MRPII must also be put under the spotlight. This appendix is therefore concerned with defending this treatment of MRPII, and it is here, and only here, that outright criticism of the MRPII standard system and its promoters is voiced. What is needed is the debunking of the mythology of MRPII in order to reduce it to what is in fact valid, and this we will now do. Dr Barekat, the promoter of distributed MRP (DMRP) once coined the headline: 'MRPII is dead. Long live MRPII.' This is in many ways the agenda of this work also.

As MRPII is indelibly associated with the pioneering work of Oliver Wight, only the word of the master himself will be challenged—Wight (1984), and works of subsequent authors in the Oliver Wight Publications school will be disregarded.

Oliver Wight's justification for a standard system

This simple logic will make good sense to most manufacturing people:

- Different manufacturing situations need different control systems.
- Different control systems need different information systems.
- The production management system is the key to the competitive manufacturing operation. Its choice may therefore influence success or failure.

This is the underlying message conveyed by Bertrand *et al.* (1990). It implies a choice of systems method to fit the specific manufacturing environment.

This is in stark contrast to the message conveyed by Wight (1984): 'What's the alternative [to the MRPII standard system]? There is no other system that simulates reality in a manufacturing business.' It is a theme that is repeated at least five times, and its underlying rationale runs as follows:

- There is a universal manufacturing equation, because the logic inherent in manufacturing is universally applicable. The problems of manufacturing are common to all businesses, rather than unique to specific businesses.
- There is therefore a standard logic applicable to the process of planning and control in all manufacturing businesses.
- There must therefore be a standard planning and control system, rather than systems that are unique to specific companies. Wight reinforces this by asserting that the systems that actually work all look identical. This is quite simply not true.
- MRPII—the standard system—is the *only* system that simulates the real logic of the manufacturing equation.
- Therefore there is no alternative system to MRPII.

It is an extremely prescriptive message.

Was Wight really saying that Toyota got it all wrong? That simple comparison between the realism and pragmatism of Bertrand *et al.* (1990) and the preaching of Wight (1984) sums it all up. The standard system is prescriptive: there is no alternative. It is the dogma of an evangelist; in different contexts wars would have been fought over it—and won, or lost. It is the philosophy of the judge as opposed to the perceiver. In the management culture of the 1990s, prescriptive judgemental solutions are avoided at all costs; they are widely and correctly perceived not to work. But a framework based on good practice does work.

Another interpretation of Wight's logic

Let us therefore seek an alternative view. This quotation, also from Wight (1984), relates not to MRPII but to MRP:

> What are we going to make? What does it take to make it? What do we have? What do we need to get? That is exactly the logic of MRP. That's why MRP works. That's why the question, 'What are the other systems besides MRP?' is invalid. Any *formal* system that answers these questions *is* MRP.

If that is true of MRP then it must also be true of MRPII. *Any* formal system that addresses the same questions as MRPII *is* MRPII. The master's own logic may be used with impunity by many software suppliers who, because they had not followed the prescriptive logic of the standard system, do not brand their packages as MRPII. If their solution addresses the same questions as MRPII, then by Wight's own reasoning they *are* in fact MRPII.

Wight (1984) was extremely critical of what we generically refer to as project management systems. He advocated MRPII as the alternative to these and predicted that before long such systems would be completely replaced by MRPII. His prediction has not been fulfilled. In complex one-off engineering projects, people still use project management systems. They use them because they are a more appropriate tool for their production environment. The end objectives of a project management system and MRPII are one and the same. It is only the methodology that differs. It is a classic case in support of the basic premise of Bertrand *et al.* (1990). If you can accept that premise, project management systems are not only a valid technique, as countless thousands of users have proved to their benefit, but are a *better* technique in that environment than MRPII. Use Wight's logic, and you can redefine project management systems as MRPII if you so wish.

The same argument can be applied to the famous Toyota system. It too is MRPII, because it addresses the same objectives. Many American writers are critical of Japanese methods. JIT and the kanban system are frequently relegated to the status of *en passant*. There is a fairly extensive school of

American thought which says that per capita productivity is higher in the USA than in Japan, therefore we have nothing to learn from the Japanese. Their facts are correct. Per capita productivity *is* higher in the USA. Tables 2 and 3 in UK Manufacturing (IEE 1992) indicate that in 1990 US per capita productivity was almost 14 per cent higher than the Japanese (compared to 24 per cent higher in 1980). The main surge in productivity growth in Japan occurred in the first half of the 1980s; in the second half that growth was only 8% higher than in the USA. On that basis it would be well through the 21st century before Japanese productivity equalled that of the USA.

The trouble is that this is too often used as a justification for discarding what the Japanese have to teach us, and more alarmingly it is very often used as the justification for promoting MRPII as a superior alternative to a kanban system.

The classic myopic viewpoint is given superbly in Tompkins (1989). Tompkins contrasts the MRPII order-based master production scheduling technique with the Toyota rate-based method. He shows a conventional block diagram of the MRPII system, and he shows the equivalent block diagram of the Toyota system. The blocks are identical, with two exceptions. In place of MPS, the Toyota system has 'establish uniform plant load', and in place of MRP it has 'material replenishment cycle'. Tompkins then uses a very simple example to demonstrate how the two systems work. He uses the example of the milkman making home deliveries.

We leave a note each night telling the milkman how many pints of milk to deliver the next morning. It is normally one pint. It is an order-based system. When we go on holiday and there is no demand, or if the entire family descend upon us and we instead require three pints, the MRPII system copes with this change in demand as it was designed to do.

He then contrasts this with the Toyota rate-based system. In that case we do not leave an order for the milkman. We simply leave an empty bottle for each pint of milk we require. The empty milk bottle becomes instead the kanban. For weeks on end we leave one empty bottle each night and it gets replenished without problem the following morning. That is rate-based scheduling. When the family descend and we put out, not one empty bottle but three, then rate-based scheduling has been deviated from and the only system which can cope with the change in demand is MRPII.

It is a wonderful illustration of how illogical one can be in defence of one's chosen system, and it is quite typical. It ignores the many real-life variables, such as my family's arrival coinciding with my neighbour's departure on annual vacation. It ignores the possibility of short- or medium-term adjustments to the rate of production to cater for seasonal demand. It is typical of the arguments used to persuade readers that MRPII is better than the Toyota system. By Wight's own logic, as we have already shown, the Toyota system *is* MRPII, although Toyota may not consider that a compliment.

MRPII was conceived before the widespread adoption of Japanese methods in Western manufacturing. That is one of its crucifixes. It needed a *post facto* adaptation to cater for repetitive manufacturing. But probably of much greater significance is the fact that MRPII predated both Lotus 1–2–3 and pocket mathematical calculators. The advent of spreadsheets has provided most companies with a very much more flexible tool for higher-level planning systems than MRPII can offer, and in many cases even for demand forecasting. Provided computer systems are sufficiently open, data may very easily be transferred between spreadsheets and mainstream systems. The very essence of Wight's concept of closed loop MRP loses part of its rationale. If we use a spreadsheet for higher-level planning, say for everything above the level of master production scheduling, then we have deviated from the standard system but have gained immeasurably in terms of both flexibility and transparency. Yet again, by Wight's own logic, it *is* MRPII.

Transparency

Mention of transparency brings us to Wight's oft-repeated assertion. If the planner cannot answer the question: why did the computer tell me to do that this time?, then the systems logic is not transparent. The logic *must* be transparent if the planner is to use the computer, otherwise he will revert to using the *informal* as opposed to the *formal* system. The plant will once more be controlled by the shortage list and not by the schedule. In the 1960s and 1970s this was certainly a very valid point of view. Many over-sophisticated algorithms for scheduling to finite capacity were certainly being adopted, and many did not work. Wight therefore rejected scheduling to finite capacity because it lacks transparency. There are many simple algorithms in use today which a planner, by experience, can relate in terms of end result to what he would have himself achieved on his planning boards. Is it justifiable that they should be so rejected out of hand by the standard system? In Part Three of this book, we see situations in which a technique like this is essential to help address situations of high contention between capacity and workload.

Wight made the valid point that computer systems work best when they supply the information to help people make decisions. Many of the techniques Wight rejected are nonetheless capable of being subjected to a yes or no decision. If the result looks good to the planner, why not accept it? If it does not, then he can always fall back on MRPII. If state-of-the-art demand forecasting can use multiple forecasting techniques, what Wight called focus forecasting, and select the best fit, surely with the almost unlimited computer processing power we have today we ought not to be constrained by just *one* scheduling method. That is like telling the forecasters they may *only* use simple moving averages.

The same is true of part-period balancing, a lot-sizing technique which requires knowledge of basic arithmetic as opposed to advanced mathematics, but which in terms of processing logic is not as transparent as lot for lot, economic order quantity, or period order quantity. The truth of the matter is that part-period balancing is never out-performed by those other three techniques, very often performs up to 40 per cent better than them, and is only marginally lagging in performance terms compared to the more complex algorithms often described in textbooks. It takes only a few minutes to simulate part-period balancing on a spreadsheet. The proof of seeing the results in that way gives me at least as much confidence in the results as I have in multiplication tables learned from memory at school. But because of Wight's prejudice you will have to look long and hard before you find MRPII software offering part-period balancing as a lot-sizing option.

With the wisdom of hindsight, Wight's position on the subject of transparency seems firmly entrenched in the battle that raged during the late 1960s between the operations research analysts and the data processing systems engineers to gain the ascendancy as the lead body in manufacturing systems design. It was a battle the data processing people won, helped to a large extent by the apostles of MRPII; they spoke a language the users—the planners—understood, although they may not in the final analysis have had the best solutions. It all happened before partnership was the natural thing, and we are not exactly better off as a result.

The same is true of more complex mathematics. Today, where demand forecasting is relevant and applicable, forecasting techniques are based on some form of exponential smoothing. Wight (1984: 441) derided exponential smoothing as 'a rather pretentious name for a moving average'. For anyone with a mathematical calculator the calculation becomes almost as transparent as multiplication, for which we nowadays typically also use our calculators.

The real point of this expose is not to quibble with every statement made by the apostle of MRPII. It is simply to show just how many points there are on which his logic can be faulted. Each time we do this it undermines the credibility of his own bigger picture—the standard system, the one and only true way, and paves the way for the more reasoned approach of adopting only his framework, and then filling out the details to fit the specific manufacturing environment.

A branded product—for commercial gain

The definitive works on both MRP and MRPII were *post facto*. In the case of MRP the definitive work (Orlicky 1975) was published a decade or so after MRP systems had begun to become commonplace. Orlicky was an IBM systems engineer, and his work on MRP was written during sabbatical leave from IBM for that very purpose. Prior to that, MRP had been documented quite extensively, especially in the *IBM Systems Journal*, and Orlicky acknowledged these seminal prior works.

It is very different with MRPII. Wight was Manufacturing Industry Education Manager for IBM. It is extremely difficult today to pinpoint the origin of MRPII to a specific period in time. When and where did the standard system emerge? And how did it emerge? I do not know, because Wight did not give me backward signposting.

Systems very similar to MRPII were in existence in the late 1960s within IBM and elsewhere, but the earliest reference Wight gave us is from 1978. The fingerprints have all been removed. Take this in conjunction with the commercial vested interests which the Wight school went on subsequently to acquire in publication and education, and it poses this question: Was MRPII really an a priori solution to what Wight described as the manufacturing equation, or was it not instead a simple core concept—MRP as defined by Orlicky, and perhaps with the extensions into capacity requirements planning available as standard applications software with the IBM 360 series of computers in the late 1960s—subsequently dressed up to be promoted for commercial gain?

Whichever way we look at this the influence of IBM is all pervading, and challengeable. Both Orlicky and Wight were employees of IBM. Much of the complexity in both MRP and MRPII appears almost tailormade to fit the specific production environment of IBM in the latter part of the 1960s, so much so that it is legitimate to view IBM as the birthplace of MRPII. A quarter of a century later what is significant is that, of all the major suppliers of IT platforms, IBM stands virtually alone in as much as the approved or badged software for its mid-range series *all* conforms to the standard system. As Figure 27.1 indicates, this is in marked contrast to DEC and the many suppliers of UNIX platforms. It is almost as if IBM is still telling us there is no alternative. It would be fascinating today to hear IBM's justification for this.

Commercial vested interests have loomed large in the promotion of MRPII to the exclusion of other competing systems techniques. Oliver Wight left IBM to found a commercial empire involved in both publishing and education. APICS, who helped promote MRP in the 1970s, went on to act as the lead body for certification of MRPII users according to Wight's classification, and not only charge for this certification but also franchise this business across the globe. However much they believed in their mission, these became powerful vested interests. Where did IBM stand in relation to this? Perhaps one day it will tell us. There is at least strong circumstantial evidence to suggest that the combined preaching of the gospel of MRPII by its various allies from the 1980s onwards was primarily driven by commercial considerations. Not only that, MRPII's market share by that time was sufficiently strong to squeeze many competitive systems techniques out of the market altogether.

It would have been nice if we had instead been able to look back on **MRPII** and see clearly the strands of objective and unbiased research or a priori academic reasoning underpinning the logic of the standard system. Because none is signposted we can reasonably infer that none exists. That leads us to examine in still more depth what Wight's real stance was, at least at the outset. A number of things *are* clear:

- A model system existed at some point in time.
- It was a closed loop system.
- It became promoted as the standard system.

It is a classic example of Baconian logic, well trusted by English and American schools of thought: work back from the observed results to infer the theoretical basis for the model. Mainstream European thinking from the time of Thomas Aquinas onwards, based on a priori reasoning forwards from first principles to practice, may instead have led to a very different and non-prescriptive model.

A replacement for the shortage list

There are some recurring themes in Wight's works which are worthy of our attention. The first is his genuine concern for the users of the computer system; his was a world in which systems were focused on people, and not on the computer, and this was in stark contrast to the attitude of many of his contemporaries. To make the computer system understandable to the planners, the systems logic had to be transparent.

This ties in with the second recurring theme. In many pre-MRPII environments the formal system was disregarded by the users in favour of the informal system, typically driven by the shortage list. In many instances computerizing the formal system led to disaster because the formal system was not the system in use. The epitome of the informal system was the shortage list. It was the shortage list which in the finality drove production, and firefighting in this way accounted for a disproportionately great part of the time of production management.

The reason the informal system prevailed was because the formal system was not based on a *valid schedule*. The keystone of MRPII is a valid schedule, which is why MRPII is the sole example (in Wight's view) of a formal system which can be made to work.

In Wight (1984: 68) we find the most extraordinary statement: 'If forecasts were perfect, MRP wouldn't be needed'. The logic behind this statement reveals a great deal. In Wight's mind MRP was the alternative to the shortage list. The shortage list was the result of there not being a valid schedule. We are reminded many times just how fundamental scheduling is, and that the logic of master production scheduling is designed to create a valid schedule.

The biggest problem with a schedule is that inaccurate forecasting at independent demand level can impair the validity of the schedule, but the logic of MRPII overcomes this by being designed to cope with the problems of emerging demand. If everything were set in the tablets at the outset, and all demand was firm beyond the planning horizon, the inference of Wight's statement is that the logic of MRPII would be unnecessary.

It is difficult to avoid the conclusion that in Wight's mind MRPII was a replacement for the shortage list. We could extend his reasoning to say that if there is no *need* for forecasting then there is therefore no need for MRPII. Contrast this, if you will, with simple a priori reasoning which says that we still need a systems mechanism for calculating the constituent parts and material content of the finished product, for placing orders for these on suppliers, and for planning production capacity, and for loading, scheduling and releasing production orders. Is not all that needed whether forecasts are perfect or imperfect?

Master production scheduling—the Achilles' heel

In many ways master production scheduling is the Achilles' heel of MRPII. The concept of order-based master production scheduling is the keystone of the MRPII standard system, a true reflection of Wight's assertion that scheduling is fundamental. In a proper perspective that type of master production scheduling is appropriate only in production environments similar to that in which MRPII was itself conceived. Given a high degree of homogeneity of work content by product, together with a relative stability of demand and manufacturing leadtimes reduced to the minimum, rate-based scheduling is not only more appropriate but simpler and more transparent.

Tompkins (1989) disagrees; he asserts that Toyota could not operate rate-based scheduling if they offered as wide a range of customer options as US motor manufacturers do. Making items like stereo radios, electric sunroof, central locking, anti-lock braking systems, and power steering standard features reduces the number of variables in a Japanese car and supports rate-based scheduling. The inference is that this is wrong, but the marketing success of the Japanese manufacturers tells otherwise. Henry Ford would have been a natural convert to rate-based scheduling. The lesson is clear: the greater the degree of homogeneity of work and part content, the less need there is for the complexity of order-based master production scheduling.

At the other end of the spectrum, in a jobbing shop where there is little or no homogeneity of work content from one order to the next, master production scheduling of the MRPII type is almost a waste of time. The balance between workload and capacity can only be struck at the level of detailed operational workload in individual resource centres, and this is best achieved by a high degree of interaction between MRP and scheduling to finite capacity, at least on bottleneck resources.

Wight (1984) recognized that there would be divergences in the application of master production scheduling, but he qualified this by his assertion that such divergences between different companies' use of master production scheduling would be in terms of how they handled the schedule. By this he was referring to the options described in Chapter 16: whether the schedule is regarded as a production plan or as a set of planned order releases. He was adamant that such differences did not extend to the design of the master production scheduling logic. He was only partially correct. The major divergence is in fact whether or not the MRPII form of order-based master production scheduling is appropriate or not. Even Orlicky accepted, by inference, that it was not always so.

The cynical, but perhaps not unjustified view, is therefore to regard an embryonic MRPII indeed as a logically based alternative to the shortage list, and to view the subsequent add-ons as the necessary appendages for the creation of a branded product which was the key to the exploitation of a wide-open commercial opportunity.

Wight's view of the evolution of MRPII

It is these appendages that gave MRPII its brand identity. Wight himself described three steps in the evolution of the brand:

- *MRP*: material requirements planning, the original MRP, and the core of MRPII. This was defined *post facto* by Orlicky (1975).
- *Closed loop MRP*: what Wight defines as closed loop MRP is in reality what the vast majority of computer software packages today offer as MRPII.
- *MRPII*: in Wight's view it was both systems integration and management practice that transformed closed loop MRP into MRPII.

The most important aspect of systems integration was linking the financial systems and the operational systems. MRPII achieved this; it is a system that supports not only manufacturing, but also finance, marketing, engineering, purchasing and distribution. Wight observed that the technical differences between closed loop MRP and MRPII were minor, and that the major difference was the way in which management used the system. And that, of course, led conveniently into the Wight and APICS classification system and a commercial opportunity.

In defining the technical differences between closed loop MRP and MRPII, Wight cited three characteristics of MRPII:

- The operating and financial system are one and the same.
- It has a what if? capability.
- It is a whole company system.

Of these the what if? or simulation capability is the most significant. It is possible, albeit clumsy, to use almost any computer system as a simulation tool by feeding different sets of numbers or data to copies of the database files, and in Wight (1984) there are several allusions to using the core MRP system in this way as a simulation tool.

What marks out the state of the art, however, is when the software offers the planner an on-line interactive simulation facility at the level of rough-cut capacity planning. Given the advance in technology since Wight's time, this should be construed as being most in keeping with the *spirit* of Wight's thinking. It is an acid test which, if applied rigorously, would result in at best a mere handful of software packages fulfilling the essential technical difference that Wight used to define MRPII as distinct from closed loop MRP.

Systems integration has moved on since Wight's time. Today we accept the interfacing of manufacturing planning and financial planning data as a *sine qua non*, and in a wider context this degree of systems integration moved forwards independently of MRPII. Open systems concepts and techniques ensuring the transparency of data interchange have made it possible to integrate or cross-refer data, not just between mainstream systems but more importantly between mainstream systems and spreadsheets, in a way that was simply not possible when MRPII was conceived.

An overarching system?

In hindsight the inference that MRPII is the overarching system—the *company* system or the keystone of the company's game plan—is a concept that the general manager of the 1990s is quite likely to associate more as a bid from the company's manufacturing division for the position as lead body in the company. Despite the validity at the time for ensuring that the same numbers were used by manufacturing, marketing, finance, etc., there was undoubtedly an underlying hint in the promotion of MRPII of a struggle for power in the business.

The same thing has happened in more recent times as ISO 9000 has been adopted. Many quality systems aimed at fulfilling the requirements of ISO 9000 have strayed into procedures well beyond the specific requirements of the standard, often beginning with the business plan, and extending into the entire realm of personnel management. The justification offered by quality managers has typically been that this is necessary to attain TQM, despite the fact that the company objective was to attain ISO 9000 registration. It is an example of the quality function's bid for power in the 1990s, in much the same way as the application of MRPII represented the manufacturing function's bid for power in the 1980s.

The wise general manager always keeps specific functional systems within their proper bounds, and seeks independent overarching systems to attain integration of planning at a businesswide level. The emerging buzzword now is that of ERP—enterprise resource planning—which seeks to offer such an overarching methodology. It is being promoted as the step beyond MRPII. It remains to be seen whether or not a standard system emerges.

MRPII—a non-prescriptive framework

MRPII is therefore a valid systems framework outlined by Wight (1984) for a manufacturing planning system, within which the detailed systems methodology is adapted to specific manufacturing environments as suggested by Bertrand et al. (1990). This leads to the generic classification of commercially available software packages suggested in Part Three, in which the prime distinction is between:

- packages that fully conform to the MRPII standard system;
- those that conform in part, but yet nonetheless claim to be MRPII;
- non-standard systems, which ensure integration of the manufacturing planning function, but which deviate from the MRPII standard system, although fulfilling identical objectives.

All of these have a proper place in different manufacturing environments. All of these are MRPII, and the logic of Wight (1984) has been produced to validate this assertion. This book therefore unreservedly uses MRPII as the framework for defining an integrated but *non-prescriptive* manufacturing planning system.

MRPII, the standard system, all too often fails to result in the benefits anticipated. This is explored in more detail in Part Four. Of the many causes of this failure, the one that has seldom been satisfactorily explored is the inappropriateness of the MRPII standard system to certain manufacturing environments. The role of management consultants has to be challenged in this respect. There is a famous adage that no one ever got fired for buying IBM. Management consultants are not unaware of this. The problem it poses is that of IBM's apparent bias in favour of the standard system, which may not be the most appropriate systems method for many environments. The result is a polarization of viewpoints, with at least one reviewer of this book claiming that his consultancy practice had not recommended MRPII in years. The redefinition of MRPII will heal this polarization.

MRPII—a tool, not a strategy

Finally, in the context of benefits, it has always to be borne in mind that MRPII is purely a systems technique. It is *not* a manufacturing strategy, and this is amplified in Chapters 5 and 29. It is from the application of better manufacturing strategy that the real benefits accrue, not from the systems methods. Wight (1984), in describing DRP, noted that 'a student who fell asleep in a distribution inventory management class in the 1950s and woke up in the 1980s would hear very little that was new'. What Wight failed to foresee was that a student who fell asleep in a manufacturing strategy class in the 1970s and woke up in the 1990s would quite simply be several generations out of date.

In a very real sense MRPII simply computerized the complex production environment of the 1960s, and was already strategically past its sell-by date before it became so widely promoted in the 1980s. As an instance of this, we can examine Wight's views on WIP. Work-in-process inventory, like any inventory, is a function of demand over leadtime (see Appendix C), and is strategically addressed by JIT methods. But Wight sees WIP in a very different light:

- The volume of WIP inventory is determined by the balance between input and output. If you issue materials to the shop floor at a faster rate than they can be consumed the level of inventory rises. Wight saw MRP as the means of avoiding this, and paraphrased Parkinson's first law by saying that if an MRP system is not being used, then WIP expands to fill the space available on the factory floor.
- The function of WIP is to avoid stoppage of production when the rate of input fluctuates. A major cause of input fluctuations is of course material shortages.
- The major variable in the level of WIP inventory is how large a queue in process safety stock is needed. In other words, how many works orders are needed in the work queue to ensure that throughput is maintained. Wight advocated a highly empirical means of determining just how large the work queue should be: sample the actual queues at major work centres, and the difference between the high and the low is the size of queue needed to avoid the work centre running out of work!

The effect of this on manufacturing leadtime and customer service is not addressed. It illustrates how signally Wight and MRPII failed to address manufacturing strategy.

It is all the more galling when you take heed of the many important words of wisdom that Wight had to offer, especially in the context of understanding people and what must be done to make systems work. He understood the value of teamwork better than the rest of his generation. He understood what drove ordinary people on the shop floor, in particular the comfort they derive from seeing a physical queue or backlog of work, and the insecurity they feel when improved control over manufacturing reduces or eliminates these queues, a fact of life that every production manager has faced at one time or another in the drive to improve shop-floor performance.

He shared some beliefs with the JIT philosophy. He had foresight of supply chain partnerships and recommended using forward delivery schedules as a means of overcoming supplier leadtime problems. Like Orlicky, his philosophy centred on inventory flow as opposed to inventory management. Their shared view was that MRP was the planning tool that made the concept of inventory level redundant, and forced planners to think instead in terms of inventory flow.

But it was the blindness of Wight and his colleagues to the advances in manufacturing strategy that occurred in Japan in his own lifetime, and the belief that a planning system alone would unlock the key to benefits, that remains the essential crucifix of MRPII, and the most important reason for discarding the over-prescriptive MRPII standard system. While the Oliver Wight school is reported to have adopted a more enlightened stance towards manufacturing strategy by the start of the 1990s, too much of the dogma remains and is still enshrined in both the published word and in too many computer software packages, especially on the IBM mid-range platform.

That is why this book was written. As Dr Barekat said, 'MRPII is dead! Long live MRPII!'

Appendix B
Exercises and answers

Exercise B1 Bill of materials structure

1. Birdhomes Ltd manufacture luxury accommodation for garden birds.
2. They make both wall mounting and freestanding models.
3. Both models comprise a common basic housing unit, which consists of a house base, three sides, a front, and a roof. These components are all externally purchased, and are sourced in a standard colour. The house base is a moulding which incorporates a twist clip fitting for a stalk.
4. On both models there is a choice of red roof or green roof. The painting of the roof is done in plant.
5. Freestanding models also comprise a stalk and a ground base. There is a choice between a short stalk (1000 mm) and a long stalk (2000 mm). The ground base is purchased and is common to both stalk heights. The stalk is cut in-plant from tube which is purchased in standard four-metre lengths.
6. Fixing of the roof to the sides and front is by clip-on assembly. The sides, front and house base are glued together using a bird-friendly glue which has an extensive curing time.
7. On freestanding units, one end of the stalk is machined in plant to give a twist clip fit to the base of the housing unit. The other end is welded to the ground base to comply with RSPB safety regulations.

Construct Birdhomes' parts master file and bills of materials, assuming a manufacturing strategy designed to maximize commonality of subassembly operations.

A suggested parts master file is given in Table B1.1 and the matching bills of material is indicated in Table B1.2. For comments on these, please return to Chapter 7.

Answers to exercise B1

Table B1.1   Birdhomes' parts master file

Part no.	Description	Level	UM	Make/Buy
A123	Wall mounting, red roof	2	Each	Make
A124	Wall mounting, green roof	2	Each	Make
A125	Freestanding, red roof, short stalk	1	Each	Make
A126	Freestanding, red roof, long stalk	1	Each	Make
A127	Freestanding, green roof, short stalk	1	Each	Make
A128	Freestanding, green roof, long stalk	1	Each	Make
B234	House subassembly	3	Each	Make
B235	Red roof	3	Each	Make
B236	Green roof	3	Each	Make
B237	Short stalk subassembly	2	Each	Make
B238	Long stalk subassembly	2	Each	Make
C345	Roof	4	Each	Buy
C346	Side	4	Each	Buy
C347	Front	4	Each	Buy
C348	House base	4	Each	Buy
C349	Short stalk	3	Each	Make
C350	Long stalk	3	Each	Make
C351	Ground base	3	Each	Buy
C352	Tube	4	Each	Buy

Table B1.2   Birdhomes' bills of materials

Parent part no.	Child part no.	Quantity per unit of parent
A123	B234	1
A123	B235	1
A124	B234	1
A124	B236	1
A125	A123	1
A125	B237	1
A126	A123	1
A126	B238	1
A127	A124	1
A127	B237	1
A128	A124	1
A128	B238	1
B234	C346	3
B234	C347	1
B234	C348	1
B235	C345	1
B236	C345	1
B237	C349	1
B238	C351	1
B238	C350	1
B238	C351	1
C349	C352	0.25
C350	C352	0.50

Exercise B2 MRP analysis

Table B2.1 shows Birdhomes' master production schedule from current week plus 14 to current week plus 18. Table B2.2 shows the current stock and on-order position of part numbers on Birdhomes' inventory master file. For the part numbers not specified in Table B2.2 it should be assumed that stock and scheduled receipts are both zero.

Prepare a full MRP analysis for all parts on the master file. In planning order releases, assume that the order will be generated 'lot for lot', i.e. one week's net requirements equals one order release.

A summary of Birdhomes' planned order releases is given in Table B2.3, and the MRP analyses for each of Birdhomes' part numbers is given in Table B2.4.

Table B2.1   Birdhomes' master production schedule

Part no.	13	14	15	Week no. 16	17	18	19
A123	0	22	0	46	0	18	0
A124	0	0	37	5	0	0	0
A125	0	28	20	0	44	0	0
A126	0	0	0	60	0	0	0
A127	0	0	36	0	0	12	0
A128	0	54	0	26	48	26	0

Table B2.2   Birdhomes' inventory and on-order position

Part no.	Actual inventory	Allocated inventory	Scheduled receipts	Week due
A123	40	0	0	
B234	0	0	100	4
C345	37	0	0	
C346	350	300	196	6
C347	175	100	82	6
C348	145	100	82	6
C349	20	0	0	

Answers to exercise B2

Table B2.3   Birdhomes' planned order releases

Part no.	1	2	3	4	5	6	7	8	9	10	11	12	13	14	15	16	17	18	19	20
A125	0	0	0	0	0	0	0	0	0	0	0	0	28	20	0	44	0	0	0	0
A126	0	0	0	0	0	0	0	0	0	0	0	0	0	0	60	0	0	0	0	0
A127	0	0	0	0	0	0	0	0	0	0	0	0	0	36	0	0	12	0	0	0
A128	0	0	0	0	0	0	0	0	0	0	0	0	54	0	26	48	26	0	0	0
A123	0	0	0	0	0	0	0	0	0	0	0	0	0	30	60	90	0	18	0	0	0
A124	0	0	0	0	0	0	0	0	0	0	0	54	36	63	53	38	0	0	0	0
B237	0	0	0	0	0	0	0	0	28	56	0	44	12	0	0	0	0	0	0	0
B238	0	0	0	0	0	0	0	0	54	0	86	48	26	0	0	0	0	0	0	0
B234	0	0	0	0	0	0	20	123	143	38	18	0	0	0	0	0	0	0	0	0
B235	0	0	0	0	0	0	0	0	0	30	60	90	0	18	0	0	0	0	0	0
B236	0	0	0	0	0	0	0	0	54	36	63	53	38	0	0	0	0	0	0	0
C349	0	0	0	0	0	0	28	56	0	44	12	0	0	0	0	0	0	0	0	0
C350	0	0	0	0	0	0	54	0	86	48	26	0	0	0	0	0	0	0	0	0
C351	0	0	0	0	0	82	56	86	92	38	0	0	0	0	0	0	0	0	0	0
C345	0	0	0	17	66	123	143	38	18	0	0	0	0	0	0	0	0	0	0	0
C346	0	0	183	429	114	54	0	0	0	0	0	0	0	0	0	0	0	0	0	0
C347	0	0	0	129	38	18	0	0	0	0	0	0	0	0	0	0	0	0	0	0
C348	0	0	16	143	38	18	0	0	0	0	0	0	0	0	0	0	0	0	0	0
C352	0	0	0	0	14	14	43	35	16	0	0	0	0	0	0	0	0	0	0	0

Table B2.4 Birdhomes' MRP analyses

										Week no.									
	0	1	2	3	4	5	6	7	8	9	10	11	12	13	14	15	16	17	18
Part no. A123																			
Planning leadtime 1																			
Gross requirements		0	0	0	0	0	0	0	0	0	0	0	0	28	42	60	90	0	18
Actual inventory	40																		
Allocated inventory	0	0	0	0	0	0	0	0	0	0	0	0	0	0	0	0	0	0	0
Scheduled receipts	0	0	0	0	0	0	0	0	0	0	0	0	0	0	0	0	0	0	0
Projected inventory	40	40	40	40	40	40	40	40	40	40	40	40	40	12	0	0	0	0	0
Net requirements		0	0	0	0	0	0	0	0	0	0	0	0	0	30	60	90	0	18
Planned order receipts		0	0	0	0	0	0	0	0	0	0	0	0	0	30	60	90	0	18
Planned order releases		0	0	0	0	0	0	0	0	0	0	0	0	30	60	90	0	18	0
Part no. A124																			
Planning leadtime 1																			
Gross requirements		0	0	0	0	0	0	0	0	0	0	0	0	54	36	63	53	38	0
Actual inventory	0																		
Allocated inventory	0	0	0	0	0	0	0	0	0	0	0	0	0	0	0	0	0	0	0
Scheduled receipts	0	0	0	0	0	0	0	0	0	0	0	0	0	0	0	0	0	0	0
Projected inventory	0	0	0	0	0	0	0	0	0	0	0	0	0	0	0	0	0	0	0
Net requirements		0	0	0	0	0	0	0	0	0	0	0	0	54	36	63	53	38	0
Planned order receipts		0	0	0	0	0	0	0	0	0	0	0	0	54	36	63	53	38	0
Planned order releases		0	0	0	0	0	0	0	0	0	0	0	54	36	63	53	38	0	0

(continued)

Table B2.4 *Continued*

										Week no.									
	0	1	2	3	4	5	6	7	8	9	10	11	12	13	14	15	16	17	18
Part no. A125																			
Planning leadtime 1																			
Gross requirements		0	0	0	0	0	0	0	0	0	0	0	0	0	28	20	0	44	0
Actual inventory	0																		
Allocated inventory	0	0	0	0	0	0	0	0	0	0	0	0	0	0	0	0	0	0	0
Scheduled receipts		0	0	0	0	0	0	0	0	0	0	0	0	0	0	0	0	0	0
Projected inventory	0	0	0	0	0	0	0	0	0	0	0	0	0	0	0	0	0	0	0
Net requirements		0	0	0	0	0	0	0	0	0	0	0	0	0	28	20	0	44	0
Planned order receipts		0	0	0	0	0	0	0	0	0	0	0	0	0	28	20	0	44	0
Planned order releases		0	0	0	0	0	0	0	0	0	0	0	0	28	20	0	44	0	0
Part no. A126																			
Planning leadtime 1																			
Gross requirements		0	0	0	0	0	0	0	0	0	0	0	0	0	0	0	60	0	0
Actual inventory	0																		
Allocated inventory	0	0	0	0	0	0	0	0	0	0	0	0	0	0	0	0	0	0	0
Scheduled receipts		0	0	0	0	0	0	0	0	0	0	0	0	0	0	0	0	0	0
Projected inventory	0	0	0	0	0	0	0	0	0	0	0	0	0	0	0	0	0	0	0
Net requirements		0	0	0	0	0	0	0	0	0	0	0	0	0	0	0	60	0	0
Planned order receipts		0	0	0	0	0	0	0	0	0	0	0	0	0	0	0	60	0	0
Planned order releases		0	0	0	0	0	0	0	0	0	0	0	0	0	0	60	0	0	0
Part no. A127																			
Planning leadtime 1																			
Gross requirements		0	0	0	0	0	0	0	0	0	0	0	0	0	0	36	0	0	12
Actual inventory	0																		

(continued)	OH	1	2	3	4	5	6	7	8	9	10	11	12	13
Allocated inventory	0	0	0	0	0	0	0	0	0	0	0	0	0	0
Scheduled receipts		0	0	0	0	0	0	0	0	0	0	0	0	0
Projected inventory	0	0	0	0	0	0	0	0	0	0	0	0	0	0
Net requirements		0	0	0	0	0	0	0	0	0	36	0	0	12
Planned order receipts		0	0	0	0	0	0	0	0	0	36	0	0	12
Planned order releases		0	0	0	0	0	0	0	0	36	0	0	12	0

Part no.   A128
Planning leadtime   1

	OH	1	2	3	4	5	6	7	8	9	10	11	12	13
Gross requirements		0	0	0	0	0	0	0	0	0	0	26	48	26
Actual inventory	0	0	0	0	0	0	0	0	0	0	0	0	0	0
Allocated inventory	0	0	0	0	0	0	0	0	0	0	0	0	0	0
Scheduled receipts		0	0	0	0	0	0	0	0	0	0	0	0	0
Projected inventory	0	0	0	0	0	0	0	0	0	0	0	0	0	0
Net requirements		0	0	0	0	0	0	0	0	0	0	26	48	26
Planned order receipts		0	0	0	0	0	0	0	0	0	54	54	48	26
Planned order releases		0	0	0	0	0	0	0	0	54	54	0	26	0

Part no.   B234
Planning leadtime   6

	OH	1	2	3	4	5	6	7	8	9	10	11	12	13
Gross requirements		0	0	0	0	0	0	0	0	54	66	123	143	18
Actual inventory	0	0	0	0	0	0	0	0	0	0	0	0	0	0
Allocated inventory	0	0	0	0	0	0	0	0	0	0	0	0	0	0
Scheduled receipts	0	0	100	100	0	0	0	0	0	0	0	0	0	0
Projected inventory	0	0	100	100	100	100	46	0	0	0	0	0	0	0
Net requirements		0	0	0	0	0	0	20	20	123	143	38	18	0
Planned order receipts		0	0	0	0	0	0	20	20	123	143	38	18	0
Planned order releases		0	0	0	0	0	0	20	20	123	143	38	18	0

(continued)

Table B2.4 *Continued*

									Week no.										
	0	1	2	3	4	5	6	7	8	9	10	11	12	13	14	15	16	17	18
Part no. B235																			
Planning leadtime 3																			
Gross requirements		0	0	0	0	0	0	0	0	0	0	0	0	30	60	90	0	18	0
Actual inventory	0																		
Allocated inventory	0	0	0	0	0	0	0	0	0	0	0	0	0	0	0	0	0	0	0
Scheduled receipts	0	0	0	0	0	0	0	0	0	0	0	0	0	0	0	0	0	0	0
Projected inventory	0	0	0	0	0	0	0	0	0	0	0	0	0	0	0	0	0	0	0
Net requirements		0	0	0	0	0	0	0	0	0	0	0	0	30	60	90	0	18	0
Planned order receipts		0	0	0	0	0	0	0	0	0	0	0	0	30	60	90	0	18	0
Planned order releases		0	0	0	0	0	0	0	0	0	0	30	60	90	0	18	0	0	0	0
Part no. B236																			
Planning leadtime 3																			
Gross requirements		0	0	0	0	0	0	0	0	0	0	0	54	36	63	53	38	0	0
Actual inventory	0																		
Allocated inventory	0	0	0	0	0	0	0	0	0	0	0	0	0	0	0	0	0	0	0
Scheduled receipts	0	0	0	0	0	0	0	0	0	0	0	0	0	0	0	0	0	0	0
Projected inventory	0	0	0	0	0	0	0	0	0	0	0	0	0	0	0	0	0	0	0
Net requirements		0	0	0	0	0	0	0	0	0	0	0	54	36	63	53	38	0	0
Planned order receipts		0	0	0	0	0	0	0	0	0	0	0	54	36	63	53	38	0	0
Planned order releases		0	0	0	0	0	0	0	0	54	36	63	53	38	0	0	0	0	0	0
Part no. B237																			
Planning leadtime 4																			
Gross requirements		0	0	0	0	0	0	0	0	0	0	0	0	28	56	0	44	12	0
Actual inventory	0																		

Allocated inventory	0	0	0	0	0	0	0	0	0	0	0	0	0	0	0	0	0	0	0
Scheduled receipts	0	0	0	0	0	0	0	0	0	0	0	0	0	0	0	0	0	0	0
Projected inventory	0	0	0	0	0	0	0	0	0	0	0	0	0	0	0	0	0	0	0
Net requirements		0	0	0	0	0	0	0	0	0	0	0	0	28	56	0	44	12	0
Planned order receipts		0	0	0	0	0	0	0	0	0	0	0	0	28	56	0	44	12	0
Planned order releases		0	0	0	0	0	0	0	0	28	56	0	44	12	0	0	0	0	0
Part no. B238																			
Planning leadtime 4																			
Gross requirements		0	0	0	0	0	0	0	0	0	0	0	0	54	0	86	48	26	0
Actual inventory	0																		
Allocated inventory	0	0	0	0	0	0	0	0	0	0	0	0	0	0	0	0	0	0	0
Scheduled receipts	0	0	0	0	0	0	0	0	0	0	0	0	0	0	0	0	0	0	0
Projected inventory	0	0	0	0	0	0	0	0	0	0	0	0	0	0	0	0	0	0	0
Net requirements		0	0	0	0	0	0	0	0	0	0	0	0	54	0	86	48	26	0
Planned order receipts		0	0	0	0	0	0	0	0	0	0	0	0	54	0	86	48	26	0
Planned order releases		0	0	0	0	0	0	0	0	54	0	86	48	26	0	0	0	0	0
Part no. C345																			
Planning leadtime 5																			
Gross requirements		0	0	0	0	0	0	0	0	54	66	123	143	38	18	0	0	0	0
Actual inventory	37																		
Allocated inventory	0	0	0	0	0	0	0	0	0	0	0	0	0	0	0	0	0	0	0
Scheduled receipts	0	0	0	0	0	0	0	0	0	0	0	0	0	0	0	0	0	0	0
Projected inventory	37	37	37	37	37	37	37	37	37	0	0	0	0	0	0	0	0	0	0
Net requirements		0	0	0	0	0	0	0	0	17	66	123	143	38	18	0	0	0	0
Planned order receipts		0	0	0	0	0	0	0	0	17	66	123	143	38	18	0	0	0	0
Planned order releases		0	0	0	17	66	123	143	38	18	0	0	0	0	0	0	0	0	0

(continued)

Table B2.4 *Continued*

									Week no.										
	0	1	2	3	4	5	6	7	8	9	10	11	12	13	14	15	16	17	18
Part no. C346																			
Planning leadtime 5																			
Gross requirements		0	0	0	0	0	0	60	369	429	114	54	0	0	0	0	0	0	0
Actual inventory	350																		
Allocated inventory	300																		
Scheduled receipts	0	0	0	0	0	0	196	0	0	0	0	0	0	0	0	0	0	0	0
Projected inventory	50	50	50	50	50	50	246	186	0	0	0	0	0	0	0	0	0	0	0
Net requirements		0	0	0	0	0	0	0	183	429	114	54	0	0	0	0	0	0	0
Planned order receipts		0	0	0	0	0	0	0	183	429	114	54	0	0	0	0	0	0	0
Planned order releases		0	0	183	429	114	54	0	0	0	0	0	0	0	0	0	0	0	0
Part no. C347																			
Planning leadtime 5																			
Gross requirements		0	0	0	0	0	0	20	123	143	38	18	0	0	0	0	0	0	0
Actual inventory	175																		
Allocated inventory	100																		
Scheduled receipts	0	0	0	0	0	0	82	0	0	0	0	0	0	0	0	0	0	0	0
Projected inventory	75	75	75	75	75	75	157	137	14	0	0	0	0	0	0	0	0	0	0
Net requirements		0	0	0	0	0	0	0	0	129	38	18	0	0	0	0	0	0	0
Planned order receipts		0	0	0	0	0	0	0	0	129	38	18	0	0	0	0	0	0	0
Planned order releases		0	0	0	129	38	18	0	0	0	0	0	0	0	0	0	0	0	0
Part no. C348																			
Planning leadtime 5																			
Gross requirements		0	0	0	0	0	0	20	123	143	38	18	0	0	0	0	0	0	0
Actual inventory	145																		

	1	2	3	4	5	6	7	8	9	10	11	12	13	14	15	16
Allocated inventory	100	0	0	0	0	0	0	0	0	0	0	0	0	0	0	0
Scheduled receipts	0	0	0	0	0	0	82	0	0	0	0	0	0	0	0	0
Projected inventory	45	45	45	45	45	107	127	0	0	0	0	0	0	0	0	0
Net requirements	0	0	0	0	16	0	0	143	16	38	18	0	0	0	0	0
Planned order receipts	0	0	0	0	16	0	0	143	16	38	18	0	0	0	0	0
Planned order releases	0	0	16	0	0	143	16	38	18	0	0	0	0	0	0	0

Part no. C349
Planning leadtime 2

	1	2	3	4	5	6	7	8	9	10	11	12	13	14	15	16
Gross requirements	0	0	0	0	0	0	0	0	28	56	0	44	12	0	0	0
Actual inventory	0															
Allocated inventory	0	0	0	0	0	0	0	0	0	0	0	0	0	0	0	0
Scheduled receipts	0	0	0	0	0	0	0	0	0	0	0	0	0	0	0	0
Projected inventory	0	0	0	0	0	0	0	0	0	0	0	0	0	0	0	0
Net requirements	0	0	0	0	0	0	0	0	28	56	0	44	12	0	0	0
Planned order receipts	0	0	0	0	0	0	0	0	28	56	0	44	12	0	0	0
Planned order releases	0	0	0	0	0	0	28	56	0	44	12	0	0	0	0	0

Part no. C350
Planning leadtime 2

	1	2	3	4	5	6	7	8	9	10	11	12	13	14	15	16
Gross requirements	0	0	0	0	0	0	0	0	54	86	0	48	26	0	0	0
Actual inventory	0															
Allocated inventory	0	0	0	0	0	0	0	0	0	0	0	0	0	0	0	0
Scheduled receipts	0	0	0	0	0	0	0	0	0	0	0	0	0	0	0	0
Projected inventory	0	0	0	0	0	0	0	0	0	0	0	0	0	0	0	0
Net requirements	0	0	0	0	0	0	0	0	54	86	0	48	26	0	0	0
Planned order receipts	0	0	0	0	0	0	0	0	54	86	0	48	26	0	0	0
Planned order releases	0	0	0	0	0	0	54	86	0	48	26	0	0	0	0	0

(continued)

Table B2.4 Continued

<table>
<tr><td></td><td colspan="19" align="center">Week no.</td></tr>
<tr><td></td><td>0</td><td>1</td><td>2</td><td>3</td><td>4</td><td>5</td><td>6</td><td>7</td><td>8</td><td>9</td><td>10</td><td>11</td><td>12</td><td>13</td><td>14</td><td>15</td><td>16</td><td>17</td><td>18</td></tr>
<tr><td colspan="20">Part no. C351</td></tr>
<tr><td colspan="20">Planning leadtime 3</td></tr>
<tr><td>Gross requirements</td><td></td><td>0</td><td>0</td><td>0</td><td>0</td><td>0</td><td>0</td><td>0</td><td>0</td><td>82</td><td>56</td><td>86</td><td>92</td><td>38</td><td>0</td><td>0</td><td>0</td><td>0</td><td>0</td></tr>
<tr><td>Actual inventory</td><td>0</td><td></td><td></td><td></td><td></td><td></td><td></td><td></td><td></td><td></td><td></td><td></td><td></td><td></td><td></td><td></td><td></td><td></td><td></td></tr>
<tr><td>Allocated inventory</td><td>0</td><td>0</td><td>0</td><td>0</td><td>0</td><td>0</td><td>0</td><td>0</td><td>0</td><td>0</td><td>0</td><td>0</td><td>0</td><td>0</td><td>0</td><td>0</td><td>0</td><td>0</td><td>0</td></tr>
<tr><td>Scheduled receipts</td><td>0</td><td>0</td><td>0</td><td>0</td><td>0</td><td>0</td><td>0</td><td>0</td><td>0</td><td>0</td><td>0</td><td>0</td><td>0</td><td>0</td><td>0</td><td>0</td><td>0</td><td>0</td><td>0</td></tr>
<tr><td>Projected inventory</td><td>0</td><td>0</td><td>0</td><td>0</td><td>0</td><td>0</td><td>0</td><td>0</td><td>0</td><td>0</td><td>0</td><td>0</td><td>0</td><td>0</td><td>0</td><td>0</td><td>0</td><td>0</td><td>0</td></tr>
<tr><td>Net requirements</td><td></td><td></td><td></td><td></td><td></td><td></td><td></td><td></td><td></td><td>82</td><td>56</td><td>86</td><td>92</td><td>38</td><td></td><td></td><td></td><td></td><td></td></tr>
<tr><td>Planned order receipts</td><td></td><td>0</td><td>0</td><td>0</td><td>0</td><td>0</td><td>0</td><td>0</td><td>0</td><td>82</td><td>56</td><td>86</td><td>92</td><td>38</td><td>0</td><td>0</td><td>0</td><td>0</td><td>0</td></tr>
<tr><td>Planned order releases</td><td></td><td>0</td><td>0</td><td>0</td><td>0</td><td>0</td><td>82</td><td>56</td><td>86</td><td>92</td><td>38</td><td>0</td><td>0</td><td>0</td><td>0</td><td>0</td><td>0</td><td>0</td><td>0</td></tr>
<tr><td colspan="20">Part no. C352</td></tr>
<tr><td colspan="20">Planning leadtime 2</td></tr>
<tr><td>Gross requirements</td><td></td><td>0</td><td>0</td><td>0</td><td>0</td><td>0</td><td>0</td><td>34</td><td>14</td><td>43</td><td>35</td><td>16</td><td>0</td><td>0</td><td>0</td><td>0</td><td>0</td><td>0</td><td>0</td></tr>
<tr><td>Actual inventory</td><td>20</td><td></td><td></td><td></td><td></td><td></td><td></td><td></td><td></td><td></td><td></td><td></td><td></td><td></td><td></td><td></td><td></td><td></td><td></td></tr>
<tr><td>Allocated inventory</td><td>0</td><td>0</td><td>0</td><td>0</td><td>0</td><td>0</td><td>0</td><td>0</td><td>0</td><td>0</td><td>0</td><td>0</td><td>0</td><td>0</td><td>0</td><td>0</td><td>0</td><td>0</td><td>0</td></tr>
<tr><td>Scheduled receipts</td><td>0</td><td>0</td><td>0</td><td>0</td><td>0</td><td>0</td><td>0</td><td>0</td><td>0</td><td>0</td><td>0</td><td>0</td><td>0</td><td>0</td><td>0</td><td>0</td><td>0</td><td>0</td><td>0</td></tr>
<tr><td>Projected inventory</td><td>20</td><td>20</td><td>20</td><td>20</td><td>20</td><td>20</td><td>20</td><td>0</td><td>0</td><td>0</td><td>0</td><td>0</td><td>0</td><td>0</td><td>0</td><td>0</td><td>0</td><td>0</td><td>0</td></tr>
<tr><td>Net requirements</td><td></td><td></td><td></td><td></td><td></td><td></td><td></td><td>14</td><td>14</td><td>43</td><td>35</td><td>16</td><td></td><td></td><td></td><td></td><td></td><td></td><td></td></tr>
<tr><td>Planned order receipts</td><td></td><td>0</td><td>0</td><td>0</td><td>0</td><td>0</td><td>0</td><td>14</td><td>14</td><td>43</td><td>35</td><td>16</td><td>0</td><td>0</td><td>0</td><td>0</td><td>0</td><td>0</td><td>0</td></tr>
<tr><td>Planned order releases</td><td></td><td>0</td><td>0</td><td>0</td><td>0</td><td>14</td><td>14</td><td>43</td><td>35</td><td>16</td><td>0</td><td>0</td><td>0</td><td>0</td><td>0</td><td>0</td><td>0</td><td>0</td><td>0</td></tr>
</table>

Exercise B3 MPS analysis

In the case of Birdhomes' part number A123, the current status relating to inventory and actual customer orders is given in Table B3.1. Also given in Table B3.1 is the forecast demand for part number A123, and the firm planned orders confirmed after the previous MPS run. The frozen zone on the schedule extends two weeks ahead, i.e. to the end of week 2.

Calculate projected inventory, net requirements and available to promise for each period on the master schedule.

The answer to this exercise is in Table B3.2.

Table B3.1 Birdhomes' MPS analysis (incomplete)

								Week no.									
	0	1	2	3	4	5	6	7	8	9	10	11	12	13	14	15	16
Part no. A123																	
Forecast		30	30	30	35	35	40	40	40	40	40	45	45	45	50	50	50
Customer orders		28	34	26	22	18	9	0	5	0	0	0	0	0	0	0	0
Total demand																	
Planned orders		35	35	35	40	40	40										
Initial inventory	25																
Projected inventory																	
Net requirements																	
Available to promise																	
Cumulative ATP																	

Answer to exercise B3

Table B3.2 Birdhomes' MPS analysis (complete)

								Week no.									
	0	1	2	3	4	5	6	7	8	9	10	11	12	13	14	15	16
Part no. A123																	
Forecast		30	30	30	35	35	40	40	40	40	40	45	45	45	50	50	50
Customer orders		28	34	26	22	18	9	0	5	0	0	0	0	0	0	0	0
Total demand		28	34	30	35	35	40	40	40	40	40	45	45	45	50	50	50
Planned orders		35	35	35	40	40	40										
Initial inventory	25																
Projected inventory		32	1	5	5	5	0	0	0	0	0	0	0	0	0	0	0
Net requirements		0	0	0	0	0	0	40	40	40	40	45	45	45	50	50	50
Available to promise		32	1	9	18	22	31	0	0	0	0	0	0	0	0	0	0
Cumulative ATP		32	33	42	60	82	113	113	108	108	108	108	108	108	108	108	108

The action that the planner may now take could include:

- raising new planned orders beyond week 6;
- changing existing planned orders to increase or decrease projected inventory.

Exercise B4 CRP analysis

The list of Birdhomes' production operations by part number has already been given (Table 17.1). The MPS is now expressed in daily time buckets, and is given in Table B4.1. Day 18 is the demand time fence. From day 19 onwards, the schedule includes level forecasts as far as day 100 for each of the six finished products. The revised planned receipts schedule, incorporating the forecast element, is given in Table B4.2. This takes account of inventory, allocated inventory and scheduled receipts, just as it did in Exercise B2.

Table B4.1 Birdhomes' master production schedule

Part no.	14	15	16	Day no. 17	18	19	20
A123	22	0	46	0	18	17	17
A124	0	37	5	0	0	8	8
A125	28	20	0	44	0	18	18
A126	0	0	60	0	0	12	12
A127	0	36	0	0	12	10	10
A128	54	0	26	48	26	30	30

Table B4.2 Birdhomes' planned receipts

Part no.	8	9	10	11	12	13	Day no. 14	15	16	17	18	19	20
A123	0	0	0	0	0	0	30	60	90	0	48	47	47
A124	0	0	0	0	0	54	36	63	53	38	40	48	48
A125	0	0	0	0	0	0	28	20	0	44	0	18	18
A126	0	0	0	0	0	0	0	0	60	0	0	12	12
A127	0	0	0	0	0	0	0	36	0	0	12	10	10
A128	0	0	0	0	0	0	54	0	26	48	26	30	30
B234	0	0	0	0	0	20	123	143	38	88	95	95	95
B235	0	0	0	0	0	30	60	90	0	48	47	47	47
B236	0	0	0	0	54	36	63	53	38	40	48	48	48
B237	0	0	0	0	0	28	56	0	44	12	28	28	28
B238	0	0	0	0	0	54	0	86	48	26	42	42	42
C349	0	28	56	0	44	12	28	28	28	28	28	28	28
C350	0	54	0	86	48	26	42	42	42	42	42	42	42

Calculate Birdhomes' workload in standard hours by department and by day from day 8 through to a horizon of day 20.

The calculated workloads for each department are given in Table B4.3.

Table B4.3 Birdhomes' workload by department

Part no.						Day							
	8	9	10	11	12	13	14	15	16	17	18	19	20
Department A													
A123	0.0	0.0	0.0	0.0	0.0	0.0	2.3	4.3	6.3	0.0	3.5	3.4	3.4
A124	0.0	0.0	0.0	0.0	0.0	3.9	2.7	4.5	3.8	2.8	2.9	3.5	3.5
A125	0.0	0.0	0.0	0.0	0.0	0.0	0.9	0.7	0.0	1.5	0.0	0.6	0.6
A126	0.0	0.0	0.0	0.0	0.0	0.0	0.0	0.0	2.0	0.0	0.0	0.4	0.4
A127	0.0	0.0	0.0	0.0	0.0	0.0	0.0	1.2	0.0	0.0	0.4	0.3	0.3
A128	0.0	0.0	0.0	0.0	0.0	0.0	1.8	0.0	0.9	1.6	0.9	1.0	1.0
B234	0.0	4.8	25.4	29.4	8.4	18.4	19.8	19.8	19.8	0.0	0.0	0.0	0.0
Total	0.0	4.8	25.4	29.4	8.4	22.3	27.5	30.5	32.8	5.9	7.7	9.2	9.2
Department C													
C349	0.0	2.0	0.2	0.0	0.6	1.1	1.1	1.1	1.1	1.1	1.1	1.1	0.2
C350	0.0	0.2	0.0	1.8	1.0	1.6	1.6	1.6	1.6	1.6	1.6	1.6	0.2
Total	0.0	2.2	0.2	1.8	1.6	2.7	2.7	2.7	2.7	2.7	2.7	2.7	0.4
Department P													
B235	0.0	0.0	0.0	4.0	7.0	10.0	0.0	5.8	5.7	5.7	5.7	0.0	0.0
B236	0.0	0.0	6.4	4.6	7.3	6.3	4.8	5.0	5.8	5.8	5.8	0.0	0.0
Total	0.0	0.0	6.4	8.6	14.3	16.3	4.8	10.8	11.5	11.5	11.5	0.0	0.0
Department W													
B237	0.0	0.0	0.0	0.0	2.3	4.2	0.0	3.4	1.2	2.3	2.3	2.3	0.0
B238	0.0	0.0	0.0	0.0	4.0	0.0	6.2	3.6	2.2	3.2	3.2	3.2	0.0
Total	0.0	0.0	0.0	0.0	6.3	4.2	6.2	7.0	3.4	5.5	5.5	5.5	0.0

Exercise B5 Capacity utilization

Birdhomes work seven days per week. The normal working day is 10 hours per day after subtraction of meal breaks, and there are no holidays or shutdown periods over the horizon of day 20. There are three people in the assembly area, and one manning the paint shop. One employee mans both the welding shop and the cutting shop, with his time allocated two thirds to welding and one third to cutting.

The prevailing department production efficiency levels are:

Department	Production efficiency %
Assembly	78.0
Painting	85.0
Welding	80.0
Cutting	80.0

Using the results from Exercise B4, calculate capacity utilizations, over/ under load, and cumulative over/under load by day by department.

The worked example is given in Tables B5.1 (below) and B5.2 (on page 331).

Answers to exercise B5

Table B5.1   Birdhomes' effective resources

Work centre	Resource quantity	Hours per day	Total hours	Efficiency (%)	Hours available
A	3	10.0	30.0	78.0	23.4
C	1	3.3	3.3	80.0	2.6
P	1	10.0	10.0	85.0	8.5
W	1	6.7	6.7	80.0	5.4

Table B5.2   Birdhomes' capacity utilization

						Day no.							
	8	9	10	11	12	13	14	15	16	17	18	19	20
Work centre A													
Available hrs	23.4	23.4	23.4	23.4	23.4	23.4	23.4	23.4	23.4	23.4	23.4	23.4	23.4
Load hrs	4.8	25.4	29.4	8.4	22.2	27.4	30.3	32.7	25.6	27.4	28.9	28.9	28.9
Utilization	21%	109%	126%	36%	95%	117%	129%	140%	109%	117%	124%	124%	124%
Difference hrs	18.6	−2.0	−6.0	15.0	1.2	−4.0	−6.9	−9.3	−2.2	−4.0	−5.5	−5.5	−5.5
Cumulative	18.6	16.6	10.6	25.6	26.8	22.8	15.9	6.6	4.4	0.4	−5.1	−10.6	−16.1
Work centre C													
Available hrs	2.6	2.6	2.6	2.6	2.6	2.6	2.6	2.6	2.6	2.6	2.6	2.6	2.6
Load hrs	3.1	2.0	3.0	3.4	1.6	2.7	2.7	2.7	2.7	2.7	2.7	2.7	2.7
Utilization	117%	76%	114%	129%	61%	102%	102%	102%	102%	102%	102%	102%	102%
Difference hrs	−0.5	0.6	−0.4	−0.8	1.0	−0.1	−0.1	−0.1	−0.1	−0.1	−0.1	−0.1	−0.1
Cumulative	−0.5	0.2	−0.2	−0.9	0.1	0.0	0.0	−0.1	−0.1	−0.2	−0.3	−0.3	−0.4
Work centre P													
Available hrs	8.5	8.5	8.5	8.5	8.5	8.5	8.5	8.5	8.5	8.5	8.5	8.5	8.5
Load hrs	0.0	6.4	8.6	14.3	16.3	4.8	10.4	11.5	11.5	11.5	11.5	11.5	11.5
Utilization	0%	75%	101%	168%	192%	56%	122%	135%	135%	135%	135%	135%	135%
Difference hrs	8.5	2.1	−0.1	−5.8	−7.8	3.7	−1.9	−3.0	−3.0	−3.0	−3.0	−3.0	−3.0
Cumulative	8.5	10.6	10.5	4.7	−3.1	0.6	−1.3	−4.3	−7.3	−10.3	−13.3	−16.3	−19.3
Work centre W													
Available hrs	5.4	5.4	5.4	5.4	5.4	5.4	5.4	5.4	5.4	5.4	5.4	5.4	5.4
Load hrs	0.0	0.0	0.0	6.3	4.2	6.2	7.0	3.4	5.5	5.5	5.5	5.5	5.5
Utilization	0%	0%	0%	118%	78%	116%	131%	63%	103%	103%	103%	103%	103%
Difference hrs	5.4	5.4	5.4	−0.9	1.2	−0.8	−1.6	2.0	−0.1	−0.1	−0.1	−0.1	−0.1
Cumulative	5.4	10.7	16.1	15.1	16.3	15.5	13.8	15.8	15.6	15.5	15.4	15.2	15.1

Exercise B6 Standard costs

The Birdhomes' parts master file is as previously defined in Table B1.1, and the bills of materials are as defined in Table B1.2. Birdhomes' production routing file is the one suggested in Chapter 17, and is repeated below in Table B6.1. The standard batch quantities are based on the forecast demand towards the latter part of the planning horizon used in Exercise B3, assuming that the lot-sizing method is lot-for-lot, and these are summarized in Table B6.2 below. Birdhomes' work-centre cost rates are given in Table B6.3 opposite, and the current purchase prices for the bought in components are given in Table B6.4.

Calculate the 'rolled up' standard cost for each part number on the Birdhomes' parts master file.

Table B6.1   Birdhomes' production routings

Part no.	Work centre	Setup (mins)	Run (mins)	Move (days)	Production operation
A123	A	15	4	0	Assemble red roof to house s/assy
A124	A	15	4	0	Assemble green roof to house s/assy
A125	A	0	2	0	Assemble short stalk to red house unit
A126	A	0	2	0	Assemble long stalk to red house unit
A127	A	0	2	0	Assemble short stalk to green house unit
A128	A	0	2	0	Assemble long stalk to green house unit
B234	A	45	12	4	Glue sides and front to house base
B235	P	60	6	2	Paint roof red
B236	P	60	6	2	Paint roof green
B237	W	25	4	1	Weld short stalk to ground base
B238	W	25	4	1	Weld long stalk to ground base
C349	C	10	2	0	Cut short stalk from 4 m tube
C350	C	10	2	0	Cut long stalk from 4 m tube

Table B6.2   Birdhomes' standard batch sizes

Part no.	Standard batch quantity
A123	15
A124	15
A125	18
A126	12
A127	10
A128	30
B234	45
B235	60
B236	60
B237	25
B238	25
C349	10
C350	10

Table B6.3   Birdhomes' work centre cost rates

Work centre	Direct rate (£ per hour)	Overhead rate (£ per hour)
A	7.50	10.00
C	7.25	9.75
P	12.75	17.00
W	15.00	20.00

Table B6.4   Birdhomes' current purchase prices

Part no.	Purchase price (£ per unit quantity)
C345	4.50
C346	1.50
C347	2.75
C348	1.65
C351	3.50
C352	28.00

Answers to exercise B6

In Table B6.5 are shown the standard costs attributable to each part number. These are not the 'rolled up' standards costs, but only the costs attracted at that single level in the product structure. The calculation basis used in Table B6.5 is as follows:

– *Material cost*: this applies to the bought-in items, and is the current purchase price given in Table B6.4.
– *Labour cost*: this applies to the items manufactured or assembled in plant, and is the sum of setup cost and production cost.

The production cost has been calculated as:

$$\text{Run time} \times \text{work centre direct cost}$$

The run time was given, by part number, in the production routings in Table B6.1, and this also gave the work centre in which the production operation is carried out, thus enabling the work centre direct rate to be extracted from the table of work centre rates in Table B6.3.

Table B6.5   Standard costs at single level

Part no.	Material cost	Direct cost	Overhead cost
		(£ per unit quantity)	
A123	0.00	0.63	0.83
A124	0.00	0.63	0.83
A125	0.00	0.25	0.33
A126	0.00	0.25	0.33
A127	0.00	0.25	0.33
A128	0.00	0.25	0.33
B234	0.00	1.63	2.17
B235	0.00	1.49	1.98
B236	0.00	1.49	1.98
B237	0.00	1.25	1.67
B238	0.00	1.25	1.67
C345	4.50	0.00	0.00
C346	1.50	0.00	0.00
C347	2.75	0.00	0.00
C348	1.65	0.00	0.00
C349	0.00	0.36	0.49
C350	0.00	0.36	0.49
C351	3.50	0.00	0.00
C352	28.00	0.00	0.00

The setup cost has been calculated in two steps as follows:

1. Batch setup cost = setup time × work centre direct rate.
   The setup time is taken from the production routing in Table B6.1. Table B6.1 also identifies the work centre, and the appropriate direct rate has been extracted from Table B6.3.
2. Setup cost per unit = batch setup cost ÷ standard batch size.
   The standard batch size was given in Table B6.2.

As both setup and run times were given in minutes, and the direct rates were expressed as the cost per hour, both setup and run times in this example have been divided by 60 to convert from minutes to hours.

– *Overhead costs*: this calculation is identical to that for the direct costs, except that overhead rate is substituted for direct rate.

In Table B6.6 are given the rolled-up costs at each level in the product structure. The difference between the costs in Table B6.6 and those given in Table B6.5 is that the standard costs in Table B6.6 are the total standard costs for each part number. They have been arrived at by working upwards

Table B6.6 Rolled-up standard costs

Part no.	Material cost	Direct cost	Overhead cost	Total cost
		(all costs are in £ per unit)		
A123	13.40	3.74	4.98	22.12
A124	13.40	3.74	4.98	22.12
A125	23.90	5.60	7.47	36.97
A126	30.90	5.60	7.47	43.97
A127	23.90	5.60	7.47	36.97
A128	30.90	5.60	7.47	43.97
B234	8.90	1.63	2.17	12.69
B235	4.50	1.49	1.98	7.97
B236	4.50	1.49	1.98	7.97
B237	10.50	1.61	2.15	14.27
B238	17.50	1.61	2.15	21.27
C345	4.50	0.00	0.00	4.50
C346	1.50	0.00	0.00	1.50
C347	2.75	0.00	0.00	2.75
C348	1.65	0.00	0.00	1.65
C349	7.00	0.36	0.49	7.85
C350	14.00	0.36	0.49	14.85
C351	3.50	0.00	0.00	3.50
C352	28.00	0.00	0.00	28.00

from the lowest levels in the bill of materials structure, accumulating or 'rolling up' the standard costs in the process.

For example, the calculation in respect of part number B234 has been made as follows. The bill of materials (Table B1.2) shows that the component parts of part number B234 are:

C346—quantity of 3
C347—quantity of 1
C348—quantity of 1

For each of the three cost buckets—materials, direct and overhead—the rolled-up standard cost is calculated as follows, using the appropriate single-level costs given in Table B6.5:

1 × the costs for B234 itself

+ 3 × the costs of C346

+ 1 × the costs of C347

+ 1 × the costs of C348

Appendix C
What drives inventory?

In this appendix, simple a priori reasoning is used to identify the real determinants of inventory and, because a major driver of inventory levels is shown to be leadtime, the key drivers of manufacturing leadtime are then also identified. In the process of analysing the three components of inventory—finished goods, WIP and production inventories—and manufacturing leadtime, the common elements become identified and in turn help identify a strategy for inventory reduction. Not surprisingly, this bears a remarkable similarity to the goals of just-in time (JIT), which were summarized in Table 4.8.

The effect of leadtime on inventory

In its most elementary form, the level of inventory in a business is a function of demand over leadtime. In the case of WIP inventory this can be demonstrated quite simply by the examples in Tables C1 and C2. In these examples, the assumption is made that:

- Technological leadtime remains constant, and the difference in actual leadtime is the result of queue times ahead of manufacturing processes and/or

Table C1 Effect of manufacturing leadtime on inventory

Factory output	Manufacturing leadtime	Average units in WIP	WIP inventory
100 units per week	1 day	20	$20 \times r1$
100 units per week	10 days	200	$200 \times r2$

r1 and r2 are the respective rates of attraction of cost

Table C2 Effect of demand on inventory

Factory output	Manufacturing leadtime	Average units in WIP	WIP inventory
100 units per week	10 days	200	$200 \times r2$
200 units per week	10 days	400	$400 \times r2$

move times between processes. The cost of value-adding activity—the labour or machine cost components of final WIP—remains constant irrespective of actual leadtime.

- The rate of attraction of cost will vary with actual leadtime, but where the major attraction of cost occurs at the start of production, for example where *all* materials are issued before production begins, then r1 and r2 in the tables will tend towards equality.

In conclusion, other things being equal, the level of inventory is determined primarily by both the level of demand and the manufacturing leadtime. Demand is an externally determined factor, and is the variable in the equation. Manufacturing leadtime is a factor that can be controlled internally, and is therefore the fixed component of the equation. Minimizing leadtime will therefore be fundamental to minimizing the level of inventory at the prevailing level of demand. Similar reasoning may be applied to finished product inventory.

In the case of production inventories the use of MRP's time-phased order scheduling techniques serves to decouple the suppliers' manufacturing leadtime from the equation shown above, but there is nevertheless an *internal* leadtime—the replenishment leadtime, and this is a function of both planning time buckets in the MRP system and the frequency of replanning. This relationship is illustrated in Table C3, which uses numbers identical to those in Table C1, but substitutes replanning interval for manufacturing leadtime. In an MRP system, r1 and r2 will of course be determined by the particular lot-sizing technique in use.

The *elemental* determinants of inventory are therefore demand and leadtime. There are then other factors which in the real world are *superimposed* on this relationship. Some, like lot-sizing formulae and safety stocks, are intentional; others, such as internal rejection rates, are unintentional. In Tables C4 to C6, we expand the inventory equation to become

$$\text{demand} \times \text{leadtime}$$

$$\text{plus effect of other factors}$$

Table C3   Effect of replenishment leadtime on inventory

Factory input	Replanning interval	Demand through planning period	Inventory level
100 units per week	1 day	20	20 × r1
100 units per week	10 days	200	200 × r2

r1 and r2 represent the planned rate of inbound flow of materials

Table C4   Finished inventory

Determinants	Influence	Source
Demand	Independent demand	4
Leadtime	Manufacturing leadtime (see Table C7)	
Safety stock	Customer service level	3/4
	Demand pattern	4
	Uncertainty	4
Unplanned	Lack of demand visibility	4
	Inaccuracy of forecasts	2
	Padding of safety stocks	2

Table C5   Production materials inventory

Determinants	Influence	Source
Demand	Dependent demand	4
Leadtime	Replenishment leadtime:	
	– time buckets	2
	– replanning frequency	2
Lot size	Perceived economics	2
Safety stock	Supplier performance	4
Unplanned	Uncertainty of schedules	2/4
	Disregard for demand dependency	1
	Inaccuracy of bills of materials	3
	Inaccuracy of inventory records	3
	Padding of lot size	2
	Padding of safety stock	2
	Padding of planning leadtime	2

As this is done we will identify from which of four sources of influence each of these other factors stems:

1. the logic of the MRP or MRPII system;
2. the management of the MRP or MRPII system;
3. internal influence, but beyond the MRP or MRPII system;
4. external influence.

Factors that are either intentional *or* expected, and are therefore planned for as a conscious act of company policy, are identified separately. Those that are normally neither intentional *nor* expected, including the manipulation of MRP system parameters by the users of the system, and therefore not consciously planned for as part of company policy, are grouped as unplanned. In

Table C6   Work in process inventory

Determinants	Influence	Source
Demand	Dependent demand	4
	Production lot size	2
Leadtime	Manufacturing leadtime (see Table C7)	
Quality loss	Process capability	3
	Quality assurance system	3
Unplanned	Bad planning or scheduling	2
	Material shortages	1/2
	Capacity bottlenecks	2
	Production efficiency deviations	3
	Machine breakdown	3
	Absenteeism	3
	Inaccuracy of routings	2
	Padding of leadtimes	2

each table the influence source is keyed to one of the four sources listed above.

What drives manufacturing leadtime

Manufacturing leadtime appears as a key determinant of both WIP inventory and finished inventory. Table C7 expands the make-up of this in a similar manner to that used in Tables C4 to C6.

Summary

The list of influences, and their source, shown in Tables C4 to C7, although not exhaustive by any means, illustrates a number of significant points:

- The MRP or MRPII system itself has remarkably little influence on inventory. Its real contribution is as a planning tool, specifically as a tool which enables decisions at execution level to reflect dependency of demand.
- There are very many ways in which the *management* of an MRP or MRPII system has a direct influence on inventory. Of especial note are the many opportunities for events to be constrained by the parameters given to the system. Padding of leadtimes, queue or move times, and safety stocks by the planner, to counter the stress factor and add an element of comfort to what may otherwise often be less than absolute data, is potentially a major variable.

Table C7 Manufacturing leadtime

Determinants	Influence	Source
Queue time	Uncertainty	2
	Management policy	3
Setup time	Process technology	3
Production time:		
– quantity	Demand	4
	Lot sizing	2
– run time	Process technology	3
	Production efficiency	3
Move time	Process technology	3
	Materials handling technology	3
Unplanned	Padding of queue times	2
	Padding of setup times	2
	Padding of run times	2
	Padding of move times	2
	Poor management of work flow	3
	Panic deviations to schedule	3

– The influence of internal factors beyond the scope of the MRP system is clearly indicated. For the most part these influences derive directly from aspects of the company's manufacturing strategy, supporting the contention that it is the choice of strategy which influences the level of inventory, and not the planning system.
– External factors apply at both ends of the supply chain. Not only is independent (or customer demand) the major variable, supplier performance is also a key area of influence.

Table C8 Inventory reductions

Inventory driver	Corrective
Manufacturing leadtime	Reduce manufacturing leadtime:
	– reduce setup time
	– reduce queue and move time
	– reduce production lot size
Demand uncertainty	Reduce manufacturing leadtime
Replenishment leadtime	Bucketless net change MRP, or kanban system
Lot size	Reduce lot size
Supplier performance	Supplier quality assurance
	Supplier partnership
Quality loss	Process capability
	Quality assurance system

Conclusion

The level of independent demand is the major variable determining inventory. As it is an external factor it may be controlled only artificially, for example by a buffer stock of finished inventory or by constraints on order acceptance. The major controllable in the equation is manufacturing lead-time, and the factors that influence the planned or expected additional elements. Table C8 lists these, the drivers of inventory, along with the a priori corrective leading to inventory reduction.

The similarity between the correctives indicated in Table C8 and the goals of JIT shown in Table 4.8 should be noted. These correctives will at the same time help to reduce or eliminate the extensive list of unplanned influences given in Tables C4 to C7.

Appendix D
Glossary of terms

ABC
Activity-based costing.

Aggregating
The consolidation of demand at item level into demand by product group for longer term demand forecasting and production planning purposes.

APICS
American Production and Inventory Control Society.

APL
Accreditation of prior learning.

ATP
See **Available to promise**

Available to promise
The quantity of a part at a specific date which is covered by stock or planned orders in excess of existing requirements within the leadtime at that date.

Back order
An order which is past its due receipt or despatch date.

Back flushing
The method of automatically generating stores issue transactions for component parts in a paperless (e.g. kanban) system.

Backward scheduling
The process of scheduling from required date backwards and offsetting by leadtime to arrive at start date.

Bill of materials
A hierarchical and structured list of component parts, raw materials and sub-assemblies.

Bill of production
See **Production routing**

Bill of resources
A summary of key resources time required to make a product; for use in rough-cut capacity planning.

Blanket order
A purchase order which covers a forward period and provides for variable order quantities to be scheduled for call-off on a regular basis.

BOM
See **Bill of materials**

BPICS
British Production and Inventory Control Society.

BS 5750
The British Standard defining a quality assurance system.

BS 7750
The British Standard defining an environmental management system.

BS 7850
The British Standard defining total quality management.

Bubble number
A sequence number determining the sequence in which the component parts of a bill of materials will be listed.

Bucketless
An MRP system in which the discrete due day of a requirement is preserved, rather than combining the requirement into a time bucket.

Buckets
Discrete spans of time used in material requirements planning to consolidate or group together the requirements.

Business process re-engineering
A fundamental reappraisal and redesign of the processes in a business in order to achieve substantial improvements in performance criteria.

CAD
Computer-aided design.

CAM
Computer-aided manufacturing/Computer-assisted manufacturing.

Cascading
A technique for allocating available materials to works orders in order of priority by lateness of works order, and sometimes for directing receipts directly to the appropriate work centre.

CFM
See **Continuous flow manufacturing**

Chase strategy
A scheduling technique aimed at following or 'chasing' the demand profile, the opposite of a 'levelling' strategy.

CIM
Computer-integrated manufacturing: the application of integrated computerized solutions to manufacturing planning and to the manufacturing processes.

Cleardown
The removal of obsolete records from a database.

Closed loop
A system in which feedback from a system module or physical activity is captured by the system module initiating the planned action.

CMLT
See **Cumulative manufacturing leadtime**

Configure to order
A systems technique providing for the definition of permissible customer features and options on a customized product and for ensuring the compatibility of product structures which may be determined by the presence or absence of customer options.

Consumption of forecast
A technique for the replacement of forecast orders by actual customer orders in the master production schedule.

Continuous flow manufacturing
The organization of the manufacturing process so that materials flow continuously from first operation to the last final assembly operation without intermediate queues or inter-process buffer stocks.

Critical ratio
The ratio of time required to time remaining, used as a means of prioritization of outstanding orders.

CRP
Capacity requirements planning.

CTO
See **Configure to order**

Cumulative manufacturing leadtime
The total leadtime to manufacture a finished product if the quantity in stock of component parts at all levels in the product structure is zero.

Cut-off time fence
The boundary in a master production schedule beyond which detailed planning will not be carried out.

Demand time fence
The boundary in a master production schedule between a frozen zone in which forecasts are ignored and the remainder of the schedule.

Dependent demand
Demand which is dependent upon and generated by the demand for a higher level product or component.

DFA
Design for assembly: a design concept aimed at simplifying the process of assembly.

DFM
Design for manufacturing; similar to DFA.

DFMA
Design for manufacturing and assembly; similar to DFA.

Direct line feed
The process of having component parts delivered directly to a production process in line with short-term requirements, rather than through a physical buffer store.

Disaggregating
The process of breaking down demand forecasts or production plans by product group into detailed forecasts by individual item at master production schedule level.

Distribution routing
The definition of how each distribution location is supplied with each finished product by which supplying location(s), and how long it takes.

DMRP
Distributed MRP or MRPII, where the computer resource is distributed at factory or department level, with a centralized resource providing the higher-level coordination.

DMS
Distribution management system.

Dock to stock
An inventory recording system which maintains visibility from factory gate receipt through all intervening movements to stores location.

Downsizing
In business strategy, the process of contracting onto a lower fixed cost base. In specific IT terminology, the process of re-engineering away from central mainframe computers towards distributed minicomputers.

DRP
Distribution resource planning.

Earliest finish date
The earliest date by which an order could be completed if it were started now and took priority over all other orders.

EBQ
Economic batch quantity. See **EOQ**

EDI
Electronic data interchange.

EDM
See **Engineering data management**

Effective date
The date on which an engineering change to a bill of materials has to come into effect.

Electric kanban
A switch on an automated line which automatically signals a need for component replenishment to a supply or feeder line, and thus acts in lieu of a kanban card.

Electronic kanban
The process whereby the system automatically triggers the 'pulling' of component parts instead of using an actual kanban card.

EN 29000
The European standard defining a quality assurance system.

Engineering bill of materials
The structures and versions of the bill of materials existing within product design prior to release for manufacturing purposes.

Engineering change
A change to the structure or content of a bill of materials.

Engineering data management
A systems technique for transferring engineering data from one discrete computer system to another, for example from a CAD system to the bill of materials module of MRP.

EOQ
Economic order quantity. A calculation which aims to minimize the total of ordering or setup costs and inventory carrying costs.

Expedite
The MRP term used to signal to the materials planner orders that are overdue or planned orders needed in less than the specified leadtime in order to meet a requirement.

Explosion
The technique used in generating lower-level component part requirements from higher-level requirements using parent/child relationships defined in a bill of materials.

FIFO
First in first out.

File server
The computer or PC in a multi-user network which hosts the databases and provides the platform for application software.

Firm planned order
In MRP an order which has quantity and date predetermined by the materials planner, and which will not be altered by the MRP logic.

FMEA
Failure modes and effects analysis.

FMS
Flexible manufacturing system. An automated and computer-controlled form of group technology.

Forward scheduling
The process of scheduling forwards from earliest start date and offsetting by production leadtime in order to arrive at a planned finish date.

Frozen zone
The part of a schedule which lies within critical leadtimes and in which it is planned to avoid further changes in order to achieve stability of plans.

Global replacement
See **Mass replacement**

Gross requirements
The time-phased requirements of component parts needed to satisfy a master production schedule (or equivalent), before taking account of stock in hand or on order.

Group technology
Organization of work into a balanced and typically U-shaped group of machines, based on commonality of operations, and through which work flows or is transferred.

Horizon
See **Planning horizon**

IMM
The Institute of Materials Management; now The Institute of Logistics.

Inbound logistics
Management of the physical flow of incoming materials from the supply chain.

Indented
Applied to bill of materials and where used listing, where the level number is indented to more clearly indicate the level in the overall hierarchy. See **Level**

Independent demand
Demand for a product or component which is independent of and has not been generated by the demand for a higher-level product or component.

In-transit leadtime
In DRP, the shipping leadtime from a supplying location to a receiving location.

Investors in People
A UK standard for human resource development.

ISO 9000
The international standard defining a quality assurance system.

IT
Information technology.

ITT
Invitation to tender.

JIT
Just-in-time.

Kanban
The Japanese word for card. A kanban is used to 'pull' materials from a buffer stock into a manufacturing process, or to 'pull' the replacement of buffer stock through a manufacturing process.

Kitting
The issuing of materials from stores to newly released works orders.

LAN
Local area network. A data communications network linking together file servers and client terminals within a local physical site.

Latest start date
The latest date on which a works order can be started in order to meet its due date, even if it were given priority over all other orders.

Level
The lowest level at which a part number appears in the hierarchy of any or all bills of materials of which it is a component part.

Levelling strategy
A scheduling technique aimed at producing a level load; the opposite of a 'chase' strategy.

Line of balance
(a) Within some MRP systems, a shortage list which indicates that there will be a shortage of a component on the date shown and by the quantity shown; (b) a scheduling technique based on the calculation of requirements at intermediate dates in order to achieve a final delivery date.

Linkages
The series of parent/child relationships between a part number and its immediate lower-level components.

Lot sizing
The method by which net requirements are converted into planned order quantities.

Lot traceability
A process of recording individual receipts of a part, and recording to which works orders it was issued. Also known as batch traceability.

Mass release
The automatic release of orders which are due for release on or before a specified date.

Mass replacement
Engineering change at part number level which has to be effected on all bills of materials containing that part number.

MCI
Management charter initiative.

MOM
McLaren order moment. A lot-sizing technique, similar to part-period balancing.

MPS
Master production schedule.

MRP
Materials requirements planning.

MRP1
See **MRP**

MRPII
Manufacturing resource planning.

MSP
Master schedule programming.

Net change
The MRP method which takes account of changes at master production schedule level since the previous planning run, and expresses these as net changes at component part net requirements schedule level.

Net requirements
The time-phased requirements of component parts needed to satisfy a master production schedule (or equivalent), after taking account of stock in hand and on order.

Netting
The process of subtracting from gross requirements the quantity of stock in hand and on order to give net requirements.

NVQ
National vocational qualification.

O&M
Organization and methods.

OEM
Original equipment manufacturer. An OEM product is one which satisfies final customer demand as opposed to being used or consumed in the manufacture of another higher-level product.

Open systems
Computer environments in which application software is portable from one platform to another, and in which there is a multi-user network allowing freedom of file server/client terminal combinations.

OPT
Optimized production technology. A production scheduling technique which concentrates on bottlenecks. (OPT is a registered trademark of Scheduling Technology Group Ltd.)

Order-point system
A stock control system in which reordering takes place when a reorder point, normally predetermined in relation to historical usage, is reached.

PAC
Production activity control. The American terminology for production control and shop-floor data collection systems.

Part-period balancing
A lot-sizing technique based on an approximation to an EOQ technique, but which allows variable order quantities dependent on the actual data.

PC
Personal computer.

Pegging
The process of matching orders placed or planned with the orders which generate the requirement.

PFMEA
Process failure modes and effect analysis.

Phantom
An imaginary subassembly in a bill of materials which does not constitute a physical subassembly. Also known as a ghost or dummy.

Planning bill of materials
A product structure similar to the main bill of materials, but showing instead the forecast percentage occurrence of optional features, and used to generate planned orders at MPS level.

Planning horizon
The future time limit to production, materials or capacity planning.

Planning leadtime
A leadtime in MRP which is offset from due date to give required date. It is normally a fixed leadtime, regardless of order or batch quantity.

Planning time fence
The future period in the master production schedule up to which the planner should now be planning firm planned orders.

Platform
The combination of computer file server hardware and its associated operating system.

Playground
A term denoting a temporary working file area where changes (e.g. to a bill of materials) may be input and validated prior to file updating.

PMS
Project management system.

Production routing
A structured definition of the sequence of production operations involved in manufacture, and the time required for and between each operation.

QFD
Quality function deployment. A method of relating to the users' views of existing and competing products and deriving from these technical parameters and priorities for new product specification.

Quality loss
The difference between 100 per cent good product and the actual level of good product, after taking account of both customer dissatisfaction and internal wastage.

R&D
Research and development.

Rate-based scheduling
The scheduling technique whose objective is to maintain a predetermined production or assembly rate, as distinct from the technique of time-phased order point adopted by MRP.

RCCP
Rough-cut capacity planning. The balancing of order workload with a limited subset of critical capacity elements in order to test the feasibility of a production plan or schedule.

Regeneration
The MRP technique which ignores the result of previous runs, and completely recalculates component net requirements based on the current master production schedule (or equivalent).

Repetitive manufacturing
A production environment adapted to assemble or manufacture high volume standard or customized products in small batches on a short leadtime.

Residual scheduling
A technique used when scheduling to finite capacity which allows a new order to be fitted around the existing schedule as an alternative to a complete rescheduling.

RF
Radio frequency.

Roll up
The process of accumulating standard material costs through a bill of material from bottom–up, or for accumulating standard costs of production through a production routing from bottom–up.

Rough cut
A 'rough' or approximate guide, for example, an approximate statement of loading applied to capacity planning.

Routing
See **production routing**

Safety leadtime
An addition to planned leadtime to cover the failure of a supplier or works to deliver on time.

Safety stock
A quantity of stock which is specifically planned to cover shortages arising from failures in delivery or quality performance and which will not otherwise be used. May also be planned to cover variability in demand.

SCADA
Supervisory control and data acquisition. An industry standard for data collection systems.

SFDC
Shop-floor data collection.

Simultaneous engineering
An approach to product or process development which involves all functions together. As opposed to serial engineering, where each function performs a discrete task in sequence.

SKU
Stock-keeping unit. The identifier of discrete items in a materials planning system, most commonly the combination of location and part number.

SOP
Sales order processing.

SPC
Statistical process control.

SQA
Supplier quality assurance.

Stage kitting
The preparation of picking lists by discrete work centres or up to a certain stage in manufacture for materials to be issued to a works order.

STEP
Standard for the Exchange of Product model description, an ISO standard that may in the future form the basis for a universal product descriptor database.

Supply chain management
A concept of integrating the management of supplies beyond the company and in partnership with suppliers.

Time buckets
See **Buckets**

Time fence
A notional barrier separating different parts of a planning horizon into 'frozen' or 'firm' periods depending on both the leadtime and the firmness of demand.

Time-phased order point
The technique used by MRP to offset lot-sized net requirements by leadtime in order to arrive at a planned order release.

TQM
Total quality management.

Trial kitting
A procedure for testing whether or not all materials are available prior to releasing a works order.

UM
Unit of measure. The measure of unit quantity within the MRP and inventory system, e.g. each, metres, square metres, kilograms, etc.

VAN
Value-added network.

Wagner–Whitin algorithm
A lot-sizing technique aimed at producing a minimum cost ordering plan.

WAN
Wide area network. A data communications network linking together remote sites.

Where used
A structured listing showing either the immediate or all higher level usage(s) of a lower level component part.

WIP
Work in process, or work in progress.

Work cell
A discrete shop-floor work unit, which is organized on the basis of group technology.

Work to list
For a production department or operation, the list of works order in the order of priority in which they should be carried out.

Appendix E
Bibliography

Anscombe, A., 'Benchmarking—a tool for business excellence', *Logistics Today*, November/December, 1992.

AT&T Istel, 'Factory management at Short Brothers', *In Touch*, Issue 3, 1992.

AT&T Istel, 'Provisa supports decisions', *In Touch*, Issue 1, 1993.

Barekat, M. M., 'Think cellular and be an MRPII winner', *Works Management*, June, 1990.

Barekat, M. M., 'A shopfloor solution to MRPII blues', *Accountancy*, August, 1991.

Bennett, R., 'Bringing corporate IT systems together', Management Consultancy, October, 1993.

Bertrand, J. W. M., Wortmann J. C. and Wijngaard, J., *Production Control: A Structural and Design Oriented Approach*, Elsevier, Amsterdam, 1990.

Browne, J., Harhen, J. and Shivnan, J., *Production Management Systems*, Addison-Wesley, Wokingham, 1988.

Burcher, P., 'Closing the loop in manufacturing resource planning systems', *BPICS Control*, August/September, 1991.

Cassidy, J., 'The Rise and Fall of IBM', *Sunday Times*, 28 March, 1993.

Caulkiner, S. and Ingersoll Engineers, 'The new manufacturing, Special Report no. 1171', *The Economist & Computer Weekly*, February, 1989.

Codling, S., *Best Practice Benchmarking*, DTI/Industrial Newsletters Ltd, Toddington, Beds, 1992.

Comber, P. R., 'Textbook MRPII implementation in the pharmaceutical industry', *BPICS Control*, October/November, 1992.

Daily Telegraph, 'UNIX adopted', *Daily Telegraph*, 31 August, 1993.

Dear, A., *Working Towards Just In Time*, Kogan Page, London, 1988.

DTI, *Competitive Manufacturing*, IFS Publications, Bedford, undated.

DTI/CBI, *Innovation—The Best Practice*, the Report, London, 1993.

Employment Department, *Investor in People—How Will We Gain Recognition?* Sheffield, 1991.

The Fellowship of Engineering, *The Management of Technology in United Kingdom Manufacturing Companies*, London, 1991.

Goldratt, E. and Cox, J., *The Goal: Excellence in Manufacturing*, North River Press, Norwich, Connecticut, 1986.

Gough, P. H., 'Training for excellence', *BPICS Control*, October/November, 1992.

Gunn, T., *Manufacturing For Competitive Advantage*, Ballinger, Cambridge, MA, 1987.

Hammer, M. and Champy, J., *Reeingineering the Corporation*, Nicholas Brearley, London, 1993.

Harrison, M., 'Finite scheduling in perspective', *BPICS Control*, December 1992/ January 1993.

Hartley, J., 'EDI: the route to lean production', *DTI/Industrial Newsletters Ltd*, Bedford, 1992.

Hill, J. F., Costa, R. S. and Jardim, E. G. M., 'Strategic management and shop floor control in jobbing industries', *BPICS Control*, February/March, 1992.

Hurst, N., 'Suppliers in the logistics chain', in *Time is Money*, Institute of Materials Management, Cranfield, 1991.

Institution of Electrical Engineers, *UK Manufacturing, a Survey of Surveys and a Compendium of Remedies*, London, 1992.

Irwin, N., 'Introducing partnership sourcing at ICL', *Logistics Today*, May/June, 1993.

Johnson, P., 'Focus on the materials that matter', in *Time Is Money*, Institute of Materials Management, Cranfield, 1991.

A. T. Kearney Ltd, *Leaders and Laggers in Logistics*, Institute of Materials Management, A. T. Kearney Ltd, London, 1991.

Little, D. and Jarvis, P. C., 'Survey of current UK shop floor scheduling practice', *BPICS Control*, December 1992/January 1993.

Logistics Today, 'Electronic trading data interchange growth continues', March/April, 1993.

Love, D. and Barekat, M., 'Decentralised, distributed MRP: solving control problems in cellular manufacturing', *Production and Inventory Management Journal*, third quarter, 1989.

Luscombe, M., *MRPII: Integrating The Business*, Butterworth-Heinemann, Oxford, 1993.

Martin, A. J., *Distribution Resource Planning*, Oliver Wight and Prentice-Hall, Essex Junction, Vt., USA, 1983.

McKenzie, A., 'Responding to change: materials strategy at IBM Greenock', *Logistics Today*, January/February, 1991.

Merke, P., 'What makes a world-class manufacturer?', *Logistics Europe*, June, 1993.

Mitchell, V., 'A goal-based finite scheduling decision support system', *BPICS Control*, June/July, 1992.

Mundy, K., 'Making the right choice', *Logistics Today*, September/October, 1992.

Nicholls, J., 'TQM's direction shifts paradigms', *Management Consultancy*, May, 1993.

Norton, N. G., Parsons, T. and Skinner, I. S., 'Control? Is management afraid of the unknown?' *BPICS Control*, December 1992/January 1993.

Orlicky, J., *Material Requirements Planning*, McGraw-Hill, New York, 1975.

Parsons, D., 'The principles of distribution resource planning (DRP)', *BPICS Control*, April/May, 1991.

Ralston, D. and Reddy, F., 'World-class manufacturing resource planning', *BPICS Control*, April/May, 1993.

Schonberger, R. J., *World-class Manufacturing: The Lessons of Simplicity Applied*, Free Press, New York, 1986.

Schonberger, R. J., *World-class Manufacturing: Implementing JIT and TQC*, Free Press, New York, 1987.

Stene, E., 'The continuing evolution of manufacturing industry and MRP', *BPICS Control*, August/September, 1992.

Sunday Times, Business Computing, 25 April, 1993, page 13.

Tompkins, J. A., *Winning Manufacturing*, McGraw-Hill, New York, 1989.

Vollmann, T. E., Berry, W. L. and Whybark, D. C., *Manufacturing Planning and Control Systems*, Irwin, Homewood, Ill., 1992.

Wallace, T., *APICS Dictionary*, American Production and Inventory Control Society, Washington, DC, 1980.

Wallace, T., *MRPII: Making It Happen*, Oliver Wight Publications, Essex Junction, Vt., USA, 1986.

Wight, O., *Manufacturing Resource Planning—MRPII*, Oliver Wight Publications, Essex Junction, Vt., USA, 1984.

Wild, R., *Essentials of Production and Operations Management*, Cassell, London, 1990.

Wilson, M., The demise of MRP as a non-value adding tool', *BPICS Control*, April/May, 1993.

Woodhead, R., 'Rate-based master production scheduling for repetitive make-to-stock manufacturing', *BPICS Control*, February/March, 1992.

Xerox Computer Services Ltd, *Software Selection in British Industry*, 1992.

Index